José de Acosta, S.J.

(1 5 4 0 – 1 6 0 0)

His Life and Thought

CLAUDIO M. BURGALETA, S.J.

Foreword by John W. O'Malley, S.J.

an imprint of
Loyola Press

Chicago

an imprint of

Loyola Press
3441 North Ashland Avenue
Chicago, Illinois 60657

Map of Peru on front cover is from Abraham Ortelius, *Theatrum Orbis
Terrarum*, 1588. Photo courtesy of Edward E. Ayer Collection, The
Newberry Library, Chicago.

Cover and interior design by Amy Evans McClure

Library of Congress Cataloging-in-Publication Data
Burgaleta, Claudio M.
    José de Acosta, S.J. (1540–1600) : his life and thought / by Claudio M.
Burgaleta.
        p.   cm.
    Includes bibliographical references and index.
    ISBN 0-8294-1063-5 (pbk.)
    1. Acosta, José de, 1540–1600.   2. Jesuits—Biography.   I. Title.
BX4705.A238B87   1999
271'.5302—dc21
    [B]   98-33511
                                                                        CIP

Printed in the United States of America
99 00 01 02 03 / 10 9 8 7 6 5 4 3 2 1

To my two families, the Burgaletas and the Society of Jesus,

for so many consolations:

life, love, traditions, the faith, an education,

reconciliation, friendships in the Lord.

Por todo esto y tanto más,

siempre estaré adeudado y profundamente agradecido

CONTENTS

LIST OF ILLUSTRATIONS

Note: Title pages were reproduced from copies in Loyola
    University Chicago Archives, Rare Book Collection, E. M.
    Cudahy Library.

FOREWORD

After Bartolomé de las Casas, José de Acosta was perhaps the most important missionary to Spanish South America in the sixteenth century, and he has other claims to fame as well. He wrote the first book in Peru. He headed off a disasterous proposal by a fellow Jesuit that Spain mount an armed invasion of China. And he was instrumental in the convocation of a pivotal Jesuit general congregation. But in spite of a life of accomplishment, he is virtually unknown.

While the literature about him in Spanish is relatively extensive, it is practically nonexistent in English. In fact, three excellent reference works have recently been published in which, in a just and equitable world, one would reasonably expect to find an entry for him—*The Oxford Dictionary of the Christian Church, The Oxford Encyclopedia of the Reformation* (four volumes), and *The HarperCollins Encyclopedia of Catholicism*. Yet Acosta's name does not appear. How does one explain this curious, but not untypical, oblivion?

The explanation is, on the surface level, rather simple. Scholarship is guided by rudders set long ago that keep the ship moving in the same direction and following the same routes—over and over again. The setting of the rudders on a given course often occurred as a result of prejudices that with the passage of time might almost be forgotten, but the scholarship sails on without deviation to right or left. The great German Lutheran historians of the nineteenth century established that the Reformation was important and "modern," while the Catholic and Mediterranean world was retrograde and uninteresting. The great English historians, with their more immediate impact on all anglophone interpretation, proclaimed the same message. It is no wonder José de Acosta never got discovered by these ships. He had three characteristics that made him remote to the trade routes: he was Spanish, he was

Catholic, he lived much of his life in Latin America, an unimportant part of the world. Sad to say, he was not the only person to be thus bypassed.

Especially in the past decade, the rudders have shown much more flexibility, as from many quarters the Eurocentrism of traditional scholarship has been challenged and searching questions raised about "modernity" and similar wisdoms. In this situation especially younger scholars have turned in increasing numbers to Catholic figures from the sixteenth century. The Carmelites, for instance, have lost their monopoly on Teresa of Avila. She has been discovered by "the world" she so resolutely renounced—not the world she knew of hidalgos and chivalric romances but the world of literary criticism, feminist critique, and social history theory. Partly in the wake of the celebrations, or countercelebrations, of the five-hundredth anniversary of the discovery of America, las Casas, surely not yet a household name, has begun to get the attention he deserves.

It is time, therefore, for the English-speaking world to be introduced to José de Acosta. That is precisely what Claudio Burgaleta does in this volume, especially by sketching the career of this brilliant man who in both Spain and the New World moved in the highest circles of Church and state. But Father Burgaleta does more. He takes us into the cultural and theological milieu in which Acosta was formed and which he in turn helped form through his writings. Among the writings, he focuses attention on the *De procuranda*, which takes us into one version of European attitudes toward the newly discovered peoples. The *De procuranda* was widely read and known in the sixteenth century, even as far as Japan, China, and the Philippines.

Acosta's is an exciting story, a story of which we have long been deprived. To it Father Burgaleta provides lucid access. We are grateful.

John W. O'Malley, S.J.
Weston Jesuit School of Theology

ACKNOWLEDGMENTS

I wish to acknowledge my gratitude to a number of people and institutions that made this book possible. First among these is the Jesuit Historical Institute in Rome for the research fellowship that they awarded me during 1994–95, which allowed me to be in residence and pursue my investigations at ARSI and the general's and IHSI libraries. The hospitality of the director of the IHSI at the time, László Szilas, S.J., the advice, assistance, and recommendations of Joaquín Domínguez, S.J., director of the Jesuit Encyclopedia project, and especially the patience, liberal photocopying privileges, and generous assistance and advice of Hugo Storni, S.J., prefect of the IHSI library, and his assistant, Dottoressa Nicoletta Basilotta, made my investigations in the Eternal City most profitable and expedient.

Boston College has also made this work possible through its magnanimous financial support by way of a University AHANA Fellowship during the four and a half years of my doctoral studies and through the assistance provided by a number of the university's constitutive parts. The Interlibrary Loan Office of the O'Neill Library could always be counted upon for obtaining elusive and obscure foreign journal articles and books. The Theology Department was, from the beginning, most flexible and accommodating in allowing me to pursue my interests, and the Acosta project in particular.

A number of scholars were most helpful during the course of my investigations, particularly in its initial moments. They often provided timely responses to my correspondence seeking counsel and orientation about various issues related with Acosta scholarship. I am thankful to Drs. Carlos Baciero, S.J., Javier Baptista, S.J., Ernesto Cavassa Canessa, S.J., Juan Guillermo Durán, Eduardo C. Fernández, S.J., Juan Luis Hoyos, S.J., Estanislao Just, S.J., Jeffrey L. Klaiber, S.J., Jesús López Gay, S.J., Mark A. Lewis, S.J., Joseph F. MacDonnell, S.J., Luis Martin, Manuel M. Marzal, S.J., Fermín del Pino Díaz,

Mario Aurelio Poli, Virginia Reinburg, Toon Van Houdt, and Juan José Villegas, S.J., for their advice and assistance.

The Society of Jesus is a large group of men, and in my eighteen years in the order I have met and lived with many Jesuits who have supported me in countless ways. But several communities and individual Jesuits deserve special recognition for their direct assistance during the writing of my doctoral dissertation that has now turned into this book. First, I am thankful to the New York Province of the Society of Jesus and to its provincial during my years as a graduate student, the Very Rev. Joseph P. Parkes, S.J. Father Parkes missioned me to graduate studies and kept the checks coming during those four and a half years. For his confidence in my academic potential and his other moral and financial support, I will always be beholden and appreciative. Special thanks too goes to Father Parkes's *socius*, Rev. Thomas E. Smith, S.J., for it was through him that I most often approached the province for various needs. These exchanges were ever cordial and expeditious.

I would also like to express my gratitude to my Jesuit friends, Daniel R. Sweeney, S.J., Philip G. Judge, S.J., Edward F. Salmon, S.J., and Michael A. Zampelli, S.J. Their assistance transporting research materials, frequent telephone calls, e-mails, and visits during these years of doctoral studies, and particularly during the hidden life that characterizes the writing phase of the dissertation, have kept me sane.

The Jesuit Community at Boston College—and in particular the Barat House Jesuit Community on the Newton Campus—has been a home, a faithful place of support remarkably forgiving of my idiosyncrasies. Thank you Barat Boys, past and present, for your love and support during the last four and a half years. Other Jesuit communities have also extended their hospitality during the research phase of this work for which I am appreciative, especially the St. Peter Canisius House of Writers in Rome, the Diego Laínez Juniorate Community in Salamanca, and the Blessed Peter Favre Community in Madrid. The Jesuit Community of St. Peter's College, my home as I prepared this volume for publication, and its leader, Rev. John F. Wrynn, S.J., have been most supportive by encouraging me in this endeavor and making it possible for me to return to Spain to continue my research on Acosta. Lastly, but not least, a word of thanks to my current community at the Jesuit novitiate in Syracuse, N.Y., and its superior, Fr. Bruce A. Maivelett, S.J., for all their support.

The young–priest graduate student does not live by research and writing alone. A very important part of the four and a half years that I researched this book have been the various faith communities I have regularly had the privilege to serve as a presider, homilist, and/or teacher. My contact with the men and women of these believing communities has confirmed and helped me keep focused on one of the principal reasons for undertaking this study of Acosta's Jesuit theological humanism, that is, to be of service, as a scholar, to the Hispanic Catholic communities in the United States by documenting and investigating *lo nuestro*, our theological heritage as Latin American Catholics. My thanks to my colleagues and students in the Spanish certificate program in pastoral studies of Loyola Marymount University and the Hispanic Catholic communities of St. Mary's Chapel, Boston College; St. Gabriel's Parish, Brighton, Mass.; and M.C.I. Norfolk, and to the coordinators of these respective programs and faith communities, Rev. Allan Figueroa Deck, S.J., Rev. Gary M. Gurtler, S.J., Rev. Alvaro Silva, and Sr. Kathleen Denevan, O.S.F.

A penultimate word of deeply felt gratitude and esteem for my readers, Francis X. Clooney, S.J., and Francis A. Sullivan, S.J. Your generosity to me during the dissertation phase of my doctoral work, but really well before this time, has never ceased to amaze me. Thank you for your long hours poring over my writing, making recommendations, correcting grammar. Thank you especially for the unique example each one of you gives of being a Jesuit priest and a scholar. My indebtedness and gratitude to my director, John W. O'Malley, S.J., even if I could articulate it, would require much more space than these acknowledgment pages allow. Thank you, John, for your ever perspicacious guidance, but above all thank you for your warm friendship. It has so very much made me feel *en buena compañía*.

In conclusion, the people of Loyola Press deserve specific mention for all their assistance in this endeavor, especially Ruth E. McGugan, Senior Editor, and Edward W. Schmidt, S.J., of *Company* magazine, for their support, encouragement, and suggestions for the dedissertationizing process that led to the book that you now have in your hands.

INTRODUCTION

A New Biography and Interpretation of Acosta's Thought

José de Acosta (1540–1600) was one of the most renowned Spanish Jesuits of his time; he was also one of the most despised. At the age of twelve he ran away from home and entered the Society of Jesus at Salamanca. Before realizing his dream of going to the Indies to save souls, he had acquired a reputation as a fine sacred orator, theologian, and playwright. In 1571 he disembarked in Peru, where he would minister for close to fifteen years. As preacher, theologian, consultor to the Inquisition, and confidant of bishops and viceroys he became a luminary of Andean colonial society.

In 1576, when Acosta was the second provincial superior of the Jesuits in Peru, he made a decision of profound importance for the Society of Jesus and the Church of Latin America. He accepted, from Viceroy Francisco de Toledo, the reduction, or mission, at Juli on the Peruvian shores of Lake Titicaca to minister to the native peoples of that area. Juli became the model for the more famous Jesuit reductions of Paraguay.

However, Don José is best known for his books. He wrote about the flora, fauna, and culture of the peoples of the Indies as well as their evangelization. His American trilogy, the *De Procuranda Indorum Salute*,[1] the *Historia Natural y Moral de las Indias*,[2] and the *Doctrina Christiana y Catecismo para Instrucción de los Indios*,[3] earned him the title of the "Pliny of the New World."[4] Before his death, Acosta's books about the Indies had been published in Dutch, French, German, Italian, Latin, and Spanish editions.

In 1587 Don José returned to Spain and became involved in the internal governance of his order and in the intrigue of Philip II's court. In 1592, serving as the agent of the Spanish king, he persuaded Pope Clement VIII to order the superior general of the Jesuits, Claudio Aquaviva, to convoke a general congregation of the order. It was Philip's hope that this international meeting of Jesuits would back his plans to exert more control over the Society of Jesus in his domains. The *memorialista* affair, as this crisis is also known, failed to curtail Aquaviva's power over the Spanish Jesuits. For his part in the affair, Acosta earned the derision of his brother Jesuits attending the Fifth General Congregation and won the esteem and loyalty of Philip II. With the monarch's support and against the wishes of Fr. General Aquaviva, Don José was named superior of the Jesuits at Valladolid and later rector at Salamanca, where he died on February 15, 1600.

The preceding highlights of Acosta's life reveal an energetic, talented, and morally complex individual. Don José exemplifies many of the facets of the proverbial Renaissance man. His interests and activities seemed to know no bounds. They encompassed the literary and the scientific, the religious and the political, the high profile of court life and the solitude and stability of the writer's room and desk. The accomplishments of this remarkable colonial figure have been studied by a number of scholars from a wide variety of disciplines.

Articles and books abound about Acosta the diplomat,[5] the economist,[6] the geophysicist,[7] the natural scientist,[8] the philosopher of nature,[9] the proto-evolutionist,[10] the pedagogue,[11] the jurist,[12] the scholar of Amerindian tongues,[13] and the precursor to such varied topics and fields as the modern Latin American novel,[14] travel writers,[15] inculturation,[16] ethnography,[17] and liberation theology.[18] Yet despite this dizzying array of articles and books on the contributions of Acosta, his life awaits a biography that will do him justice.[19] Building on the existing foreign-language biographies of Acosta, especially León Lopetegui's *El Padre José de Acosta, S.J., y las misiones*, the first part of this book is such an attempt. It is the most complete Acosta biography that exists in English.

The second part of this book seeks to correct certain shortcomings in the studies of Acosta's thought that are detailed in the first appendix. It brings greater clarity to Don José's way of doing theology by taking into account a number of neglected characteristics of his thought. In the past, scholars have either focused on the missiological content of Acosta's writings or its humanist form, but have failed to understand that in Acosta's thought these and other characteristics, such as his Jesuit spirituality, comprise a whole. By arguing that Acosta's theological writings are best classified as Jesuit theological humanism, it situates his thought in the context of his day and both identifies similarities and dissimilarities with other sixteenth-century theological movements. Informed by my reconstruction of Don José's life and times, particularly his intellectual and religious formation, and by examining his American theological works on their own terms, I describe these neglected characteristics of Acosta's thought.

I have coined the term *Jesuit theological humanism* as an instrument of exploration to account for these neglected characteristics. As I conceive it, Jesuit theological humanism is composed of a highly rhetorical style that is concerned with moving the audience's heart to work on behalf of the salvation and evangelization of the Amerindians. It employs both the methods and sources of humanist theology and of scholasticism as well as a ministerial spirituality that is characteristically Ignatian. Chapters five through seven provide a lengthier explanation of Jesuit theological humanism and point out its similarities and differences with sixteenth-century theological movements it resembles.

Sources

As part of the research for this biography, I worked at archives in Italy and Spain since not everything that Acosta wrote has been published or is available in contemporary editions. I examined some of Acosta's books not available in modern editions,[20] some of his correspondence with the Jesuit generals, and a few letters from and to Acosta's parents from Frs. General Laínez and Borja.[21] All of these were located at the Roman Archives of the Society of Jesus (ARSI).

The correspondence written by Don José to which I paid close attention includes various quarterly letters to the Jesuit superior general in Rome that he wrote when he was a scholastic, or young Jesuit in training, at Segovia (1559)[22] and Alcalá (1559–67).[23] These quarterly letters were required to be sent to the superior general in Rome by the local superiors of Jesuit houses and reported the most important events that had occurred in the community since the last quarterly letter.

I was also interested in two letters[24] written by Acosta to Fr. General Claudio Aquaviva, S.J., around the time that Don José played a crucial role in the convocation of the Fifth General Congregation of the order as the agent of Philip II and against the wishes of Aquaviva. As we shall see in chapter four and in appendix one, these two letters raise some questions about the way that Acosta's motivations for aiding Philip II in the convocation of the congregation have been interpreted in the past.

The research phase of this book also took me to the Biblioteca General de la Universidad de Salamanca to investigate several volumes of Acosta's sermons[25] and the unfinished manuscript of his last theological work, a commentary on the psalms.[26] Acosta died as rector of the Jesuit college in that city in 1600 and according to various Jesuit bibliographies[27] many of his papers remained at the college until 1767. At that time, the year of the first expulsion of the Society from Spain, they were transferred to the library of the University of Salamanca. Sadly, many of the original manuscripts of Acosta's works, especially the many sermons he delivered during his years in Peru, have not survived.

Felicitously, the occasion of the fifth centenary of the Columbian event has led the Consejo Superior de Investigaciones Científicas (CSIC) of the Spanish government to edit a number of excellent Latin-Spanish translations of some of the most important texts of the colonial period. These have been published in its series *Corpus Hispanorum Pace* (CHP), and among them are several of Acosta's major works.[28] The CHP edition of the *De Procuranda* is particularly useful since it reproduces the original text in its entirety before deletions were made by the censors of the Inquisition. I have made use of these critical editions for my work.

LIST OF ABBREVIATIONS

AGI	Archivo General de Indias, Seville, Spain
AHN	Archivo Histórico Nacional, Madrid, Spain
AHSI	*Archivum Historicum Societatis Iesu*
ARSI	Archivum Romanum Societatis Iesu, Rome, Italy
BAC	Biblioteca de Autores Cristianos
BAE	Biblioteca de Autores Españoles
CEHILA	Comisión de Estudios de Historia de la Iglesia en América Latina
CELAM	Consejo Episcopal Latinoamericano
CEP	Centro de Estudios y Publicaciones, Lima, Peru
CHP	*Series Corpus Hispanorum Pace*
CSIC	Consejo Superior de Investigaciones Científicas
IHSI	Institutum Historicum Societatis Iesu, Rome, Italy
Lima III	Third Provincial Council of Lima, 1582–1583

GLOSSARY

a la española Literally, in the Spanish style or way. It refers to the mindset prevalent in Spain during the Early Modern Period that, because of Spain's status as a Catholic world power, its customs and way of doing things were better than and deserved preeminence over the customs of other nations or peoples.

accommodation A central characteristic of the Jesuit way of proceeding, that is, adapting Christianity to different times, places, persons, and circumstances so that it is not in conflict with non-Christian cultures. This approach is based on the insight of St. Ignatius of Loyola expressed in the Spiritual Exercises that God deals directly with his creatures and accommodates his way of dealing with us to our capacities.

Acosta's American trilogy The three books written by Acosta while in the New World: *De Procuranda Indorum Salute, Historia Natural y Moral de las Indias*, and *De Doctrina Christiana*.

altiplano The Andean highlands of Bolivia and Peru.

alumbrados Literally, illuminists. A group of men and women condemned by the Inquisition as heretics in sixteenth-century Spain both for their morality and theological positions. Among other things, they advocated the superiority of their faith and piety that was said to be directly inspired by the Holy Spirit and disparaged the role of the Roman Catholic Church, its sacraments, and other forms of external religious observance.

Angelic Doctor A title often given to St. Thomas Aquinas.

Angelus A traditional Catholic prayer recited at noon honoring the Blessed Virgin Mary and recalling the words spoken to her by the Archangel Gabriel according to the Gospel of Luke.

Assistancy In the Society of Jesus, the jurisdictional unit comprising a number of provinces that often share a common language. The Father Assistant was the Jesuit priest in Rome charged by the superior general of the order with attending to the business of a given assistancy or group of provinces.

auto sacramental An allegorical religious play.

auto-de-fe A public religious ceremony in which those convicted by the Inquisition had their sentences decreed.

ayllu The basic kin unit of Andean social structure.

Aymara An Indian language spoken in Peru.

Blessed Sacrament The name given by Catholics to the Sacrament of the Eucharist when it is reserved, that is, when the bread or host that has been consecrated at the Mass is kept for adoration and for the communion or consumption of those who for serious reason cannot attend mass. The host is kept in a tabernacle or special place of reposition in the church. The tabernacle is indicated by a solitary perpetually burning candle that is kept nearby.

brother A nonordained member of the Jesuit order who is not a scholastic. Brothers were also referred to as temporal coadjutors.

cacique The Spanish word for an Andean ethnic lord, or *kuraka*.

cases of conscience The matter of casuistry, that is, the study of individual moral dilemmas or cases to assist the confessor in his role as judge and doctor of the soul. The study of such cases was the origins of the field of moral theology and it sought to clarify complicated moral issues by sorting out competing moral obligations in such a way that the context of ethical behavior, that is, time, places, and circumstances, was taken into account.

catedrático The holder of chair at a Spanish university. At the University of Alcalá in the Early Modern Period, these chairs were associated with a particular school of thought and were awarded for a fixed period of time on the basis of a competitive process. The holder of the chair was expected to deliver lectures in the tradition of the particular school of thought that he represented, for example, Scotist, nominalist, Thomist.

chicha Andean alcoholic beverage, usually made of fermented corn.

Christianitas The basic beliefs and practices of Christianity common in the Middle Ages and the Early Modern Period such as the catechism, the sacraments, the spiritual and corporal works of mercy, popular devotions of a personal and communal nature both public and private such as prayers, processions, and the veneration of images and statues.

chuño Freeze-dried potatoes commonly consumed in the Andes.

clerks regular Religious orders of men who are neither monastic nor mendicant and who follow a particular rule, but in externals closely resemble the clergy of a diocese or parish priests.

comisario An office that existed in the Spanish Assistancy of the Society of Jesus during the generalates of St. Ignatius and Diego Laínez. The comisario was appointed by the superior general of the Society and served as his intermediary between the king and the provincials. The office functioned as the national provincials or presidents of provincial conferences in the order today. It was abolished during the generalate of St. Francisco de Borja much to the chagrin of the king and many Spanish Jesuits.

confessor The name used to refer to a priest who administers the sacrament of penance on a regular basis to the same individual.

confraternity Religious associations of laypeople that had their origins in the Middle Ages and were initially modeled on the mendicant orders from which they drew inspiration and guidance. They would proliferate throughout Christian Europe, the Americas, and Asia pursuing the sanctification of their members through a variety of religious observances and the practice of the spiritual and corporal works of mercy.

congregation of procurators In the Society of Jesus, an international meeting of delegates chosen at provincial congregations to represent the Jesuit provinces from throughout the world at a meeting regularly held at the Jesuit headquarters in Rome. The purpose of the meeting was to inform the superior general of the state of the Society and to determine whether it was expedient to convoke a general congregation of the order.

Constitutions The ten-part document written by Ignatius of Loyola and collaborators, from 1540 until the time of his death in 1556, governing the organization and spirit of the Jesuit order. It was approved by the First General Congregation of the order in 1558.

consultor In the Society of Jesus, the canonical advisors to a Jesuit superior appointed by the superior immediately over said superior. In case of the superior general, the consultors are elected by a general congregation.

Contemplatio ad Amorem The Contemplation to Obtain Divine Love. The final meditation exercise in the Spiritual Exercises of St. Ignatius of Loyola. In this meditation Ignatius has the person praying contemplate how God is at work for his or her welfare throughout the chain of being that is creation, from inanimate objects through spiritual beings to God's very self.

contemplative in action A term explaining the goal of the spirituality of the Jesuit. He is to be a man who is able to find God in all things because he is attuned to the action of God in the world.

conversos Spanish Jews or Muslims who had recently converted to Christianity. Also referred to as New Christians.

corporal works of mercy Assistance rendered to alleviate material suffering in imitation of the ministry of Jesus, e.g., feeding the hungry, clothing the naked, etc.

corregidor The crown-appointed official charged with the administration of a civil province. In Latin America, this meant that he was the royal official charged with overseeing the native peoples in the countryside.

Council of the Indies The royal council founded in 1524 and invested with the authority to administer the affairs of the Spanish crown in the Americas.

After the king himself, it was the highest legislative and administrative authority for Spain's American Empire.

criollo Someone of pure-bred Hispanic ancestry born in the Americas.

daily order The schedule followed on a regular basis by members of a Jesuit community or house.

De Auxiliis **controversy** A theological debate that raged in Catholicism from the late sixteenth century through the early seventeenth century that pitted the Dominicans against the Jesuits concerning free will, predestination, and God's sovereignty. The central question but by no means the only one in this debate was how to reconcile human freedom with the universal knowledge and power of God. The Jesuits defended the freedom of the human person in responding to God's grace, while the Dominicans safeguarded the sovereignty of God by emphasizing the impotence of human beings before the power of the Creator. The debate came to preoccupy more than just theologians and led to heated and acrimonious public accusations of heresy by both parties and their supporters throughout the Catholic world. The matter was abated with the decision of Pope Paul V in 1607 to impose silence about the issue on both orders.

discernment of spirits The ancient Christian practice of prayerfully scrutinizing one's interior movements to determine God's presence in one's soul. St. Ignatius of Loyola placed this discipline at the center of his way to God and formulated rules for such a prayerful scrutiny based on his spiritual journey that he included in his Spiritual Exercises.

Distinguished Doctor A title often given to Jesuit theologian and philosopher Francisco Suárez.

doctrina An Indian parish.

doctrinero Someone entrusted with the Christian religious education of the native peoples, sometimes a priest but not necessarily.

eloquentia perfecta Literally, perfect eloquence. This refers to one of the hallmarks of Jesuit education borrowed from the humanists' emphasis on elegant writing and convincing rhetoric.

encomendero Spanish colonist who received a grant of land and the charge of looking after the spiritual welfare of a number of native peoples living on the land grant from the crown. Tribute or labor services were exacted from these Indians by the encomendero in lieu of the "services" rendered by the encomendero.

encomienda The grant of land and of the native peoples living on that land made by the crown and received by the *encomendero*.

evangelization The spread of the gospel of Jesus Christ through preaching, catechizing, art, or other means.

examination of conscience A form of prayer proposed by St. Ignatius of Loyola in the Spiritual Exercises involving the review of one's day to discern God's presence in it and become aware of one's resistances and rejection of that presence.

externs The term used in Jesuit documents to refer to all those who were not members of the Jesuit order.

final vows In the Society of Jesus, the profession of solemn vows of poverty, chastity, obedience and full incorporation into the order with the grade or status of a brother, spiritual coadjutor, or professed father. This occurs at the end of the third probation or tertianship after the Jesuit's spiritual and academic preparation of over ten years has been completed.

first vows In the Society of Jesus, vows of poverty, chastity, obedience, and to be incorporated into the Jesuit order according to the grade that the superior general decides at the end of the Jesuit course of studies, pronounced at the end of the two-year novitiate. In the Society of Jesus these vows are perpetually binding on those pronouncing them but not on the order; thus, they do not expire after a period of time, as in most other religious communities. At the end of his training the Jesuit pronounces them again after his final status or grade in the order has been determined by the superior general.

formation The term used in religious orders to refer to the general period and program of training of its recruits.

fray Literally, brother. A title given to friars of certain mendicant religious orders, such as the Franciscans and Dominicans.

general confession A pious practice promoted by the Jesuits of reviewing one's life and confessing all of one's sin on a frequent basis with the end of experiencing the greatness of God's love and forgiveness over and against one's infidelity and sins.

general congregation In the Society of Jesus, the highest governing body in the Jesuit order. It is composed of elected delegates from Jesuit provinces throughout the world and the governing provincial of those provinces, in addition to the council of the governing superior general of the order. General congregations meet to either elect a new superior general upon the death of the existing one or to deal with matters of grave import in the order. Since the founding of the Jesuits there have been only thirty-four of these international gatherings.

gravitas See *patres graviores*.

huaca A native Andean god that was often associated with nature and one's ancestors such as hills, waters, caves, stones, ancestor mummies, etc.

the Institute More generally a synonym for the Society of Jesus, but more specifically the foundational documents of the Jesuit order such as The Formula of the Institute and the Constitutions.

Jesuit theological humanism A term coined by the author of this volume to account for the hybrid theological style and method of José de Acosta, S.J. It is composed of a highly rhetorical style that is concerned with moving the audience's heart to work on behalf of the salvation and evangelization of the Amerindians. It employs both the methods and sources of humanist theology and of scholasticism, as well as a ministerial spirituality that is characteristically Ignatian.

juros Annuities paid by the Spanish crown for loans it had taken out.

kuraka Andean ethnic lord.

Lima III The Third Provincial Council of Lima (1582–1583) attended by most of the bishops of Spanish-controlled South America at the time, also known as the Trent of the Americas because of its reformist agenda similar to the European ecumenical council.

limpieza de sangre Literally, purity of blood. The freedom from any taint of Semitic blood or ancestry.

loci theologici Literally, places (sources) of theology. The important writings of Christianity and the thought of important Christian thinkers used by theologians to support their opinions, for example, the Bible, the writings of the Fathers of the Church, the decrees of Church councils, etc.

memorial Memorandum.

memorialistas The name given to a group of approximately thirty Spanish Jesuits primarily from the Jesuit provinces of Castile and Toledo who from 1586 to 1589 wrote often anonymous memoriales to Philip II and the Inquisition complaining of the chaotic state of affairs in the Society of Jesus. They blamed this state of affairs on the governance of the superior general of the order, Claudio Aquaviva. The memoranda written by these Jesuits played an important part in Philip II's decision to pressure Pope Clement VIII to order Aquaviva to convoke, against the Society of Jesus' wishes, the Fifth General Congregation of the Jesuit order to investigate his tenure as superior general. The memorialistas are also known as *perturbatores*.

mendicant orders Religious orders founded in the Middle Ages with the aim of imitating the itinerant preaching ministry and lifestyle of Jesus and his apostles. Most famous among these orders are the Franciscans and the Dominicans.

meseta Plateau.

mestizo A descendant of mixed Indian-white parents.

minister In the Society of Jesus, the Jesuit charged with the material welfare of the members of a given Jesuit house and the house's temporal administration.

ministries of the Word of God Among the early Jesuits, the broad understanding of proclaiming the gospel that included various forms of discourse, including preaching, lecturing, giving the Spiritual Exercises, publishing books, engaging in spiritual conversation and spiritual direction or guidance, teaching the catechism, popular missions, etc.

missiology The branch of theology that deals with questions related to the Church's mission of evangelization. Traditionally, missiology was concerned with questions that arose in the Church's missionary activities. Contemporary missiology is more globally concerned with questions of inculturating or presenting the gospel message in ways that are relevant to different cultures.

mita The colonial forced labor institution providing rotations of native laborers to different endeavors, perhaps the most famous and infamous being the silver mines in the outskirts of present-day Potosí, Bolivia.

modus parisiensis The pedagogical method or way followed by the University of Paris and adopted by the Jesuit order in its schools. Among other elements, it involved an orderly progression of courses and subjects that built and presupposed each other's content and included a number of academic exercises such as lectures, disputations, repetitions, etc., to facilitate the students' mastery of the matter.

monastic orders Religious orders founded as early as antiquity which sought to imitate the evangelical counsels of Christ through a perpetual commitment to a particular community or monastery. In the West, the most famous of these monastic orders is the Benedictines.

mystical theology The term used by Jerónimo Nadal, S.J. (1507–80), Ignatius of Loyola's right-hand man in explaining the Constitutions and Jesuit spirit throughout Europe, for the theology that should characterize the Society of Jesus. This theology would be *spiritu, corde, practice*, that is, inspired by the Holy Spirit, from the heart, and pastorally useful.

natural philosophy The branch of Aristotelian philosophy that dealt with questions related to material objects and movement. Natural philosophy was the forerunner of modern science.

nominalism A type of scholastic philosophy and theology that was inspired by the thought of the Franciscan, William of Ockham. Among other positions, the nominalists were concerned with safeguarding the sovereignty of God and like the Scotists defended the superiority of the will over the intellect. In contrast to the realist, or Scotist, school though, the nominalists rejected the existence of universals and saw them as terms that signify individual things.

novice In the Society of Jesus, a member of the order undergoing a two-year program of probation and spiritual formation before being admitted to first vows of perpetual poverty, chastity, obedience, and openness to whatever grade in the group the superior general selected him for at the end of his training. After the two-year novitiate, or noviceship, a novice is received in the order as either a scholastic or a brother.

novitiate The building that houses the novices during their two-year period of training; also, the program of training itself.

nuncio The name given to the pope's ambassador.

Open Thomism of the First School of Salamanca A termed coined by the Spanish historian of theology, Melquíades Andrés Martín, to describe the Thomism of the generation of Dominicans of the Convent of San Esteban at the University of Salamanca from 1526 to 1580. Initiated by Fray Francisco de Vitoria, O.P., this type of Thomism is called "open" because it was characterized by its flexibility and openness to the critiques that humanists had made of the Angelic doctor and a willingness to depart from his opinions when they thought it was merited.

patres graviores Literally, weighty fathers. Term used to refer to the oldest professed Jesuits of a given community or province who by virtue of their seniority composed the membership of provincial congregations. Often their virtue and prudence, or *gravitas*, merited their opinions and counsel great respect.

Patronato Real The authority granted by late fifteenth-century and sixteenth-century popes to Spanish monarchs to oversee all aspects of the Church in their domains such as the appointment of bishops, the convocation of provincial councils, the collection of Church taxes, etc., in exchange for the crown's protection, propagation, and financing of the Catholic faith and Church particularly in its foreign possessions.

perturbatores See *memorialistas*.

popular missions Programs of preaching, catechesis, confession, and reform or establishment of confraternities that involved several missioners who were often priests. These missions originated in the sixteenth century and at first took place in the countryside. In the seventeenth century they were extended to cities. Protestants also adopted them, and much later would often call them "revivals."

positive theology A term coined by John Major of the University of Paris in the early sixteenth century referring to the study of the Bible and the Fathers of the Church for use in preaching and practical instruction in living the Christian life.

probation Another term used to refer to the training period in religious orders. In the Society of Jesus, reference is made to the first, second, and third probations. The first probation corresponds to the first days in the novitiate, the second probation to the period including most of the two-year novitiate, and the third probation, or tertianship, to the final period of intense spiritual preparation before full incorporation into the Society.

procurator In the Society of Jesus, the elected delegate from a province to a congregation of procurators. However, this term is also more generally applied to a Jesuit who served as a business agent of either a house or school or who represented the order at a given royal court.

professed father In the Society of Jesus, a Jesuit priest who has finished his training and has been selected to form part of the group within the order that in addition to the vows of poverty, chastity, and obedience, vow special obedience to the pope in matters of the missions for which he may select them. It is from this group distinguished in virtue and learning that the religious superiors of the Jesuit order are selected.

professed house A Jesuit community or house composed only of the professed members of the order. Unlike other Jesuit communities composed of members who were not professed, professed houses were required by the rules of the order to subsist only from alms and to have no fixed revenues. Very few of these communities ever actually existed.

provincial In the Society of Jesus, the priest appointed by the superior general in Rome to govern a province or national jurisdictional unit of the order for a once renewable term of three years.

provincial congregation In the sixteenth-century Society of Jesus, the meeting of a given province's professed fathers convoked by order of the superior general. Such meetings usually had a very restricted agenda that involved electing a delegate to a general congregation or congregation of procurators held at the Jesuit order's headquarters in Rome.

provincial council A meeting of Roman Catholic bishops from a given ecclesiastical province or jurisdiction headed by a metropolitan or archbishop. Usually the agenda of such meetings involved the drafting of canons or ecclesiastical decrees to deal with issues or problems common to the assembled bishops of the region.

Puquina An Indian language spoken in Peru.

quaestio disputata Literally, a disputed question. The disputed questions were published summaries of disputations or debates about philosophical and theological issues frequently utilized in the pedagogical method of scholasticism. The professor summarized his opinion on a disputed issue taking into account the positions expressed by his students who had been assigned the role of defenders of a given position and objectors to it during a given disputation or debate.

quarterly letters Letters written four times per year to the superior general in Rome from Jesuit houses throughout the world describing the state of these communities and their activities. Later the frequency of this correspondence was reduced.

Quechua An Indian language spoken in Peru.

quipu A knotted cord used by the Incas to store numerical and other information. Also rendered as *kipu*.

Ratio Studiorum The document, first officially promulgated by the superior general of the Society of Jesus in 1599, detailing the program of studies to be followed in Jesuit schools throughout the world.

rector In the Society of Jesus, the religious superior of a Jesuit house, usually appointed by the superior general in Rome for a once-renewable term of three years.

reducción Literally, reduction. Hispanic-style villages composed of resettled native peoples who had been nomadic or scattered so as to more efficiently govern them and convert them to Christianity.

refectory The dining room of a Jesuit house.

Roman curia The members of the pope's court who assist him in administering the affairs of the Church.

sacramental ministries The administration, in most cases by an ordained minister, of one of the seven sacraments of the Roman Catholic Church, i.e., Baptism, Confirmation, Eucharist, Confession, Holy Orders, Matrimony, Holy Anointing.

scholastic In the Society of Jesus, a member of the order who has completed the novitiate or noviceship, made first vows of poverty, chastity, and obedience, and continues his formation as a student of the humanities, philosophy, and theology, before being ordained a priest and finally being definitively received in the order as a professed father or spiritual coadjutor.

scholasticism The type of philosophy and theology with origins in the schools of the Middle Ages but which continued into the modern period. This type of theology and philosophy was both characterized by certain common methods of instruction and argumentation such as the disputations and *quaestio* and a variety of schools of thought such as the followers of St. Bonaventure, St. Thomas Aquinas, Duns Scotus, William of Ockham, Siger of Brabant, etc.

Schoolmen A term used in theology and philosophy to refer to the practitioners of the various forms of scholasticism. These philosophers and theologians engaged in their academic pursuits in the medieval schools associated with the various religious orders of the time that developed into the modern university.

Scotism A type of scholastic theology and philosophy that followed the thought of the Franciscan Duns Scotus. This school of thought emphasized the superiority of the will over the intellect in contrast to the thought of St. Thomas Aquinas, for example. The school of Scotus is often referred to as Realism because it held for a formal objective distinction to explain universals.

sermonario A book composed of sermons.

soteriology The branch of theology that deals with questions related to salvation.

spiritual coadjutor In the Society of Jesus, a Jesuit priest who has been definitively received in the order and made his final profession or vows but who has not been selected to form part of the group in the order called the professed fathers.

Spiritual Exercises A manual containing a series of meditations and other forms of prayer on the life of Christ organized into four periods roughly corresponding to a chronological week written by St. Ignatius of Loyola. The purpose of the meditations is conversion and commitment to Christ and is inspired by the conversion of St. Ignatius. The Exercises form the heart of Ignatian or Jesuit spirituality.

spiritual works of mercy Assistance rendered to alleviate non-material forms of suffering in imitation of Jesus, e.g., instructing the ignorant, comforting the despondent, etc.

studium In the Order of Preachers, or Dominicans, a convent with a program of academic studies for friars in formation.

summae A comprehensive type of writing common to scholastic philosophy and theology treating a wide-ranging set of issues in a particular discipline and arranged following the *quaestio* format.

superior general In certain religious communities, the religious superior that has general jurisdiction or governance over all other superiors in the order. In religious communities of men, such as the Society of Jesus, the superior general is more popularly referred to as "Father General."

Suscipe A prayer of thanksgiving and offering of oneself to God composed by St. Ignatius of Loyola and contained in the Contemplation to Obtain Divine Love of his Spiritual Exercises. Commonly referred to as the "Take Lord Receive" prayer, St. Ignatius's most famous prayer.

temporal coadjutor See brother.

tertianship The final stage of a Jesuit's program of formation before he is fully admitted into the Society and granted final vows in the order. This usually occurs after the Jesuit's program of studies has been completed and it typically lasts for nine months. It is also known as the third probation. Its purpose is to rekindle the Jesuit's spiritual life after many years of study through a program of study of the order's foundational documents, repeating some of the experiences of the novitiate, and the making once again of the full Spiritual Exercises.

theological anthropology The branch of theology that deals with questions and issues related to the relationship between the human person and God, especially questions involving the relationship between God's action or grace and the freedom of human nature.

Thomism The school of scholasticism that followed the theological method of St. Thomas Aquinas.

Vicariato Real The theory propagated by Spanish monarchs commencing with Philip II and characteristic of the crown's ecclesiastical policies of the seventeenth century. It extended the authority and power of the *patronato* received from late fifteenth-century and early sixteenth-century popes from a limited papal concession to a vicariate of unlimited authority and powers over all types of ecclesial matters and issues concerning the crown's foreign possessions.

viceroy The royal official that exercised supreme authority within the jurisdiction of the viceroyalty as the direct representative of the Spanish crown. He was both the chief military and civil officer and had jurisdiction over justice, finances, and the *patronato*.

viceroyalty The largest civil and military jurisdiction of the Spanish Empire, composed of provinces. In the Americas, there were two viceroyalties: the Viceroyalty of New Spain, comprising all the provinces north of Panama and the provinces of the coast of Venezuela and the Philippines, and the Viceroyalty of Peru, comprising all the provinces in South America controlled by Spain.

visitation A formal tour of inspection carried out by a Jesuit priest named by the Jesuit superior general in Rome and possessing wide-ranging powers to correct abuses in the houses visited.

visitor The Jesuit priest named by the superior general in Rome to undertake the visitation of a given Jesuit house, province, mission, or region.

Vulgate The fourth-century translation of the Bible done by St. Jerome and considered inaccurate by some humanists and Protestant reformers of the sixteenth century.

way of proceeding The term used by Jesuits to describe their style or way of doing things.

Part One

José de Acosta

THE MAN AND HIS TIMES

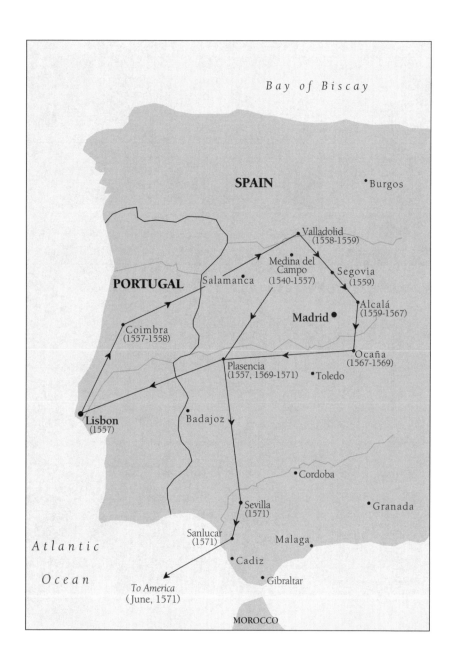

Bay of Biscay

SPAIN

•Burgos

Valladolid
(1558-1559)

Medina del
Campo
(1540-1557)

Segovia
(1559)

PORTUGAL

Salamanca

Alcalá
(1559-1567)

Madrid •

Coimbra
(1557-1558)

Ocaña
(1567-1569)

Plasencia
(1557, 1569-1571)

•Toledo

Lisbon
(1557)

•Badajoz

•Cordoba

Sevilla
(1571)

•Granada

Sanlucar
(1571)

Malaga•

•Cadiz

Atlantic

Ocean

To America
(June, 1571)

•Gibraltar

MOROCCO

José de Acosta's travels in Spain and Portugal: 1540–1571

CHAPTER 1

The Genesis of Acosta's Jesuit Vocation
1540–1552

The Medina del Campo of Acosta's Early Life

José de Acosta was born in the prosperous Castilian commercial center of Medina del Campo, northeast of Salamanca and just southwest of Valladolid, in 1540. Medina was an important center of commerce.[1] Its privileged geographical position—it was at the crossroads of north-south and east-west routes on the Castilian *meseta*—had made it an ideal place to hold trade fairs since the late Middle Ages. The town prospered from exporting raw materials, especially wool to Flanders, Italy, and France, and importing such agricultural products and manufactured goods as Baltic wheat and Dutch naval supplies and textiles. Medina's trade fairs were the biggest in Spain at midcentury and saw people from all over the peninsula and indeed all of Europe. Medina enjoyed economic and demographic ascendancy throughout most of the sixteenth century until about 1575 and reached a population of approximately 20,000.

The thriving trade fairs of the sixteenth century meant that Medina was a cosmopolitan place by early modern standards. Merchants and others came from throughout northern Spain and as far away as Portugal, Flanders, France, and Italy to buy and sell their wares. Among the people who made their way to the fairs of Medina were gangs of thieves, vagrants, charlatans, and prostitutes who hoped to eke out a living from the wealth produced by the legitimate businesses of the town. There was always a certain amount of poverty in Medina. Parish records of 1561 give evidence that some of the poorer areas of the city away from the Plaza Mayor and around the perimeter of the town wall considered as much as ten percent of their approximately five hundred parishioners as poor. The vast majority of these poor people, eighty-eight percent in 1561, were single mothers and their children. They were usually widowed, but they also included the unmarried.

An example of a poor widowed mother was the *conversa* Catalina Alvarez de Yepes, who had come to Medina from Arévalo in the hope of finding work in the shadow of the prosperous trade fairs. Catalina lived in a poor neighborhood in the northern part of the city near the Santiago Gate and tried to earn a living as a seamstress. She did not seem to have much success making ends meet for her family, and we know that from 1559 to 1563 she had to turn over her son, Juan, to the Colegio de la Doctrina, a type of orphanage and one of the town's many organisms devoted to relief of the poor and sick. Juan would later enroll in the Jesuit college of Medina and eventually would make his mark on the world as St. John of the Cross.[2]

The Castile where José grew up was the largest and most prosperous of several kingdoms on the Iberian peninsula.[3] It stretched from Galicia in the northwest to the lands of the former Muslim kingdom of Granada in the southeast, and it also included Castile's extensive possessions in the Americas and the Philippines. The lord and master of this formidable dominion at the time of Acosta's birth was the Hapsburg, Charles I of Spain, Charles V of the Holy Roman Empire. He reigned from 1517 to 1556.

In 1540, the year of José's birth, Charles I's possessions encompassed not only Castile and her foreign possessions in the Americas and Asia but also the rest of the Iberian peninsula excluding Portugal, present-day Belgium, the Netherlands, Liechtenstein, parts of southeastern France, Germany, the Czech Republic, Slovakia, the northern regions of the Balkan peninsula, Austria, Hungary, several cities in North Africa, Sardinia, Southern Italy, Sicily, and most of northwestern Italy. While Charles's empire was international, Castilians and their culture played a prominent role in the life of the monarch and his court.

Charles chose only Spanish confessors, and Spanish nobility was admitted to the Burgundian Order of the Golden Fleece and to other foreign honors. The official language of his entourage was Castilian, which he considered "so noble that it should be learned and understood by all Christian peoples."[4] This meant that Castile and her people became protagonists on the European stage as they obeyed a monarch whose political interests extended throughout the continent. Thus the Castile in which José was born and reared was the head of all the realms of the Austrias, as the Hapsburgs were known in the slowly emerging Spanish nation.

The international protagonism afforded Castile by its monarch was a mixed blessing since with it came the heavy burden of financing the emperor's extensive European military campaigns. By 1534, despite Castile's contributions to the imperial coffers from the precious metals coming from Bolivia and Mexico, the sale of aristocratic titles, the sale of public offices, the sale of royal lands and those belonging to the military orders, and all the forms of taxes on laity and clergy alike, there was a constant and mounting deficit. Charles was faced with no alternative but to borrow, especially from German and Italian bankers, who charged ever-increasing rates of interest. The consequence of this policy was that foreigners came to exercise more and more control of the Castilian economy on whose security the loans were made.

During Charles's reign, German financiers bought offices, lands, and *juros*, or annuities, yielding a yearly interest of seven percent and paid out of ordinary royal revenues, and were granted administration of three military orders and of the mercury mines at Almadén. Castile came to be viewed by foreign financiers less as a nation in which to invest and more as one from which American bullion could be easily acquired through trade. It developed a massive balance of payment problem. The kingdom's economy at the time of Acosta's birth resembled the charlatans from the great Spanish picaresque novel *Lazarillo de Tormes*: the outer trappings were those of world-class empire, but underneath, the garments of the Castilian economy were severely tattered and in disrepair.

But if the macroeconomic situation of Castile was in the long run bleak, the microeconomics of the kingdom made many very wealthy. Between 1530 and 1580 Castile saw its population increase by some fifty percent. This meant that there was a rise in demand for commodities, especially food. There was greater pressure on land use and on grain supplies; Spain became an importer of wheat. The need for food and manufactured products in America also increased demand. This, coupled with the influx of American gold and silver into the kingdom, saw a tremendous increase in prices in the first half of the sixteenth century. For the merchants, this period of inflation was a godsend. They came to have more cash to invest in trade, and manufacturers had more money to invest in production. Profits rose with this increased trade and production; and interest rates fell because of the greater amount of money in circulation. A boom hit Castile with three principal centers of economic activity: Granada, Seville, and Valladolid.

The religious panorama of Medina in the sixteenth century was no less impressive than its prosperous economic face and its wretched poverty and sanitation. Medina could easily have laid claim to the title of the Rome of Castile, for it enjoyed a larger number of clergy and religious than was typical in the region at the time. In 1591 there were over 136 diocesan priests in over 20 parishes, 220 male religious in eight religious foundations, and 254 female religious in seven convents.

Christianitas, or the typical early modern way of being a Christian with its emphasis on religious practices, especially the corporal works of mercy, was alive and well at Medina. The various guilds of the town had organized some sixty religious confraternities for the mutual religious and corporal assistance of their members. But there were other confraternities whose focus was the needs of the neighbor, particularly the sick and the homeless. All of the city's parishes and many of its male religious houses had Confraternities of the Blessed Sacrament that "offered hospitality" to the poor and the infirm.

Lay philanthropy in Medina was not limited to the confraternities. The town's economic prosperity in the sixteenth century created the possibility for a number of her citizens to distinguish themselves in this area. There were at least three hospitals founded and maintained by the beneficence of wealthy merchants. And as we shall see, it would be these prosperous merchants who would bring the Jesuits to Medina and see to it that they remained permanently by founding a college in the town.

The Acosta Family

It was to one of these prosperous and philanthropic Medina merchant families that José de Acosta Porres was born. His parents were Don Antonio de Acosta and Doña Ana de Porres. The Acostas probably lived near the commercial center of the town, the Plaza Mayor, in the parish of San Antolín, of San Facundo, or of San Juan de Sardón, where over half of the town's merchant elite and nobility lived. Besides José, the Acostas had eight other children, five sons and three daughters. This was an unusually high number of children for a Medinan family of the time, which typically numbered half that many. Five of the six sons, including José, entered the Society of Jesus, and of their three daughters two also entered religion.

Scholars are not sure of the exact date of José's birth, but the place and year of his birth are attested to by young José's own hand. He provided this information in a questionnaire he filled out for Fr. Jerónimo Nadal, S.J., in 1561, while he was a student at the Jesuit college of Alcalá de Henares.[5] This questionnaire, though brief, is an invaluable autobiographical source for Acosta's life and self-understanding as a member of the Society of Jesus.

From 1561 to 1562 Nadal was the personal representative, or *comisario*, of the general of the Society, Diego Laínez, to the Jesuit provinces of Spain and to the court of King Philip II.[6] As part of his official visit to the Jesuit houses of Spain and Portugal, Nadal composed a thirty-question form to be filled out by all Jesuits. The questionnaire was a way of acquiring biographical information about the membership of the order but also a means to evaluate what the order's Spanish and Portuguese subjects thought about their identity as Jesuits.[7]

Don Antonio, José's father, was a prosperous merchant and a generous benefactor of the Society. In 1551 he gave the Jesuits of Medina a property adjoining their first residence in the city so that they could enlarge their cramped accommodations. And again in 1553, when construction on the Jesuit college and church began just outside the walls of the city, he provided 2,000 ducats for the enterprise.[8] Don Antonio's Jewish heritage has been the source of some speculation among scholars. It has been maintained by some that his ancestors were Portuguese Jews, but there is no documentary evidence to substantiate this claim.[9]

Don Antonio was also a devout man. On October 2, 1569, he petitioned Francisco de Borja, who had become general of the Society of Jesus in 1565, for a special dispensation, which neither provincials nor rectors could concede, to enter the Society as a temporal coadjutor.[10] Don Antonio wanted to spend his remaining days on earth in the Society that he so much admired. He had the consent of his wife who like him had decided to take a vow and spend the rest of their lives in continence. At this time, he was almost eighty years old.

Of Doña Ana de Porres, José's mother, we know somewhat more. She was no retiring wallflower. On May 30, 1564, she wrote from Alcalá, where undoubtedly she was visiting her son José, to Fr. General Diego Laínez, asking that her husband and daughter Juana might be buried in the Jesuit church at Valladolid or wherever else in the world they happened to die.[11] She had taken up the matter with the Father Borja during his short-lived term as the *comisario general*, or megasuperior, of all Spanish Jesuits, but she did not receive satisfaction. The reason for this unusual request was, as she put it, "…we, the parents and daughter and our whole estate, are servants of the Society, no less that our sons are …"[12] She was not even beyond asking Laínez to instruct her youngest son, Diego, to write home more often!

Tenacity seems to have been another trait of Doña Ana. Several years later, after the death of Laínez and the election of Borja as superior general, she wrote to the new general renewing her request to be buried in a Jesuit church.[13] It did not dissuade her that the man she was writing to had not satisfied her request when he was comisario general of the Spanish Jesuits. This time she asked that not only she, her husband, and their daughter Juana receive this permission, but also Hernando, her only son who had not become a Jesuit. Doña Ana's audacity seems to have known no bounds, for she was not satisfied simply with Borja's written confirmation of Laínez's earlier permission; she also requested a letter instructing any Jesuit superior in the world, including Borja's successors in the office of superior general, that she and her relatives be buried in the Jesuit church anywhere in the world nearest to the place where they would die.

It is not clear that Borja satisfied all these conditions, but in 1592 when her son José was the rector of the professed house at Valladolid, on the occasion of the dedication of the new Jesuit church, the Acostas' remains were transferred from the old Jesuit church.[14] They were buried in the Jesuit mortuary chapel that was part of the new edifice. This day José preached the sermon and his brother Jerónimo presided at the Eucharist.

Acosta's Decision to Become a Jesuit

The Jesuits were first brought to Medina del Campo by a wealthy and influential merchant, Rodrigo de Dueñas, who had been highly impressed with Frs. Peter Faber and Antonio de Araoz at Valladolid.[15] Don Rodrigo invited the Jesuits to come to Medina during Advent of 1550 to preach at one of the trade fairs for which the town was renowned. Two fathers arrived and originally planned to stay for fifteen days preaching outdoors at the fair. However, the townspeople were so taken by their ministries that they begged them to stay until Easter. Don Rodrigo invited them to stay in his house and promised the Society that he would provide them with a house and pay for the education of a scholastic at Salamanca if they decided to establish themselves permanently in Medina.

Ignatius, still the superior general of the fledgling order at this time, recognized the importance of a base of operations in this important business center and accepted the offer. In 1551 a Jesuit residence first opened its doors in a rented house within the walls of Medina. The ministries of the first Jesuits at Medina took them throughout the city and touched a wide variety of the town's social echelons. The fathers and scholastics preached in churches, in hospitals, and even in the streets; they also catechized the young and unlettered and delivered public lectures on cases of consciences focused on business affairs.

From its genesis there were always a number of Jesuits in training who formed part of this community. These scholastics received some education in the humanities and philosophy from one of the Jesuit priests in the house while engaged in the Jesuits' usual ministries. In 1551 the Fleming Fr. Maximiliano Capella, S.J., gave classes to five Jesuit scholastics and to a few non-Jesuit students. It was probable that José was among this group of "externs," as non-Jesuits were called. From these humble beginnings in 1551, there would emerge a thriving Jesuit church and college for externs just outside the city walls, where scholastic José de Acosta would later distinguish himself in his literary pursuits.

Relatively little is known about young José's education before entering the Society in 1552. He mentions in Nadal's questionnaire of 1561 that before entering the novitiate he studied Latin grammar for a number of months. Although he does not specify whether this study of grammar was at a school or with a private tutor, it seems likely that he studied at the newly founded Jesuit residence at Medina del Campo. In early September 1552, just a few weeks shy of his twelfth birthday, the precocious José ran away from home and entered the Society at Salamanca. The reason for his flight from his native Medina seems to have been the understandable opposition of his parents, given his young age. However, Don Antonio and Doña Ana, who had ample experience with their offspring entering religious life and the Society in particular, did not persist long in their opposition. A month later José continued his novitiate at the Jesuit community in Medina.

Why did José enter the Society? From the questionnaire he filled out for Jerónimo Nadal we obtain the image of a frail young man, inclined to study and endowed with an excellent memory as well as having a propensity for recollection and piety—particularly a devotion to the souls in purgatory, for whom he frequently gave alms. He states that he entered the Society because he "saw the great charity, kindness, humility and fervor that existed in it."[16] This was not an uncommon response among his contemporaries,[17] however, what does stand out among José's understanding of his Jesuit vocation was his disponability to be sent wherever his superiors thought best. In particular he desired "to go to the Indies, but also to work among the Africans, and to work out of love of the Lord unto death."[18] Among his peers from throughout Europe who filled out Father Nadal's questionnaire the more typical response was that they had joined the Society "to save their souls by fleeing the dangers of the world and rarely indicated the desire to be sent out to convert heathen and heretic as a motive for joining."[19]

The program of formation and probation of the novitiate for those desiring to be Jesuits was modeled on some of the experiences that Ignatius and his first companions had during their student days at the University of Paris and their itinerant ministries throughout the Italian peninsula. These ministry experiences bore a great resemblance to the ministry of Jesus and the Apostles as well as to their medieval incarnation among the mendicant orders of Sts. Francis and Dominic, the so-called *vita apostolica*. They included the month-long Christocentric program of prayer and meditations in silence known as the Spiritual Exercises, and several weeks of "trials" or experiences of mortification and service in hospitals, teaching the fundamental beliefs and practices of the Christian faith to children and unlettered persons, preaching, working in lowly occupations around the Jesuit house, especially in the kitchen, and going on pilgrimage without any funds.

The goal of this initial period of the long Jesuit program of training was to determine if the candidate had the qualities necessary to be a Jesuit. Furthermore, the novitiate was meant to hone those qualities and virtues for the life of ministry that was to characterize the Jesuit vocation or "way of proceeding." The profile of the ideal Jesuit is described in the ninth part of the Jesuit Constitutions, which describes the qualities that the ideal superior general should possess. The virtues sought were prayerfulness, compassion with firmness, courage, generosity, learning, love of the Society, flexibility in the face of the varied and difficult pastoral circumstances that would be encountered, and sound judgment or prudence.

Since 1547 the experiences the novices underwent were slowly being institutionalized to bear greater resemblance to the activities that the novices of the mendicant and monastic orders had. In 1555, the Spanish Jesuits opened their first free-standing novitiate building in Simancas. But before that happened, Jesuit novices were formed in run-of-the-mill Jesuit houses and frequently participated in the ministries of the other community members of the place. This seems to have been the novitiate experience that José had at Medina del Campo from 1552 to 1554.

The Jesuit community at Medina during this time was located in a rented house within the city walls and the Jesuits numbered in the midtwenties. It included seven or eight priests and fifteen or sixteen brothers, scholastics, and novices. The rector of the house from 1554 to 1560 was José Sevillano, a scholastic, who had come to Medina in 1551 with the first group of three Jesuits to permanently settle in the city. On November 1, 1554, José pronounced his first vows, which marked the end of his novitiate; he continued on at Medina as a scholastic. He studied and taught the humanities in his home town for the next three years.

During his five-year stay in the Jesuit community at Medina, José witnessed a thriving enterprise. In 1552 their first great benefactor, Don Rodrigo de Dueñas, gave the Society the large Reguera farm just outside the city walls near the St. James gate. However, Don Rodrigo was reluctant to give any benefaction for the foundation of a school, preferring rather to fund a local hospital and other charitable works with orphans and lost women. But the Jesuits had no trouble in securing other patrons from the city's prosperous merchant class, among them Don Antonio de Acosta. In 1553 Francisco de Borja, the comisario general, came to Medina to lay the cornerstone for the new school. A very short time later the new school had an enrollment of 170 students of the humanities.

For the next decade the Reguera farm on the outskirts of Medina saw a steady transformation. In addition to a new two-floor school building with two large patios, the physical plant also included workshops, stables, pantries, wine cellars, wine and olive presses, a bakery, and a good-sized orchard with its own water wheel for irrigation. With the aid of their principal benefactors after 1553, the merchant Don Pedro Quadrado and his wife Doña Francisca Manjón, the fathers also built a new church, which Nadal described as one of the best he had ever seen in the Society.

The new house built for the Jesuit community on the Reguera plot was also impressive. In one of the regular letters sent to Rome reporting on the state of the community, the young José de Acosta, who because of his skills as a Latinist would often be charged with this task during his years of formation, described it to the general of the Society as "a house which was better [than the old one] for the religious life and for comfort."[20]

CHAPTER 2

Acosta's Formation as a Jesuit
1553–1571

Acosta's Humanistic Formation as a Jesuit

The curriculum that José de Acosta followed as a student at Medina and then imparted as a master was basically shared by all the Jesuit schools on the Iberian peninsula. This program of studies adopted the Renaissance humanist ideal of providing a classical education and a pious formation. Renaissance humanism, which arose from grammatical and rhetorical studies, was a cultural, literary, and educational movement that flourished in Europe from the fourteenth through the sixteenth century. Humanists introduced a new classicist style into a wide range of scholarly disciplines and professional fields that had already existed since medieval times. There were humanists in such wide-ranging fields and professions as theology, jurisprudence, medicine, mathematics, and philosophy.

One of the humanist concerns with which the Jesuits sympathized was to foster a more Christocentric spirituality among the faithful. But by no means did they discard all elements of the more traditional devotional Christianity of the masses, unlike some humanists who considered some of these practices to be superstitious. Sacred images were found in all Jesuit classrooms, and students were regularly instructed to say prayers before them when they entered these rooms. Jesuits took the value of relics for granted and utilized them in public rituals against all types of threats, Protestants included. The devotion to the Mother of God was particularly propagated in the schools through confraternities known as the Sodalities of the Blessed Virgin Mary. Jesuits promoted recitation of the Litany of the Saints at their schools; this was eventually adopted for all Jesuit houses as the only occasion where all Jesuits gathered regularly for prayer. Jesuits followed the piety proposed by the Spiritual Exercises. Popular practices were used pragmatically if they were approved by custom and ecclesiastical authorities and were not deemed to be overly superstitious.

The Jesuit schools were also characterized by a unified method, the *modus parisiensis*, which the founders of the Jesuit order had experienced during their education at the University of Paris. This method emphasized an orderly progression from basic disciplines to the more complicated ones, and frequent and varied pedagogical exercises to reinforce the matter of the lectures. Thus in the college of Medina del Campo, the study of Latin and Greek grammar and classical literature was organized in a four-year cycle of classes.

In the first year, "infima," the emphasis was on memorizing declensions and translating small sentences containing the verb "to be." "Media," the second year, was dedicated to syntax and the translation of Cicero's letters; and in the third year, "suprema," the past tense and supine verbs were studied and expurgated Terence and Virgil were translated. After the initial three-year cycle of Latin grammar, students usually began what was called the rhetoric year, where they would study the rhetorical theory of Cicero and his speeches and some works of Quintillian. The more accomplished students in Latin grammar skipped the rhetoric year and followed a program of studies that emphasized Latin composition and poetry-writing called "humanities." During the rhetoric and humanities years students were initiated in the study of Greek grammar and literature. Aesop's fables and the Dialogues of Lucian were the matter of the rhetoric year, and the humanities year concentrated on Aristophanes and Homer.

Students spent three hours in the morning and three in the afternoon in the classroom engaged in a wide variety of pedagogical exercises that had been adapted from the *modus parisiensis*. The goal of this humanistic formation was *eloquentia perfecta* in the spoken and written word. In this regard the curriculum of the Jesuit school at Medina del Campo resembled the humanist concern for writing that was lucid, that emulated the literary style of the Greco-Roman classics, and that above all looked to persuasion.

From the writings that Acosta has left us, most of the major ones in elegant Ciceronian Latin, we know that José mastered well the art of writing in Latin. The testimony of his contemporaries about his skills as a sacred orator and playwright also give witness to his literary and rhetorical talents. For example, on the feast of St. Barnabas, June 11, 1559, José was chosen to preach at the inauguration of the Jesuit college at Segovia. Even at the tender age of nineteen he already enjoyed something of a reputation for his literary accomplishments. Four years earlier he had composed and staged the play *Jephthah Sacrificing His Daughter* at the Jesuit college at Medina del Campo, earning the praise of those who attended. In subsequent years his productions of *autos sacramentales* would win equal adulation from their audiences. Some eighty years later, a chronicler of the Jesuits of Castile described the oration José gave at Segovia with these words:

> [the sermon] occasioned not a little admiration from the audience, that included all the nobility, the learned clergy and laity, and grave religious of the whole city, because Brother Joseph was so young, and yet had such erudition and eloquence.[1]

While the *modus parisiensis* was the heart of the Jesuit schools, it was also adapted to the needs the Jesuits saw among the students. Among these adaptations included the incorporation of catechism classes and "cases of consciences" into the curriculum, a concern for the spirituality of students, and the opportunity to engage in sports and other extracurricular activities. Students often put on different kinds of events for the public at large, such as plays, debates, poetry readings, and speeches.

The Jesuit colleges were also seen as apostolic platforms from which Jesuits could evangelize not only the students attending classes but also the town where they were located and even the local region. The colleges were the residences of teachers, preachers, and rural missionaries. Students helped these Jesuits in organizing processions and plays which had a didactic and evangelizing end. They complemented the preaching of their tutors in the public squares and churches.

The young Acosta experienced this holistic Jesuit formation in classical learning and traditional Christian devotional piety in his hometown of Medina, but in due course he was called upon to impart in other Jesuit colleges the classical knowledge he had acquired on the banks of the Zapardiel. In 1557 and for the next two years, the young Acosta, who since his entrance to the Society at Salamanca had been assigned only to the college at Medina, was posted in rapid succession to a number of Jesuit colleges throughout Old Castile and Portugal. During this time he was principally involved in teaching the humanistic disciplines he had mastered at Medina.

In the spring of 1557 he spent a month in Plasencia, from which he was quickly moved to Lisbon, where he spent the summer teaching. The fall of

1557 and winter of 1558 found him at the Jesuit college at Coimbra, where for two months he studied philosophy. The Jesuit school at Coimbra was renowned as a center of humanistic learning. In the mid-1550s it distinguished itself for being the Jesuit college to offer the largest number of Greek classes and for the critical editions of Aristotle that came to be published from the classes taught by Frs. Pedro Fonseca, S.J., and Emmanuel Goes, S.J.

Acosta's time in Portugal may have also been important for the genesis of his vocation within a vocation. At the time he studied and taught in Portugal, news of St. Francis Xavier's enterprises in India, the Moluccas, and Japan was widely known, and Jesuit scholastics had begun to be recruited and trained for these missions in a special college at Coimbra. The heroic missionary work of Xavier certainly features prominently in Acosta's first work, the *De Procuranda*.[2]

Mission fever was in the air, and it appears that it may have affected the young José, seventeen at the time. In a letter of April 23, 1569, to the superior general of the Jesuits, José mentions that his desire to offer himself for the missions had been stirring in him for eight or nine years.[3] This would date his desire for the Indies to 1560 or 1561. At that time the only Jesuit missions in existence were those in Portuguese colonies. And so it seems reasonable to postulate that the young José would have first learned about them during his stay in Lisbon and Coimbra. Perhaps the young José received firsthand accounts about them from returning missionaries whom he encountered in Portugal.[4]

In the early spring of 1558 he returned to Spain and was assigned to the college at Valladolid for a year. He probably taught the humanities here too. In the spring of 1559 he was selected to be part of the founding community of the Jesuit college of Segovia. Again he taught the classics, and he publicly distinguished himself by giving the much acclaimed inaugural sermon of the academic year before the city fathers and other notables.

Acosta's Philosophical and Theological Studies at Alcalá

After his humanistic formation and teaching experiences, in the fall of 1559 José was moved to the premier Jesuit house of studies in Spain, the college at Alcalá de Henares. This house owed its reputation to the large number of Jesuit students who lived under its roof and to the numerous candidates who came to know and enter the Society through it. Only fifty years before, Alcalá had been an agricultural town owned by the archbishops of Toledo. The ambitious and successful reformist educational and religious project of the observant Franciscan Cardinal Francisco Ximénez de Cisneros, Archbishop of Toledo and Primate of Spain, had transformed the city since the construction of the university in 1508 not only into a university town but also into a small center of industry and printing.[5]

The Renaissance Curriculum of the University of Alcalá

As a reformist educational project, the University of Alcalá was part of a more ambitious long-range plan of religious reform and centralized control at the service of national unity promoted by Cardinal Cisneros during the twenty-five-year reign of the Catholic Kings, Fernando and Isabel, from 1479 to 1504.[6] This religious reform plan included the fostering of the observantist reform among monks, nuns, and mendicants in both the kingdoms of Castile and Aragon, the education and reform of the diocesan clergy, the restructuring of the existing universities, increasing the quality of those chosen to be bishops, and an overall reform of pastoral life by the regulation of moral and religious life by means of the Inquisition and the elevation of knowledge by preaching. Many of its key elements would be continued under the reigns of Charles I and Philip II.

The University of Alcalá fit into Cisneros's ambitious plan of the religious revitalization of the emerging Spanish state by providing a center of moral and intellectual perfection which would combat ignorance through learning and propagate this learning by means of the printing medium. The university was destined to form lay and clerical elites who would concern themselves with propagating its ideal of formation in piety and the humanities in other centers of learning and in society at large throughout the peninsula. The University of Alcalá was composed of a number of schools, about eighteen, that housed several hundred students of grammar, philosophy, theology, canon law, and medicine.

The crowning jewel of the different faculties at Alcalá was, of course, the theology faculty. It was here that Alcalá's fame as a reformist and humanist center of learning most clearly manifested itself. Cisneros established three chairs for the teaching of theology at the faculty. These three chairs would be occupied by representatives of the Thomist, Scotist or realist, and nominalist schools. In addition to these three schools, students were, during the first two years of their program, required to attend lectures in Sacred Scripture and in the Sentences of Peter Lombard.

At the time of its inauguration, this system of the "three ways," as it was called, was quite innovative, and Alcalá was the only Spanish university organized in this fashion. Eventually all Spanish theology faculties would adopt it in the sixteenth century. The *catedráticos*, or holders of the chairs of theology, were appointed for limited terms and on a competitive basis with the final determination made by the votes of the students. At first they were required to lecture twice daily, in the early morning and early evening for an hour. However, this proved to be too much for one professor to handle, and after 1536 the afternoon lectures were handled by another *catedrático*.[7]

Although the cardinal would have liked to have only one school of theology reign at Alcalá so as to insure uniformity, he realized that this was not feasible given the pluralism that existed in the early sixteenth-century academy. Therefore, he settled for providing his university with the most complete program in theology available. The plurality of schools would also foment lively disputations. The academic exercise of the disputation played a central role in the pedagogical system at Alcalá, which modeled itself on the University of Paris. Completing the key elements of *lectio* and *disputatio* of the *modus parisiensis* that reigned at Alcalá was *praedicatio*. Students were required to deliver several public sermons throughout their program of studies in the faculty of theology.[8]

In addition to the innovation of teaching of theology by means of the "three ways," Cisneros's university broke new ground in other ways also. Making his own the humanist concern for translating and studying the Christian classics, he financed new critical translations and printing of the sources of theology such as the Sacred Scriptures, in the famous Polyglot Bible, and the Fathers. To facilitate this enterprise, the university had a trilingual college that trained scholars in the ancient languages. The sphere of spirituality was also cared for by Cisneros when he established an observantist Franciscan college at the university, the College of Sts. Peter and Paul, which would serve both the intellectual training of the friars and the spiritual life of the university at large. According to the statutes of the university, "preaching of the Sacred Scriptures should be the principal end of the theologian."[9] As we shall see when we examine Acosta's theological writings, this is a characteristic that they very much manifest.

Acosta's University Studies at Alcalá

Acosta commenced his study at the university in the fall of 1559 in the faculty of arts, or philosophy, continuing the two-month initiation into the subject that he had begun at Coimbra some two years earlier. The curriculum that José followed at the university during his four years of philosophy and four of theology there was solidly Thomist. In the first half of the sixteenth century the faculty of arts had been a stronghold of nominalism, but after a reform of the faculty in the mid-sixteenth century the Thomists came to have control over the program of study.[10]

The course of philosophy studies in the faculty of arts at Alcalá lasted four years. The first year, known as "súmulas," was dedicated to the study of Peter of Spain's *Súmulas logicales*. Peter was actually a thirteenth-century Portuguese, and his text served as an introduction to the study of philosophy. In the second year, known as "logic," students studied Porphyry's *Predicables* and Aristotle's *Predicaments*. The third year was devoted to the study of the Aristotelian natural sciences by means of his *Natural Philosophy*. And the final year concentrated on Aristotle's *Metaphysics*, in addition to geography, arithmetic, geometry, and perspective as expounded by other authors.

From university records it is known that during the years that Acosta studied philosophy at Alcalá Professors Rodríguez and José Villel were responsible for teaching the four-year cycle of courses.[11] It is quite probable that during those years the texts used by the professors to lecture were the same as those in favor from 1564 to 1585, when commentaries on Peter of Spain, Porphyry, and Aristotle by Francisco de Soto, O.P., Gaspar Cardillo de Villalpando, Juan Cantero, and Francisco Vallés were the required texts from which professors lectured.[12] As in the faculty of theology, the pedagogy used was the *modus parisiensis* with its mixture of morning and afternoon lectures with frequent disputations and repetitions of the lecture material.

After philosophy, the course in theology studies lasted another four years; during Acosta's time there the theology faculty included many distinguished professors. Frays Mancio de Corpus Christi, O.P., and Pedro Portocarrero, O.P., and Drs. Pedro Balbás and Diego López taught St. Thomas; Drs. Pedro Martínez de Brea, Juan Ruiz, Andrés Rodríguez, and Francisco Sánchez taught Scotus, which would later become the chair in moral philosophy; Drs. Pedro Balbás, Juan García, Juan Ruiz, and Andrés Uzquiano occupied the chair of nominalist theology, also called the chair of Gabriel Biel, which would later become the chair of Durando; Drs. Juan Méndez and Alonso de Mendoza taught Sacred Scripture, especially the fourth gospel and the epistles of St. Paul.[13]

During the years that Acosta studied theology at Alcalá, there was great fluidity among the masters with regard to the different schools of theology they taught in their lectures. So, for example, Dr. Pedro Balbás taught both St. Thomas and nominalist theology, as did Dr. Juan Ruiz from 1563 to 1567. The flexibility and openness of the representatives of the different schools indicates that during Acosta's studies at Alcalá there did not yet reign the rigidity and partisan spirit that would characterize the schools of theology in Spanish universities later in the sixteenth and throughout the seventeenth century. And while there was a plurality of schools represented in the faculty of theology at Alcalá during the early and mid-1560s, in fulfillment of the desires and statutes drafted by the founder of the university, Cardinal Cisneros, there was a perceptible trend in favor of St. Thomas. Thus it may be said that during Acosta's study of theology at Alcalá the Scotist and nominalist schools were in decline.[14]

If Scotus and Ockham were overwhelmed by the popularity of St. Thomas at Alcalá during the 1560s, it was due not in small part to the lectures of the Jesuit Alonso de Deza, known as the "teacher of teachers."[15] Deza was born in Alcalá in 1530 and studied theology at the university, where he was taught by such distinguished scholars as the Dominicans Melchior Cano and Mancio de Corpus Christi.[16] He obtained the doctorate in 1550.[17] Before entering the Society in 1558, he read Scotist philosophy and theology at the Franciscan house of studies at Alcalá.[18] Once he completed his novitiate, he began a long and distinguished career teaching St. Thomas at the Jesuit house of studies at Alcalá, where his pupils included such distinguished theologians as Francisco Suárez, S.J., and Gabriel Vásquez, S.J.[19]

Deza's lectures on metaphysics were especially popular, and in 1563 they were opened to the public, the first such lectures offered in a religious house of studies at Alcalá that were opened to other university students. So popular did Deza's teaching become that in 1567 Dr. Alonso Mendoza, who taught Sacred Scripture, procured a decree from the Royal Council which forbade the attendance of lay students at the lectures given at religious houses; this measure, however, did not have its desired effect.[20] Although Deza did not produce much by way of scholarly writings, we know from his letters[21] and from the praise of such distinguished Dominican theologians as Mancio de Corpus Christi and Domingo de Báñez that he was a convinced and respected disciple of St. Thomas.[22]

The Jesuit Program of Studies at Alcalá

In addition to the theological program stipulated for all students matriculated at the university, José and his brother Jesuits at Alcalá were required to take additional private classes, which would have included St. Thomas and perhaps positive theology.[23] What was understood by *positive theology* in Acosta's time? The first to use the term seems to have been John Major of the

University of Paris in his commentary on the fourth book of Peter Lombard's Sentences, published in 1509. He understood positive theology to be the study of the Bible and the Fathers for use in preaching and practical instruction in living the Christian life. Positive theology was in this sense distinguished from scholastic theology or purely speculative theology.

During the course of the sixteenth century certain humanists such as Erasmus came to see the distinction between positive theology and speculative or scholastic theology as an absolute separation. These humanists mocked the abstraction and dryness of the distinctions which so characterized the method and thought of the scholastics, and lauded positive theology which they considered to be the theology of Christ and the New Testament. Positive theology was more emotive and useful for the preacher who desired to move his audience to a more radical and authentic living of the gospel.

This, however, was not the position of the Society of Jesus that José de Acosta would have been exposed to during his formation in Spain during the mid-sixteenth century. When they studied theology at Paris, St. Ignatius and his first companions were exposed to the rigid separation between scholastic theology and positive theology of some within the humanist movement,[24] but they were not swayed by this position. Ignatius himself recommended in his eleventh rule for "Thinking with the Church Militant" in the Spiritual Exercises that both positive and scholastic theology should be praised because each was useful in its own way for the ministry. Furthermore, Ignatius observed that among the scholastics of his day there was both an appreciation and use of Scripture, the Fathers, and the decrees of the councils of the Church and of canon law.[25] Ignatius's exhortation to praise and study both positive and scholastic theology was reflected in the curriculum of both the houses of formation of the Society[26] and the universities[27] that it would administer according to the Constitutions of the new order.

The characteristics of the Society's theological program may be summed up as follows. It sought not to make a sharp division between scholastic and positive theology. This was facilitated by the type of scholastic theology that the early Jesuits had been exposed to at the University of Paris, which had taken seriously the critiques of the humanists and seriously attended to such sources of theology as Scripture, the Fathers, and the councils. In Spain this reformed type of scholasticism that originated at the University of Paris was propagated by the Dominicans of Salamanca such as Francisco de Vitoria, Domingo de Soto, Mancio de Corpus Christi, and Melchior Cano.[28] There is no doubt that while José was a student at Alcalá he was exposed to the early

Society's esteem of the reformed Thomism of the First School of Salamanca and of positive theology.

The Influence of Jerónimo Nadal

Part of the Jesuit governance structure was regular official correspondence between the houses of the Society and the headquarters in Rome. Acosta was commissioned by his rector at Alcalá to write many quarterly letters to Rome updating the major events that had occurred in the community. In one of them he mentioned the impact that the visitation and exhortations of Fr. Jerónimo Nadal had had.[29]

Since the time of St. Ignatius and during the generalates of Fathers Laínez and Borja, Jerónimo Nadal had played a most significant role in the life of the early Society of Jesus. Born at Palma de Mallorca on one of the Balearic Islands, Jerónimo studied at Alcalá, Paris, and Avignon, where he obtained the doctorate in theology. Distinguished in the art of disputation, he was also skilled in Sacred Scripture, positive theology, scholastic theology, Latin, Greek, Hebrew, and mathematics. His theological expertise would insure that part of his activity in life would include writing and consultation on ecclesiastical matters. Indeed, in 1562 he would be for a very short period one of the Jesuit *periti* at the Council of Trent.

In 1545 at Rome he made the Spiritual Exercises under the direction of Ignatius and then entered the Society. Shortly thereafter, in 1548, Ignatius sent him to be the rector of the first Jesuit school at Messina in Sicily. There he was responsible for organizing the school's order of studies, which would later be exported to other Jesuit educational institutions throughout Europe.

Perhaps the most important legacy of Nadal is the many talks he gave to Jesuit communities throughout Europe in his capacity as official representative of the superiors general of the Society of Jesus. He began these visitations in 1553 with his visit to the Jesuits of Spain and Portugal, and eventually he would extend his travels to France and Germany. His talks during these visitations were very popular. He would explain the history and new way of proceeding of the order willed by Ignatius and contained in the Constitutions. In this regard one of his greatest theological contributions was the development of the idea that each religious community had a particular grace or charism. This charism, according to Father Nadal, was most palpable in the life and graces that God gave the founder of the community.

Another topic concerning the Society's way of proceeding covered by Nadal's exhortations had to do with the studies of the scholastics. This twelfth of fourteen exhortations delivered to the community at Alcalá from October 1561 through early 1562[30] dealt with what kind of theology young Jesuits should study. Nadal stated clearly:

> It is necessary to combine the practical with the speculative. It is necessary to combine the spiritual life, that is, the Christian life that is anointed with piety and devotion, and proceeds guarded by divine and ecclesiastical precepts, with knowledge and theology. Those who are lacking this are missing something that is paramount. And when one's studies are like this, they are singularly efficacious and bear much fruit.[31]

Nadal's concept of theological studies that were proper for young Jesuits deeply influenced the young Acosta and his later writing; this theology will be studied in detail in chapter six.

Acosta's Daily Life at Alcalá: Formation for Ministry

José's life at Alcalá was not limited to the academic. His training as a Jesuit also involved other types of preparation for the apostolate.[32] The quarterly letters sent from Alcalá to the Jesuit superior general in Rome describing the activities of the community provide a window to glimpse the daily life of José at Alcalá. From 1560 through 1564 these letters were composed by José himself.[33] He seems to have written one in Latin and one in Spanish, and they follow a standard form. After reporting the number of Jesuits in the community and their grades and occupations, he proceeds to mention any special events that occurred since the last quarterly letter. He concludes by describing the various ministries that those in the community have been engaged in.

The Jesuit community at Alcalá was one of the largest and finest houses of formation that the Society had in Spain at the time. As in the community at Medina del Campo, the Jesuit house at Alcalá was composed of priests, brothers, scholastics, and novices. The community hovered at around fifty members, with the majority being scholastics and novices. As early as the summer of 1558, the community built one of the first Jesuit villa or vacation houses in the small mountain town of Lorcana, some twelve miles northeast of Alcalá. The house, called *Jesús del Monte*, was large enough to accommodate between fifty and sixty men and had its own church.[34] Its purpose was to serve as the summer residence of the Jesuit students, thus affording them the salubrious option of escaping the oppressive and often fatal heat of La Mancha.

Central in the daily order at Alcalá was the spiritual life. In Acosta's time the spiritual regime followed by the community members had been tempered from the intensity that characterized it in the mid 1550s. At that time, in addition to daily mass and weekly confession, Jesuit students were allowed to sleep only six hours, for their mortification, and were required to pray for two hours each day, one hour in the morning and one in the afternoon. This prayer took place in common in the house chapel. The whole community made a visit to the Blessed Sacrament after the midday and evening meals for the specified time of fifteen minutes, and it fasted Fridays and Saturdays.

In early 1554, when Jerónimo Nadal visited Alcalá to explain the newly composed Constitutions, he was unhappy with what he considered an excessively demanding spiritual regime that could jeopardize the health of the Jesuit students, and he moderated the religious practices of the community. Thus, in José's time the community was permitted seven hours of sleep and was no longer required to fast on Fridays and Saturdays; the visits to the Blessed Sacrament were shortened; and the hour of prayer in the afternoon was eliminated.[35]

José was also accustomed to renew his vows of poverty, chastity, and obedience every six months with the rest of the members of the community who had not made their final religious profession. In addition to this required practice, José derived much consolation from the practice of frequently renewing these vows in private. He also frequently engaged in a pious exercise recommended by the Spiritual Exercises and avidly promoted by the Jesuits of the time called the general confession.[36]

The general confession differed from the annual confession required by canon law for all Catholics in that it was voluntary. It was a spiritual inventory of one's life since the last confession had been made. The end of the general confession was to recognize the way in which God had manifested himself and how one had or had not responded to these initiatives with generosity. It is supposed to help one see oneself as one really is before God, i.e., as a sinful creature loved by God. The intention of this form of confession was that the penitent would be moved to start anew one's relationship with God with more fervor and generosity. This Jesuit style of confession was understood as a devout practice undertaken for spiritual progress and not as the unpopular obligation which annual confession had become in many parts of Europe.

Besides the routine of study and prayer that guided the daily life of José in Alcalá, there was much exposure to and participation in the Society's many types of ministry, or apostolic "way of proceeding." This seems to have been especially the case during the summers when scholastics were dispersed throughout the communities of the Jesuit province of Toledo to help out with the ministries of those houses.[37] Many of the ministerial activities of this first generation of Jesuits resembled many of the pastoral works that Ignatius himself and his first companions had engaged in.

During the course of his life Ignatius visited the sick and imprisoned in hospitals and prisons, engaged in spiritual conversation and direction with the laity, created the Spiritual Exercises, catechized and engaged in popular preaching, established confraternities, engaged in a ministry of writing that produced the Constitutions of the new community and hundreds of letters of subtle spiritual guidance and shrewd temporal advice, all for the greater glory of God and the help of souls. These ministries of the Word and of the corporal works of mercy, along with sacramental ministry and the works in the schools, form the core which would characterize the ministerial endeavors of the early Society.

The quarterly letters José wrote from Alcalá mention many of these ministries, but they especially take note of the ministry of the Spiritual Exercises.[38] The history of the ministry of the Exercises at the Alcalá community dated from its foundation in 1546. In 1553 the first building specifically designated to house men making the Exercises was constructed at the Jesuit college of Alcalá, and often there was a waiting list. During Acosta's days at Alcalá this ministry continued to thrive. During Lent of 1561 a dozen men made the Exercises, the largest number known to date; however, the correspondence does not indicate the duration of these retreats. These dozen men placed a strain on the accommodations set aside for them in the community, and others who wished to make the Exercises had to be turned away. During the winter and spring of 1564, however, that record was broken, and José reported that forty-five men had made the Exercises.

Associated with the ministry of the Exercises were other "ministries of the Word" that were typical of the Jesuits of this generation and that were also taking place at Alcalá. Foremost among these ministries of the Word mentioned by Acosta in the quarterly letters he wrote was preaching.[39] Just as Ignatius and the early companions engaged in a ministry of itinerant preaching in public spaces, so too did the Jesuits of Alcalá. Everyone who was able preached, not just the ordained. For example, during carnival in 1562 twenty-four priests and scholastics of the Jesuit community at Alcalá went out at the same time to preach. They divided themselves in small groups and spread themselves throughout the town singing the catechism and inviting children and adults to come and hear the word of God. Other Jesuits situated themselves in public squares and in the most travelled thoroughfares. When the groups of children and adults approached the places were the Jesuit preachers were located, the latter launched into animated and fervent exhortations. They reminded the astonished people of their Christian obligations and encouraged them not to defile themselves with the usual profane goings-on of the carnival season.[40]

In their preaching, this first generation of Jesuits took seriously the criticisms made of the penitential and university preaching of the mendicants, and they successfully attempted to combine the best of both. They preserved the rationality and subtleties of scholasticism but were much concerned that their sound and erudite doctrine move the hearts of those who heard them to an increase of faith and love of neighbor. They also avoided controversial topics such as predestination and focused on sound and accepted doctrine.

Acosta's quarterly letters are replete with news of a variety of forms and venues of Jesuit preaching. On the feast of the Holy Trinity, 1564, the solemn profession of two of the Jesuit priests in residence at Alcalá was the occasion for the organization of several public sermons. These were well attended and especially impressed the local inquisitor and his vicar, who were in attendance and after the ceremony were invited to the Jesuit community for a simple repast.[41]

But if there was one audience that the Jesuits targeted above all at Alcalá it was the university students. Acosta mentioned the oratory and success of Fr. Alonso de Madrid, S.J., in this regard on several occasions.[42] Madrid had obtained a doctorate in theology from Salamanca, where he also taught and had been a chaplain to the king before entering the Society in 1555. His primary ministry after the novitiate was that of an itinerant preacher. During the late 1550s and in the 1560s he made several visits to Alcalá. His preaching during Lent of 1562 is described by Acosta as "accompanied with many tears," "full of words with feeling," and "highly esteemed by many students because of his charism and teaching."[43] And again in the fall of 1562 Acosta notes that Madrid's sermons are exemplary because their "tenderness moved the audience to tears" and also caused many university students to go to confession.[44]

Another form of preaching the Jesuits practiced during this time was the popular missions. These missions were highly organized and orchestrated preaching blitzes that took place in the countryside, where the faithful were often neglected. They seem to have had a great impact as a method of rural evangelization. The popular missions were elaborate affairs involving a week or more of preaching in the town or village. But before that much background research went into preparing the sermons and staging the processions and other devotional acts which were part of this ministry. During the day, the mission team of several Jesuits focused on educating the catechists of the local population.

In the quarterly letter of early September 1561, Acosta makes mention of one such popular mission in the local villages around Alcalá and especially of the fruit that such a ministry produced, the reconciliation of warring local families.[45] This was another form of ministry that the early Jesuits often engaged in, the ministry of peacemaking or reconciliation especially in small towns where vendettas between rival clans severely strained civic life.

If peacemaking was a typical Jesuit work of reconciling the estranged, by far the most common form of the ministry of reconciliation that the Jesuits practiced was the ministry of the confessional. Interestingly, they considered confession not a spiritual work of mercy per se but to some extent another form of the ministry of the Word. This was so because the forum of the confessional allowed the confessor not only to reconcile but to give advice, to speak to the penitent about the mercy of God, and thus perhaps to soften his or her heart and move it by the Word of God. In short, as Nadal put it, it allowed a sort of private sermon to the penitent.

Jesuit confessors had the reputation of being masters of casuistry, and were known as compassionate and erudite confessors. They paid close attention to the offense being confessed but also to the state of mind of the penitent at the time of the sin and the circumstances surrounding the action. The Jesuit use of casuistry also had an impact in the lecture halls of the university, and their careful analysis of confessional cases became the foundation for the field of moral theology.

There is another way in which the ministry of the confessional was related to the ministry of the Word. Jesuit sermons were often crafted with the intention of moving the audience to seek out the ministry of reconciliation, and the preacher's confrere in religion was conveniently at hand as a confessor. This was especially practiced at the Jesuit church at Alcalá, where Acosta often measures the efficacy of a preacher's sermons by the number of "conversions," or confessions, that it produced.[46] Another criterion of apostolic success that Acosta mentions in his letters to Rome is the increase of alms received at the Jesuit church in Alcalá. Without going into detail, José attributes this to the fine liturgical services that the Jesuits were providing at their church.[47] Among these services were special prayers and penitential processions organized in 1561 to seek divine intervention in ending a long-lasting drought.[48]

The corporal and spiritual works of mercy also featured prominently in the ministries of the early Society. An important part of Ignatius's life while a student at Alcalá and Paris was to assist the sick and imprisoned at local hospitals and jails. The material relief he provided was often accompanied with instruction on *Christianitas*, the basic pious practices and beliefs of the Christian faith. While in Rome during the last part of his life, Ignatius continued to exercise his concern for the social problems of his day by helping to found, with the help of lay confraternities, houses for reformed prostitutes, Jewish converts, and orphans. This attention to the corporal works of mercy was also continued by the first companions of Ignatius and became a standard part of the training and ministry of the early Jesuits.

It is no surprise then that relief for the poor dispensed from the Jesuit community at Alcalá and at the local jail and hospitals is mentioned by José in his chronicle of his confreres' ministries. The material assistance that the scholastics at Alcalá distributed to widows, orphans, the sick, and the imprisoned was accompanied by sermons that moved the heart and encouraged an increase in faith and virtuous living and instruction in the catechism.[49]

It would be erroneous and incomplete if the intellectual and religious formation that young José's received at Alcalá left one with the impression that by and large it was an exciting time marked by a flurry of intellectual and apostolic activity. Despite the tremendous expansion and variety of apostolic activity that characterized the Jesuit foundation at Alcalá in the 1560s, there were times of economic hardship for the community. But it was especially in his personal life that José experienced pain and hardship. The reports sent to Rome about him by his rectors at Alcalá frequently mention two items. The first of these is his intelligence, facility in dealing with others, and virtue and prudence, which make him especially apt for preaching, teaching, hearing confessions, and governance. The second is that he is frequently sick.[50]

The sickness to which these reports refer was rather serious and often incapacitated José. He describes it as a chest sore that bled for a long time and also caused him to have a fever of long duration. The illness was so severe that it prevented him from engaging in physical labor for some time. His malady also appears to have been a chronic condition, since he says that from time to time the wound continued to bleed even if in diminished amounts.[51]

Two events that will significantly mark the life of José also took place during his time at Alcalá. It is during this time of studies that he first put down in writing a desire to go to the Indies. It is quite likely that this desire originated during his time in Lisbon and Coimbra, but it was at Alcalá that he first explicitly formulated it in these words: "I have desires to go to the Indies, but also to work among the Africans, and I am drawn to work out of love of the Lord unto death to the extent that my energies permit."[52] As we shall see these desires will continue to be present and grow during José's first assignments as a priest.

His ordination to the presbyterate sometime in the winter or early spring of 1567 was the second life-altering event of José's life during his student days at Alcalá. In a sense José's ordination may be seen as the end of both his period of formation as a Jesuit and of his youth. After his ordination he left Alcalá to begin a life of full-time ministry as a professor of theology, preacher, and confessor at the Jesuit college located in the Manchegan town of Ocaña, a small town on the New Castilian plain some eight miles from Aranjuez and just over thirty miles from Madrid on the road to Andalucia.

The issue arises of whether Acosta ever obtained the doctorate in theology. It is not clear that he did so. Normally, the courses of studies for the doctorates in philosophy and theology at Alcalá lasted four years each. Students could sit for the exams for the bachelor's in theology after two years of study and for the licentiate and doctorate after a total of four years of theological studies. The most difficult exams were those for the licentiate; the doctoral exams, usually less demanding than those for the licentiate, occurred fifteen days or so after the latter. José studied philosophy at Alcalá from 1559 to 1563, and theology from 1563 to 1567. Therefore, he completed the requisite number of years in the theology faculty that would have qualified him to sit for the doctoral exams.[53]

However, the doctoral exams and ceremonies associated with them were particularly expensive affairs. It was not uncommon in Spain at this time for poor students and especially students of religious communities to do their course work in the major universities like Alcalá and Salamanca and then sit for doctoral exams in the minor universities located at Avila and Sigüenza.[54] Since the Jesuit house of studies at Alcalá was in dire economic straits at this time, it may be that economics prevented the brilliant young theologian from obtaining the highest degree in theology available to him. In any event, it is clear from José's writings that his study of theology at Alcalá prepared him well for an academic career in the field.

Acosta's First Assignments and His Missionary Vocation

In contrast to the cosmopolitan cities of Medina del Campo, Lisbon, Coimbra, and Alcalá, where he had previously resided, the next four years of

Padre Acosta's life were spent in small provincial towns. In the fall of 1567, Acosta and a companion, Fr. Alonso de Sandoval, inaugurated classes in theology at Ocaña, where they taught some Jesuit students who had been sent there from Alcalá to relieve the overcrowding in that house. As the letters of his rectors to Rome confirm, Padre José was highly successful as a professor for his brother Jesuits. He also excelled as a preacher and confessor and was once again able to exercise his dramatic talents by staging an *auto sacramental*, *Joseph Sold into Egypt*, which he had already written and executed during his early years in the Society at Medina del Campo. The whirlwind of apostolic activities during these first years of active ministry agreed with José, for his superiors frequently mention in their correspondence to Rome that they considered his health to be better during this time.

In 1569 the rector at Ocaña learned that for economic reasons the Jesuit students of theology and with them their professors would be transferred to the college at Plasencia. He implored Fr. General Borja that since there was still a need for someone to preach and lecture on cases of conscience Padre José should remain behind while two others could go with the scholastics to teach them theology at Plasencia. The rector's pleas were to no avail, and in September 1569 Acosta took up residence in Plasencia.

At this time Plasencia was a small, mountainous Extremaduran town notorious for the clan rivalries that plagued both its civil and its ecclesial life.[55] It lay some forty miles from the Portuguese border, on the road to Andalucia between the larger cities of Cáceres and Salamanca. José was no stranger to the town, having resided in it for about a month in 1557 on his way to Portugal. As per usual, Acosta was selected to preside at a public disputation of theology in the presence of the local bishop and other dignitaries. This academic event inaugurated the theology classes at the Jesuit college, and once again Father José dazzled the audience with his learning.

An interesting episode from the ministry of Acosta while in Plasencia was his encounter with the Basque Jesuit brother and future martyr, Esteban Zuraire. Brother Zuraire was a novice and in charge of the laundry when Acosta met him at Plasencia and served as his confessor and spiritual director. José encouraged Esteban to take advantage of the opportunity to labor in the Brazilian missions. Esteban accepted this assignment and confided in Acosta that during a retreat he received the revelation that he, Esteban, would go to Brazil and be martyred there. And so it came to pass that on July 15, 1570, Brother Zuraire and thirty-nine Jesuit companions, including Fr. Ignatius Azevedo, were martyred onboard ship by Huguenot pirates. This occurred when they were off the Canary Islands on their way to Brazil.

The event of paramount significance that took place in Padre José's life during these first years of full-time apostolic ministry was the fulfillment of his "desire to go to the Indies." After he first formulated in writing this vocation within a vocation in 1561, he wrote several letters in 1569 to Fr. General Francisco de Borja requesting to be sent to the new territories of Spain in the Americas. Borja made it clear in 1569 that those interested in laboring in the Indies should write only once to Rome expressing their desire, and all subsequent petitions should be sent to one's provincial. Besides, in 1568 he had decided that no Jesuit suitable for governance, preaching, or teaching theology should be sent to the New World. As if circumventing Borja's stipulations and regulations concerning these matters, José sent his letters to Rome with fellow Jesuits who were traveling there on the order's business. On one occasion, he let Borja know that he was willing to go to the Indies even if he could not engage in direct missionary work and rather was assigned to preach and teach theology to suitable candidates for ordination in those lands.

Borja acknowledged Acosta's zeal in writing, but his plans for the talented young priest lay in Rome and not in the New World. He considered Acosta a suitable candidate to replace Francisco de Toledo, an eminent theologian at the Roman College and later the first Jesuit cardinal. Toledo had recently left his teaching position to assume the post of preacher at the papal court. When Acosta's transfer to Rome proved to be problematic because of displeasure at the Spanish court that too many talented Spanish Jesuits were being assigned overseas, Borja decided to assign him to Burgos.

Conveniently, Acosta's chest sore began to bleed shortly after the assignment to Burgos was received, and he stayed put in Plasencia. José's rector complained to Rome that he should be allowed to remain because his teaching and preaching ministries were sorely needed. The rector's request was honored for a brief time, and Acosta remained in Plasencia with only a brief journey to Alcalá, where on September 24, 1570, he made final profession of vows before his provincial. Then in early 1571 Acosta received the long-awaited news from Rome that he had been assigned to preach and teach theology in Peru.

Borja seems to have reversed his standing policy of not sending professors of theology or preachers to the missions for two reasons. First, the requests coming from Peru for missionaries stressed that precisely what was needed was men skilled in these ministries. And second, certain divisions among the Jesuits already in Peru concerning the legitimacy of their work there required men trained in theology to address the serious doubts that threatened the Society's new enterprise in that land.

After a month in Seville, where he received money and provisions from the *patronato* for the voyage to Peru and also engaged in preaching and hearing confessions, Acosta made his way to the port of Sanlúcar de Barrameda on Spain's southern Atlantic coast. After several false starts he finally set sail for the Indies on June 8, 1571. With two Jesuit companions he made the crossing in a record three months, arriving in Santo Domingo in early September. He remained several months in Santo Domingo and had the opportunity to engage in the first of many delicate diplomatic negotiations that would occupy his time during the fourteen-year stay in the New World.

The Franciscan archbishop of Santo Domingo, Fray Andrés de Carvajal, had grave reservations about the nature and way of proceeding of the Society. In particular he was concerned about the reputation the Society had acquired for avarice and wealth. Although the archbishop gave Acosta permission to preach in his diocese, few of the local clergy would invite him to do so because of the displeasure they knew their ordinary felt toward the Jesuit Institute. Acosta decided to take the bull by the horns and sought and received an audience from his grace in which he was able to answer the Franciscan's concerns about the Society and convince him of the Society's orthodoxy and good repute. A memorandum replying to the archbishop's concerns written by Acosta was sent to the Jesuit superior general in Rome.[56] After several months in Santo Domingo, the three Jesuits left for Panama. After crossing the isthmus, they set sail for Peru. They finally arrived in Lima on April 27, 1572.

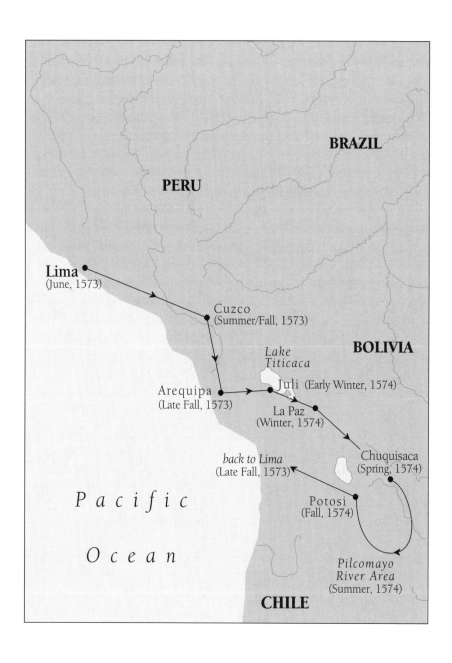

José de Acosta's first trip to the interior of Peru and Bolivia: 1573–1574
(Modern country names are indicated; the seasons are
in terms of the Northern Hemisphere.)

CHAPTER 3

The Apogee of Acosta's Life
Peru, 1572–1586

Peru at the Time of Acosta's Arrival[1]

The thirty-year-old Spanish Kingdom of Peru that José de Acosta set foot upon in 1572 was an immense domain. It encompassed all of South America with the exception of Brazil and the Caribbean coast of the continent east of Colombia. José's fourteen-year stay in the kingdom was limited to activities and travels in the southern halves of Peru and Bolivia. Even given the limited geographical area of the kingdom that Acosta was familiar with, these lands included very different topographical and climactic zones, which ran the gamut from the desert coastal zone, to the populous Andean zone with its high peaks, fertile valleys, and plains, and to the eastern tropical jungles that descend to the banks of the Amazon River and its tributaries.

Present-day Peru and Bolivia were considered Castile's most prized possessions in the Americas because of their lucrative silver and gold mines. It is estimated that at the time of Acosta's arrival in Lima in 1572, the population of what is today Peru was approximately 1,300,000 people. The vast majority of the population was composed of well over a million native peoples. Europeans, mostly from the Iberian peninsula, numbered around 25,000. Peoples of mixed race are estimated to have been around 70,000. There also seems to have been a sizable number of African slaves, who by 1570 outnumbered the European population in certain coastal areas of Peru.

Three years before Acosta's arrival in Lima, Philip II dispatched a new viceroy to the Kingdom of Peru, Don Francisco de Toledo, who implemented sweeping changes in Spain's Andean possessions.[2] From 1570 to 1575 the new viceroy undertook an ambitious *visita*, or visitation, of his domain to implement a reorganization of the kingdom. Toledo conducted public proceedings on Inca tyranny which supported the legitimacy of the Spanish conquest. He invaded the Inca kingdom of Vilcabamba and publicly executed its ruler, Tupac Amaru. He instituted the policy of reducing the native peoples to settlements, or *reducciónes*, ruled by Spanish *corregidores* and Indian *kurakas*, or native leaders loyal to the state. To insure ample manpower for the mines, he set up a system of tribute and rotating forced labor controlled by the state called the *mita*. Thus he tied the Spanish elite's economic success to the state's new social and economic institutions. He consolidated these changes by decreeing a sizable corpus of legislation to govern the politics and economics of the new order he established.

Toledo's twelve-year rule (1569–81) in Peru roughly corresponds to Acosta's fourteen years there (1572–86). The two men knew each other, but after an initially amicable working relationship which saw Toledo value Acosta's advice on religious and secular issues, the relationship soured. Toledo's resentment of the Jesuit's independence and resistance to royal manipulation of the order's internal affairs during Acosta's provincialate saw them part ways on hostile terms; more will be said later about Acosta's exchanges with Toledo. Acosta's arrival in Peru coincided with the initiation of the viceroy's reorganization, and the fourteen years of his stay would be marked by a period of economic boom which would not peter out until the 1610s and 1620s. Beginning in the 1590s, the native peoples and encomenderos allied with them made use of Hispanic justice, among other strategies, to limit the number of men assessed for the *mita*, thus severely hampering the smooth functioning of the mining economy.

The first Jesuits in Lima, a party of seven who arrived on April 1, 1568, saw a local Church that had only relatively recently begun to organize itself after an initial period of instability caused by the violence of the conquest and civil wars. It was better established in the urban areas populated by Spaniards, where it bore great similarity to what the Jesuits had left behind in Castile. The evangelization of the native peoples was under way, even if the resources for this Herculean enterprise were less than sufficient and even if its results up to that time were less than satisfactory. But more importantly, the Society entered Peru at the dawn of a new age for the patronato real. This expansionist and centralized vision of the patronato would insure that part of the Society's early years in Peru would be characterized by the tensions of an organization that had to protect its unique way of proceeding against the crown's policies of centralized control of all religious affairs in the Americas.

By the time of Acosta's arrival in 1572, the Society's presence in the king-dom had grown to over forty Jesuits, among whom were counted some mesti-zos who had been born in the viceroyalty.[3] The principal institutional ministries of the Society in Peru were the college in Lima, the residence at Cuzco, and the *doctrinas* in the province of Huarochiri and the pueblo of Santiago del Cercado just outside of Lima. The work of the college and resi-dence was very similar to the activities of their counterparts in Europe, and the community in Lima even had a novitiate. The exception in Lima was that in addition to ministering to the Spanish colonials of the city, the Jesuits also employed their traditional pastoral ministries of preaching, establishing con-fraternities, teaching catechism, and distributing relief to the poor among the sizable African slave population of the city as well as the native peoples. In ad-dition to the college, residence, and doctrinas, Jesuits were called upon to ac-company and help Viceroy Toledo on his visitation of the kingdom. This was a task they were not enthusiastic about because of the partisan way in which it embroiled them in a number of political feuds between the viceroy and other Spaniards, lay and religious, as well as the native peoples.

The work in the doctrinas was also thought to be unsatisfactory by a num-ber of Jesuits, and it created deep divisions in the new province. The problem was a canonical one, since the doctrinas were technically parishes for Indians, and those priests who served in them were assuming a curacy with all the obligations of stability and monetary privileges that such a benefice required. Such curacies were explicitly forbidden by the Jesuit Constitutions, which saw them as an obstacle to the desired poverty and mobility that St. Ignatius de-sired for his sons. Fr. General Borja had given permission to Fr. Jerónimo Ruiz del Portillo, first provincial of Peru, to accept some doctrinas, since this was the established way to minister to the Indians in Peru. The pressures being ex-erted by the crown for the Society to accept them also influenced Borja. But the general made it clear to Portillo that he should resist the crown's pressures to accept many of these Indian parishes.

Among the most vocal Jesuits against Portillo's decision to accept the doc-trinas at Huarochiri and El Cercado were those with the greatest *gravitas* and eloquence in the new province, Fr. Luis López, rector of the residence at Cuzco, and Fr. Bartolomé Hernández, former rector of the Jesuit colleges at Salamanca and Burgos. The viceroy kept the pressure up for the provincial to accept new doctrinas. In 1572 Portillo withdrew the Jesuits from the doctrina of Huarochiri because of opposition in the province to this work, seen as con-trary to the Jesuit Institute, and also because of the murder by hostile natives of two of the Jesuits assigned there. The Society would continue ministering to Indians by means of occasional missions organized from Jesuit colleges and by working with those natives who lived and worked in or near the cities where the Society was established.

Adding to these tensions, Portillo also decided to refrain from being Toledo's confessor. This decision deeply bruised the viceroy's honor, who saw it as a public commentary on his moral and spiritual life. The viceroy's sense of personal humiliation and his frustration that his pleas for more Jesuit doctrineros continued to go unheeded led him to select Fr. Diego de Bracamonte, S.J., to return to Spain and Rome and make his case before the king and the pope. Bracamonte was one of the Jesuits recently withdrawn from the doctrina of Huarochiri, and he agreed with Toledo's position that Jesuits should accept more doctrinas. The roller-coaster relations between Toledo and the Society had begun in earnest; it was during this dip in the ride, and just after Bracamonte had departed for Spain, that Acosta arrived in Lima on April 27, 1572.

Acosta's Early Years in Peru: 1572–1575

Upon his arrival in Lima in April 1572, Acosta took up residence in the Jesuit college and began teaching moral theology, hearing confessions, and preaching. He soon acquired a reputation as a remarkable theologian and sacred orator and as a prudent and wise counselor, as well as an exemplary religious. José remained occupied in these labors until June 1573, when the provincial, Portillo, sent him on a visit of the southern half of the kingdom. This would occupy him for the next year and a half, until the end of 1574, when he returned to Lima.

During his travels Acosta made a canonical visitation of the recently founded and troubled Jesuit college at Cuzco. He also toured the other principal cities of the kingdom, including Arequipa, Potosí, La Paz, and Chuquisaca, where he and his companions stayed in local hospitals. The purpose of this mission was to reform the lax religious life of the Cuzco Jesuits, to investigate the possibility of new foundations, and to examine the work among the native peoples being carried out by others in the Peruvian hinterlands. Acosta's preaching and other ministries at Potosí, Arequipa, and La Paz were warmly received, and he left those cities with promises and cash advances from leading citizens to found Jesuit colleges there.

The trip was efficacious on another count, since it provided him with invaluable knowledge of the state of the kingdom and of the Indian peoples and cultures which it comprised; at this time indigenous peoples formed most of the population of the cities he visited. This invaluable new knowledge would become the foundation of his subsequent writings and governance of the Jesuit province. Accompanied on this trek by several Jesuit brothers who knew the native languages well, it is probable that Acosta acquired some knowledge of Quechua at this time; this is implied by the many references to this tongue in his writings. However, Acosta's reliance on other Jesuits who were better "tongues" than he was in his subsequent travels throughout Peru and in the translation of some of his works into Aymara and Quechua suggests that he was less than bilingual in his grasp of the native languages.[4]

During his first visit of the kingdom, Don José was summoned to a personal audience by Viceroy Toledo, who was interested in meeting him because of the fame of his sermons. While complying with the viceroy's summons to Chuquisaca, Acosta met Don Polo de Ondegardo, one of Toledo's advisors and a renowned author on Inca culture and history. Padre José became familiar with his writings on Inca religion and society; these writings were his principal sources on Incan culture for two of his subsequent books, the *De Procuranda* and the *Historia*.

Upon his return to Lima at the end of 1574, Acosta continued his teaching, hearing confessions, and preaching. At the request of the viceroy, he began teaching at the University of San Marcos in Lima. The subject of his lectures was the sacraments, Sacred Scripture, and the Incarnation, and their content would eventually appear in his books *De Procuranda* and *De Christo Revelato*. On the insistence of the Jesuit provincial, Father Portillo, he also assumed the duties of consultor of the Inquisition; Acosta exercised this office along with the provincials of the Augustinians and Franciscans. It was during this time that he came to sit in judgment on Fray Francisco de la Cruz and two other Dominicans.

Cruz had a reputation in the kingdom as a seer and holy man; and these activities, certain indiscretions with women who sought him out for spiritual guidance, and his inflammatory preaching with Lascasian and Carranzan sympathies came to the attention of the Inquisition. Both Las Casas and Carranza were Dominicans and bishops. Carranza was the archbishop of Toledo who was arrested for heresy by the Inquisition in Spain because his catechetical writings were found to be too Lutheran in approach. On the other hand, Las Casas, bishop of Chiapas, Mexico, was never found guilty of heresy, but his denunciations of the cruelties of the Spanish colonization against the indigenous peoples made him and his sympathizers unpopular and suspect in the eyes of the Inquisition. Cruz's apocalyptic preaching would become the subject of Acosta's sermons and eventually part of his books *De Procuranda*[5] and *De Temporibus Novissimis*.[6] Cruz was eventually burned at Lima in the auto-de-fe of 1578.[7]

In the middle of 1575, Fr. Juan de la Plaza, S.J., arrived in Lima with the powers of official visitor and with the expressed instruction to seek out Padre Acosta's opinions on a host of issues related to the situation in the kingdom. The frictions within the order and with the viceroy about the legitimacy of accepting doctrinas and Portillo's other unpopular decisions as provincial made the new general of the Society, Everard Mercurian, decide to send Plaza to Peru to put things in order. Plaza's visitation would last a record four years, and he would spend long periods of time in the three houses that made up the province at this time. Much impressed with Acosta's wisdom and knowledge of Peru, Plaza quickly named him rector of the college of Lima. A few months later, on January 1, 1576, the feast of the Circumcision and the titular feast of the Society, at a festive repast and in the presence of the viceroy, Plaza appointed the thirty-five-year-old Padre José the second provincial of Peru.

As one would imagine, the circumstance of having a visitor and a provincial governing a province concurrently for such an extended time would generate jurisdictional tensions even among the most compatible of personalities. Plaza was not the easiest person to get along with because of a tendency to perfectionism. And so it would come to pass that Acosta and Plaza would part ways on unfriendly terms. On matters of substance, Acosta and Plaza disagreed about the collaboration that Jesuits should give to the Inquisition and on their judgment about Fr. Luis López, S.J., whose indiscretions with women and his opinions about the viceroy's policies would cause the Society much trouble during Acosta's provincialate. Acosta opposed López, while Plaza supported him.

They also disagreed on the legitimacy of the Spanish conquest of the New World. Plaza, like Portillo and other Jesuits in the province, had their doubts about this matter, while Acosta considered it a legitimate commission received from the Holy See to preach the gospel. Acosta did not deny that there were instances of unjust violence in the various conquests. But he also noted that all other empires in history had origins plagued by unjust violence. Besides, the Spanish conquest of the New World was, in Acosta's estimation, a fait accompli whose alteration at that time would produce more harm than good.[8]

Acosta's relations with the visitor were not always tense, and on a number of crucial issues for the life of the province they were in agreement. They both favored accepting doctrinas, and they both opposed the viceroy when he closed the Jesuit houses in Potosí and Arequipa and the Jesuit college in Lima and insisted that the Society accept the administration of the University of San Marcos in Lima.

Acosta's Provincialate: 1576–1581

Acosta's first major act as provincial was to convoke the first Jesuit provincial congregation in Peru. This gathering was a meeting of the professed fathers, those priests who had completed their training and had professed the three vows of poverty, chastity, and obedience and a special fourth vow of obedience to the pope for missions. Such a congregation was supposed to be held every six years in the missions to treat matters of import in the province. A provincial congregation would also be summoned to elect delegates to general and procurator's congregations of the order held in Rome.

The first congregation of the Peruvian province met in two sessions and in two different locations. The first session took place in Lima, January 16–27, 1576, and the second in Cuzco, October 8–16, 1576. At most, eleven fathers were present at the sessions, and among them was the official visitor, Father Plaza, who could not cast any votes in the congregation's proceedings.

There were three major issues that the general wanted this congregation to address, in accordance with his instructions to Father Plaza. Holding the congregation in two sessions and in two locations made it possible for all the *patres graviores* to be consulted on these and to be persuaded to accept the congregations's decisions. The most important issue was the acceptance of doctrinas, and it was paramount for the progress of the Jesuit enterprise that a consensus be achieved around this issue. The second issue was the specific behavior of certain Jesuits of the province; among the questions raised by some Jesuits were whether those ministering among native peoples should be accompanied by soldiers and whether *criollos* and *mestizos* should be admitted into the Society. The Society's relationship with the viceroy was the third major issue that the general wanted considered.

In addition, during its session in Lima the congregation discussed the overall ministries of the Society in Peru and the province's internal organization. Besides the doctrinas, Acosta proposed three other means the Society could employ to minister to the native peoples. One was to open Jesuit residences in towns that were more heavily populated by indigenous peoples, so as to offer them the Jesuits' traditional ministries. Another was preaching popular missions among the native populations; and the third was to open a school that would be wholly devoted to the education of the children of the *kurakas*, the native leadership.

The fathers discussed the merits of each of these ministries and decided that despite the inconveniences involved with each one the Society should continue to employ them or initiate them if it had not yet done so. With regard to the doctrinas, they agreed that they should request permission from the general to accept them because the same conditions that existed in the East Indies and Japan that allowed the Society to modify its prohibition against them existed also in Peru; it was simply the dire necessity among the native peoples. The congregation also commissioned a number of catechetical tools in Quechua and Aymara including a short and a long catechism, grammars, a confessional manual, and a primer of prayers that could be printed in Spain and then used in Peru.

One interesting point which will feature prominently later in Acosta's life that the fathers discussed was the province's internal organization. The necessity of new governmental structures not specified in the order's foundational documents would be a rancorous issue that would occupy Acosta upon his return to Spain in the late 1580s. Indeed, it would be one of the principal planks of the Spanish Jesuits, the so-called *memorialistas* or *perturbatores*, who were dissatisfied with what they perceived to be Fr. Claudio Aquaviva's distant, anti-Hapsburg, partisan, autocratic, and rule-obsessed governance. This concern for a less remote style of governance would feature prominently in the convocation of the Fifth General Congregation in 1592, and Acosta would be seen as one of its chief proponents.

As early as 1576 Acosta and the other professed fathers were willing to entertain such new possibilities in governance, just as they were willing to consider new forms of ministries forbidden by the Constitutions, such as accepting doctrinas. In so doing they manifested a certain freedom from established Roman ways of proceeding which would grow stronger in subsequent years among Spanish Jesuits. Later, as we shall see, this flexibility would come to be interpreted by the order's central leadership as disobedience to the Constitutions and a threat to the general's autonomy vis-à-vis the centralizing religious policies of Philip II.

But in 1576, the principal concern of the professed fathers of Peru was that the local provincial had too much power. To redress this imbalance they considered several options, including the naming of a *comisario*, who would have special powers over the provincial in certain specified matters. This had long been one of the principal points of Philip II's religious reform policies. The crown saw it as a means of insuring a more direct oversight of the life of religious orders that were often ruled by their leadership ensconced in Rome.

Orders with central leadership in Rome were not always quick to attend to the desires of the royal will. In any event, the option of the comisario was rejected by the Jesuit superior general in Rome precisely because of the fear that such a structure would play into the crown's hands and weaken the general's authority over the Society in Spanish lands. But the fathers in Lima agreed that it should be proposed to the general that the provincial's official advisors, or consultors, have the same power that the general's assistants were granted by the Constitutions, that is, the power to depose from office in certain cases.

During the second session of the congregation in Cuzco, the assembled fathers elected a procurator, Fr. Baltasar de Piñas, who would represent the province in Rome, and approved the acts of the first session. The catechetical tools ordered by the fathers in Lima were entrusted to Fr. Alonso Barzana with the understanding that they would be completed in time to go to Spain with the newly elected procurator in April 1577. Alas, these were not completed until 1584, when Acosta himself and a team of translators put themselves to the task by commission of the Third Provincial Council of Lima. The Fathers also considered anew the province's internal organization and decided that the provincial's visitation should take place only every two years, and recommended that dependent vice-provinces should be erected in the northern and southern parts of the province in present-day Ecuador and northern Argentina.

The first provincial congregation of Peru accomplished its goal of fixing a plan of action for the ministries of those early Jesuits in the kingdom. As we have seen, the province's ministries among the native peoples, including the administration of doctrinas, would be its principal work but not the exclusive emphasis of its pastoral endeavors. It is evident from reviewing the official acts of the province congregation, which were sent to Rome with the procurator in 1577, that the new provincial played a major role in the deliberations. And so it is no surprise that the content of these acts bears a great resemblance to Acosta's *De Procuranda*. It was probably the case that both documents— the acts of the congregation and the *De Procuranda*—mutually informed each other, since Acosta was working on the text of the *De Procuranda* throughout 1576.

Besides the acceptance of the doctrina of Juli in 1576, Acosta's provincialate also saw the establishment of new works and houses throughout the province. A new residence was opened at Potosí in 1577, and another college was established at Arequipa in 1578. It was this expansion of the Society into areas not exclusively populated by indigenous people that would unleash the wrath of Viceroy Toledo on the Jesuits. Toledo interpreted the new foundations as flagrant examples of the Society's unwillingness to dedicate more men to the work among the Indians, and thus a violation of the royal will that had approved the Society's entry into the Americas for this expressed purpose. Much of the remainder of Acosta's provincialate would be spent in doing battle with the viceroy over the ministries the Society should have under its care.

Acosta's struggle of wills with Toledo started in 1578 and involved several incidents which reveal the intransigence of both parties. Even as early as 1577 Acosta had written to Philip II complaining of what he considered very high tributes demanded of the indigenous peoples by the viceroy.[9] But it was in 1578 that the tensions between the provincial and the viceroy erupted into the public forum. Toledo ordered the Jesuits to abandon their new foundations in Arequipa and Potosí for the reasons mentioned above. Furthermore, he closed down the Jesuit college in Lima by issuing a decree that forbade students from attending classes anywhere in the city except at the University of San Marcos. At the root of this sanction was the viceroy's displeasure that the Society had refused to accept the administration of the university, which he had offered it since 1576. In 1579 the saga continued with the arrest of Fr. Luis López, S.J., by the Inquisition.

The charges against López at this time involved the opinion he expressed in writing concerning what he considered to be the illegitimate rule of Philip II and his officers in the Indies. Although it does not appear that Toledo had any knowledge of charges of sexual misconduct against López, the matter was complicated because López had previously been denounced to the Inquisition for illicit sexual relations with several women in Lima and Cuzco. Furthermore, López's office as rector of the Jesuit community in Cuzco and his personal relationship as confidant of the previous provincial, Father Portillo, and of the visitor, Father Plaza, did little for the Society's reputation. Both Portillo and Plaza had been implicated in the charges of sexual misconduct and treason to the crown, respectively.

Yet another variable in the equation was Acosta's own knowledge of the charges against López while he served as a consultor of the Inquisition before he was named provincial and later in his capacity as superior of both López and Portillo. Because of his knowledge of the events, Acosta was both well informed about the López case and tragically incapable of acting on the information he had lest he violate the confidentiality of his offices as inquisitor and as provincial. López was eventually found guilty of expressing treasonous opinions about the crown and was exiled to a life of penance in the Jesuit college of Trigueros in southwestern Spain. Both Plaza and Portillo escaped the wrath of the Inquisition, but the episode served to consolidate Viceroy Toledo's enmity against the Society in Peru. The incident also promoted the perception in royal circles both in Peru and in Spain that the Society was an ungrateful and untrustworthy servant of the crown.

Also in 1579, Acosta joined the provincials of the other religious orders working in the kingdom in writing to the king complaining of the way in which Toledo's enforcement of the royal decree of 1574 concerning the patronato made their lives impossible. They claimed that Toledo had violated many privileges obtained from the Holy See by the respective religious communities.[10] For the remainder of this year and into 1580, a good deal of Acosta's energies would be spent marshalling support from influential colonials and writing the king himself to overturn Toledo's actions against the Jesuits.

In the long run Acosta would win the day, and the king would restore to the Society its properties in Potosí and Arequipa and its right to conduct classes in Lima.[11] However, the cost of the victory to Acosta, even if not Pyrrhic, was high. Soon after finishing his term as provincial in 1581, he petitioned Rome to be allowed to return to Spain, alleging the weakened state of his health occasioned by the arduous and acrimonious tenure of his provincialate. Toledo for his part was relieved of his duties as viceroy in 1581 and returned to Spain to live out the rest of his days as one of Philip II's majordomos.

At the beginning of Acosta's provincialate in January 1576, the Jesuit province of Peru numbered 77, with no more than a handful of Jesuits who were fluent in the native languages. The Society labored at the colleges in Lima, La Paz, and Cuzco, and the doctrina of Santiago del Cercado on the outskirts of Lima. In 1581, when Acosta finished his stint as provincial, there were 113 Jesuits, 50 of whom were fluent in various native languages. This was quite a testimony to his concern, frequently expressed in the *De Procuranda*, for the importance of learning the indigenous languages so as to be able to adequately proclaim the gospel to the native peoples. During Acosta's tenure as provincial, a college had been opened in Arequipa, the doctrina of Juli was accepted and was thriving, and there were new residences in Panama and Potosí. From a purely statistical point of view, Acosta's term as provincial had been one of growth. Despite his running war with Viceroy Toledo, the Society's reputation seems not to have suffered much, and when Acosta laid down his charge as provincial there were petitions from Philip II for the Society's services in present-day Ecuador, Chile, Bolivia, and northern Argentina.

Notwithstanding these signs of success, Acosta's provincialate had its drawbacks both for him personally and for the province as a whole. As we have seen, the repeated crises with Toledo and others left him physically and emotionally exhausted. His unsuccessful dealings with Toledo, albeit not wholly his fault and despite the fact that ultimately he was vindicated, made the life of the Society anxious and precarious. For the first time there are reports of Acosta suffering from "melancholia" and leading a religious life that was lax in observing the vows of poverty and chastity.

Fr. Juan de Atienza, rector at the college of Lima when Acosta finished his term as provincial in 1581 and later provincial himself (1585–92), was sufficiently convinced of Acosta's shortcomings that he wrote the general explaining why José should never again be placed in a leadership position. Atienza's concerns included his mood swings, high lifestyle, possessiveness in material things, particular or exclusive friendships with members of the Jesuit community, excessive fastidiousness about his accommodations, and preoccupation with the affairs of the Inquisition and the new viceroy.

Such complaints about Acosta would increase once he left the position of provincial, and added to them would be charges that he showed favoritism for certain students of the college at Lima and that he spent an inordinate amount of time with certain nuns whose convents he undertook to reform during his last years in Peru. In fairness to Acosta and keeping in mind that both his predecessor, Portillo, and successor, Piñas, were more problematic in the job of provincial than he, one would judge that overall his provincialate was satisfactory but not without some spectacular mistakes on Don José's part.

It also seems that some of the charges leveled against him of living too comfortable a lifestyle may to a certain extent have been caused by his deteriorating health. While it is difficult to give a precise date to his physical deterioration, it seems that during his years in Peru Padre José put on a large amount of weight, which aggravated his chronic health problems. José's obesity seems to have unleashed his appetite, and he required more food than the average member of the communities in which he lived.

In addition, his corpulence made movement difficult, particularly travel on horseback, and he came to require the permanent accompaniment of a companion, usually a Jesuit student or brother, on his travels. Years later in his apologia[12] against charges leveled against him for playing a role in the convocation of the Fifth General Congregation of the Society, he would allude to these special requirements not as indicative of a dissolute religious observance, as his detractors alleged at that time, but as a necessity occasioned by his poor health compounded by his obesity. It is amazing, given his corpulence and the chest pains that this produced, that Acosta accomplished as much as he did while in Peru, let alone the travels and intrigues he would be involved in upon his return to Spain.

The Apple of Acosta's Eye: The Reduction at Juli[13]

Probably the most important work undertaken during Acosta's provincialate was the reduction at Juli on the southwestern shore of Lake Titicaca near Peru's current border with Bolivia. It was among those who directly ministered to the native peoples at Juli that Acosta's ideas had their greatest impact. Acosta had to argue with passion at the first provincial congregation of Peru to convince his brother Jesuits to accept this type of permanent apostolate among the Amerindians in the Peruvian hinterlands. He visited Juli twice during his official visitations of the province in 1576–77 and 1578–79. And the enthusiasm with which he wrote in his annual letters to Rome about the progress of this mission suggests that, of all the apostolates that he initiated as the second provincial of Peru, Juli was the apple of his eye. With time Juli would become the initial model and training ground for the more famous Paraguayan reductions established by the Society in the seventeenth century.[14]

The doctrina of Juli had originally been entrusted to the Dominicans, who began to staff it in 1547; but after two royal inquiries into their work in the province of Chucuito, in which Juli was located, had found their labors wanting and because of the dangers and hardships involved in ministering there they relinquished the parish in 1572. Secular priests then received pastoral care of the town until the viceroy offered Juli to the Society and the first Jesuits arrived in November 1576; Jesuits would remain laboring in Juli's churches, schools, and mission stations until the expulsion of the Society from Spanish domains in 1767.

One thing that the royal inquiries found deficient in the Dominicans' work was their failure to learn the native languages, which meant that they could catechize only in Spanish and hear the confessions only of those Indians who spoke Spanish. Furthermore, their missiological strategy favored the frequent transfer of friars from town to town, which made it all the more difficult for them to learn the native tongue and to engage in the necessary prolonged programs of instruction for the native peoples who were neophytes in the faith.

It also appears that the Dominicans were slower to incorporate the native peoples into Christianity through baptism. Whereas the standard initiation process in the Americas was baptism first and instruction afterwards, the Dominicans at Juli departed from the procedure and decided to instruct the people first and then baptize those who showed a sufficient grasp of the faith. They could do this because they believed that explicit faith in Christ was not necessary for salvation and that an implicit faith was sufficient to be saved; thus they felt no urgency for baptism. The Jesuits followed another strategy. They too catechized before baptism, of course, but emphasized an explicit faith in Christ and sought to initiate the people into the Christian religion as quickly as possible.

The Dominicans were also accused of inflicting harsh corporal punishments on the Indians for offenses that were unrelated to their evangelization. And they were reputed to have cajoled excessively large donations of lands, churches, and other tributes from the Amerindians under their pastoral care. In short, they were perceived as unusually greedy.

At the time of the arrival of the Jesuits there were approximately 14,000 Indians in the town of Juli and its environs. Most of these native peoples had been baptized but not fully catechized, and so catechesis became an immediate and perennial concern of the Jesuits who labored at Juli. There was always a good number of Jesuits assigned to the reduction, averaging around twelve priests, brothers, and scholastics. Juli became the residence for young priests of the Peruvian province who were finishing their Jesuit formation with the final stage called "tertianship."

In accord with Acosta's insistence on the importance of mastering the native languages, there was also a language school at Juli for Jesuit scholastics destined for ministry among the native peoples. Aymara, Quechua, and Puquina were taught at this school with great success. Spaniards were not allowed to reside in Juli, as was the case with most other Jesuit reductions. But because of Juli's strategic position on the road from the lowlands of Peru to the altiplano, it became a favorite stopping point for those who traveled that road. Bishops and other clerics, royal officials, miners and other businessmen were frequent visitors of the Jesuits at Juli. Guests were welcomed, but a three-day limit was usually placed on their stay.

As Acosta repeats over and over again in his writings, the scandalous behavior of Spaniards, both lay and clergy, was one of the biggest stumbling blocks for the faith of the native peoples. From the very beginning of the Jesuit presence at Juli, great efforts were made to keep those who might give bad example to the natives out of the town. Also a calculated program of winning the natives over was employed by the Society from the beginning of its presence at Juli. As Acosta insisted in the *De Procuranda* and the *Doctrina Christiana*, the integrity of the missionary, persuasion, and the collaboration with the local elites would do much more for winning the natives to the faith than coercion.

At Juli persuasion took the form of frequent catechetical instruction and sermons as well as the replacement of native sacred places and feasts with Christian substitutes. Crosses were erected on native sacred mountains and other holy places, the feast of Corpus Christi replaced Inti Raymi, new sacred dances were introduced and incorporated into Christian liturgical rituals and processions. The Jesuits of Juli worked with the *kurakas*, known in Spanish as *caciques*, seeking their permission for their preaching, catechesis, processions, and confraternities. The kurakas of Juli kept the books of all alms received and distributed. They were in charge of seeing to it that their respective clans, or *ayllus*, attended the required catechetical instruction. The kurakas also administered all punishments, physical or otherwise, to those who violated the town's laws, especially those prohibiting idolatry and drunkenness.

In accordance with their Constitutions and traditions, the Jesuits accepted no gifts from the native peoples for themselves, nor did they employ them for their personal service. Once their austere basic needs were met, the Jesuits were very careful to use the rest of the funds they received—from the crown, from the income of the sheep and llama herds set aide for the maintenance of the four parish churches of the town, or from gifts—for the relief of the poor. Juli boasted one of the best free hospitals in Peru, and its munificence to the poor made it a magnet for the needy throughout the altiplano. Of course, in keeping with the Jesuit rule, no stipend was accepted for any of the religious ministrations that the Jesuits dispensed to the native peoples.

Acosta articulated a theoretical foundation for ministry among the Amerindians in the *De Procuranda*, where he insisted that not all the Amerindians had the same degree of cultural development and that their evangelization had to be adapted to each group's particularities and capacity. Here he developed his famous tripartite typology of barbarians, discussed in detail in chapter six. How his theories worked out in practice is demonstrated by the reduction of Juli.

The governance, catechesis, and worship of Juli were organized into four parishes. Each parish was governed by native kurakas from the ethnic groups that inhabited that parish and was attended by a bilingual Jesuit priest. The

Huancollos belonged to St. Peter's parish; the Incas, Chambillas, and Chinchallas lived in Holy Cross; the Mochos, or Mojos, inhabited Assumption; and the Ayancas belonged to St. John the Baptist.

Each morning the Indian children, both boys and girls, under sixteen years of age went to one of the local parish churches, and under the supervision of an Indian catechist they repeated the short form of the catechism and various prayers. This also occurred at the Angelus each day. On Sundays the children were joined by their elders. Also on Sundays there were open-air sermons for the whole town followed by a sung solemn high mass accompanied by exquisite musical compositions. After mass alms were distributed to the needy accompanied by another period of catechetical instruction. After a few hours of free time, the whole village would once again gather at two o'clock for a massive procession and public recitation of the catechism. Once the procession concluded there was a program of native songs and religious theater in the central plaza of Juli in front of St. Peter's Church.

Participation in all the sacraments, except Holy Orders, was also a hallmark of the spiritual life of Juli. Acosta advocated this in his writings, but it was rather unusual for priests who worked among the Amerindians to encourage them to receive the sacraments, especially the Eucharist. But at Juli, most of the native peoples received Holy Communion every two months and on the principal feasts of the liturgical year. So many regularly received the Eucharist during the Easter season that often the churches of Juli could not accommodate all the communicants. Juli became known as the *pueblo santo*, or holy town, and the Amerindian Rome.

The maxim that Acosta popularized in the *De Procuranda* concerning the tack to be followed in the evangelization of the native peoples, "first humans and then Christians," also guided the efforts of the Jesuit missionaries at Juli. All were expected to work. In general, the Jesuits of Juli held their flock in high regard, considering them industrious and intelligent laborers. In theory, they believed, as did Acosta, that the natives should not be overly hispanicized in the process of evangelization. And so some social structures and cultural customs that were not thought to be in violation of the natural law and the gospel were maintained and fostered. Among the native social structures and customs that the Jesuits of Juli fostered were the use and manufacture of native dress, many of the nonreligious songs and dances, native languages, and the structure of native leadership. Native artistic potential and the use of *quipus*, or knotted strings used by the Incas as a method of recording and remembering past events, were also harnessed to decorate the churches of Juli and to teach the catechism.

The town came to have two schools run by a Jesuit brother and staffed by Indians, and from time to time one or another Jesuit priest. The children, both male and female, who were more capable were taught to read and write. All were instructed in various trades, particularly those related to the wool trade, since the principal commerce of the reduction was the raising of sheep and llamas. The children were also taught to sing, and the Juli choirs came to be renowned in southern Peru. They often performed on major feasts in the larger towns of Copacabana and La Paz. All this bore a great resemblance to the Acostan position that the native peoples could reach the levels of civilization and faith of the Europeans through education.

Don José's emphasis on persuading the natives through convincing reasons was also implemented by the fathers at Juli. As in Lima, the Jesuits of Juli established houses where natives convicted of idolatry and prostitution served out their sentences. Part of the regimen of these houses was a program of religious and moral exhortation aimed at persuading the inmates to abandon their idolatrous practices and scandalous behavior and embrace Christianity. This was accomplished through a program of instruction and preaching that was specifically tailored to the guilty parties.

The Jesuits of Juli were no less effective in providing the natives with new tools, skills, and ways of organizing and entertaining themselves that made their lives easier. We have already mentioned the famous Juli choirs. These were accompanied by Indians on musical instruments that at first the Jesuits imported from Europe and later manufactured at Juli and other Jesuit reductions. The Jesuits also spent their own funds to purchase and install several fountains and a flour mill for the town. They introduced sheep herding and plowing with oxen, and eventually Juli came to have its own printing press. They also journeyed with the Indians from Juli to the infamous silver mines at Potosí in Bolivia. Here a certain number of Indians from each clan was required to work for several months each year as payment of tribute to the crown. The Jesuits organized the natives so that those who were at the *mita* in Potosí had their lands and flocks at Juli looked after by their neighbors who remained behind there.

What the Jesuits did was subject to criticism, of course. Some of their contemporaries accused them of exercising too much control over the lives of the natives of Juli. The charge that Juli was a theocracy and that the Jesuits were paternalistic has also been made by contemporary scholars. But the fact remains that despite the regimented daily order and the various regulations and punishments that governed life at the reduction, Juli did not experience any decrease in population. Rather, its population steadily increased during the

211 years that the Jesuits staffed it. Native peoples flocked to live at Juli while the trend in the other reductions was the opposite. And there are also letters written to Philip II by the native leaders of Juli who defended the Jesuits on charges made against them and begged Philip II to send more Jesuits so that other Julis could be founded.

As for the modern charge that the Jesuits were paternalistic, it cannot be denied that they were. As is often the case in Acosta's writings, the natives were considered children, and the Jesuits basically related to them in a paternalistic fashion. But neither can it be denied that in an age when the natives were physically and psychologically abused and exploited by the Spaniards and the Indian aristocracy alike, paternalism was an improvement. Nor should one fall into the anachronistic temptation of interpreting the fact that physical punishments were decreed by the Jesuits of Juli, though never administered by them, for violations of the town's laws, especially those against idolatry and drunkenness, as a cruel and sadistic style of evangelization. Harsh physical punishment for the violation of the community's codes was an accepted part of native culture, and severe corporal punishment and shame rituals were practiced even throughout Europe at this time for heresy. The Jesuits' acceptance of harsh and often cruel native punishments was a form of accommodating themselves to native culture; these harsh punishments did not seem to them to contravene the natural law or accepted European codes.

There was also opposition from within the order to the Jesuits of Juli. There were tensions and repeated skirmishes with those who felt that the Jesuits of Juli were leading too austere a life. There were those in the province, especially provincials, who had designs on the wealth generated by the reduction. They did not approve of the policy at Juli of returning as much income as possible from gifts, salaries from the crown, or profits from the parishes' herds and haciendas to the work of the reduction, especially to relief of the poor. However, the rectors of Juli managed successfully to rebuff the designs of successive provincials to use the surplus wealth of the Juli reduction for the common good of the province. The rectors' appeals to the Jesuit superior general in Rome repeatedly brought replies that sided with them against the provincials in these disputes.

The Third Council of Lima and the Final Years in the Americas: 1581–1587

Despite his expressed desires to return to Spain at the end of his tenure as provincial, Acosta remained in the Americas for another six years. The principal reason for the delay appears to have been his appointment by the new and saintly archbishop of Lima, Toribio de Mogrovejo, as the official theologian of the Third Provincial Council of Lima, more popularly referred to as Lima III. So it seems that just as Acosta's reputation soured within the Jesuit order, a new patron, Monseñor Mogrovejo, arrived to insure that Padre José's stature as a player in the kingdom's ecclesiastical and civil affairs would not be diminished.

Archbishop Mogrovejo arrived in Peru more or less concurrently with the new viceroy, Don Martín Enríquez de Almanza, in May 1581. Both he and the new viceroy had received instructions from Philip II to convoke a provincial council; the last one had taken place in 1567. Viceroy Toledo had attempted to do this throughout his tenure in an attempt to consolidate the *vicariato real* in what pertained to the bishops and secular clergy, but the ordinaries of the ecclesiastical province dragged their feet and ignored his convocations of the meeting. It now fell to Mogrovejo and Enríquez to initiate and complete what Toledo had been unable to accomplish.[15]

Monseñor Mogrovejo convoked the council on August 15, 1581, officially inaugurated it a year later, and terminated it a year after that on August 15, 1583. This council is recognized as the most important of the colonial provincial councils because it was attended by the bishops of almost all the sees then in existence in the Spanish-controlled portion of the continent. Only the churches of Nicaragua and Panama, whose sees were vacant at the time, were not represented. The decrees and documents of Lima III consolidated Philip II's vision of the patronato over the bishops and secular clergy, and the catechism it designed for the indigenous population became the standard catechetical tool throughout the continent well into the nineteenth century. Some have even come to call Lima III the "Trent of the Americas" because of the impact of its reformist agenda, similar in many ways to the program of the great council, whose last session had ended two decades earlier.

The work of Lima III occurred in two major parts. The first of these dealt with the imposition of Philip II's vision of the patronato as a vicariato on the bishops and secular clergy of Latin America, giving him wide ecclesiastical power. It placed Archbishop Mogrovejo and Viceroy Enríquez as agents of Philip II in confrontation with most of the other bishops who attended. The catalyst for this confrontation was the case of the bishop of Cuzco, Sebastian de Lartaún, who was accused of the homicide of one of his canons and the despoliation of his goods. Lartaún denied the council's authority over him and was supported by the vast majority of the other bishops present. He was opposed by Mogrovejo, one other bishop, and the viceroy. The situation was a tense one, and it imperiled the work of the council until things resolved themselves with Lartaún's unexpected death in October 1585.

The second part of the council's work concerned itself with the evangelization of the Indians, and it pitted the bishops and viceroy against the *encomenderos* and other colonial elites who resisted the council's reformist program in favor of the indigenous peoples. Acosta was involved in both parts. However, his provincial's prohibition of any involvement in investigating charges against the bishop of Cuzco curtailed his direct participation in the intrigues of the first part of the council's agenda.

Acosta did have a direct hand in the council's work as the author of the council's acts, catechism, confessional manual, and handbook of catechetical sermons.[16] These were later translated into Quechua and Aymara by a team of diocesan priests and were printed at the press of the Jesuit college in Lima; they were the first books printed in Peru. Later, upon his return to Europe in 1587, Don José would defend the council's legislation against the secular clergy that tried unsuccessfully to have its decrees abrogated by both the crown and the Holy See. In so doing he managed the diplomatic coup of facilitating an occasion when the crown's interests in the Church in America was in tandem with the position of the Holy See and opposed to the interests of the secular clergy and other colonial elites. This victory won Acosta the respect and trust of both the crown and the pope and served as the catalyst for Fr. General Claudio Aquaviva's decision to have him return from Rome to Spain as the Society's special representative to Philip II.

Once Acosta finished composing and supervising the translation and publication of the council documents and catechetical tools, he once again insisted on returning to Spain. There was no longer a momentous task to be completed to hold him back, and no doubt the disposition of the Jesuit provincial at the time, Father Atienza, played a major role in this decision. Atienza was Acosta's former rector and the one who had written to the general detailing Acosta's unsuitability for leadership. He was not enthusiastic about having the demanding and singular Don José around.

Acosta arrived in Mexico in transit to Spain in 1586, and he remained there for almost a year. The reason for the delay was to avoid returning to Europe at the same time as or shortly after the arrival of Frs. Luis López and Miguel de Fuentes, both of whom had been condemned by the Inquisition in Lima. The general ordered Acosta to delay his arrival in Spain by some time so that there would be no suspicion about these three Jesuits traveling together or arriving in Spain within a short time of each other.

The year's delay in Mexico provided Acosta with both fortuitous and ominous occurrences. Felicitously, he was able to visit with his brother, Bernardino de Acosta, S.J., who had recently been appointed rector of the Jesuit college at Oaxaca. When not occupied with the usual ministries of preaching and hearing confessions that we have seen him exercise throughout his life, José studied the culture and religion of the Aztecs and worked on his books. His guide in the study of the Aztec civilization was Father Juan de Tovar, S.J. Acosta's work in this area would be incorporated into his second and perhaps best-known book, the *Historia Natural y Moral de las Indias*, which he completed upon his return to Spain.

We know from a letter of the provincial of Andalucia, Gil González Dávila, to Fr. General Aquaviva that when he arrived in Spain Acosta had already finished two books inspired by his American experiences, particularly his preaching ministry.[17] These two were the *De Temporibus Novissimis*, dealing with the interpretation of the predictions about the end times contained in the Bible, and the *De Christo Revelato*, a compilation of the life of Christ as contained in the Bible and meant to be an aid to preachers.

Finally, while in Mexico Acosta met the troublesome Fr. Alonso Sánchez, S.J.[18] While in the East Indies Sánchez had proved to be imprudent. On several occasions he had criticized the peaceful evangelizing work of the Jesuits in Japan and China; and he advocated the military conquest of China so that, as with the Inca and Aztec empires, Christianity could more safely and efficiently be propagated there. Letters from such famous Jesuits as Matteo Ricci and Alessandro Valignano and from the Jesuit provincial of Mexico warned Aquaviva that unless the imprudent Sánchez was somehow checked his ideas could do much damage to Society's work in the Far East. While Sánchez was on his way to the court of Philip II as agent of colonizers of the Philippines, Aquaviva acted and assigned Acosta as his personal superior.

The general forbade Sánchez to speak in public without Acosta's permission and ordered Acosta to accompany Sánchez back to Spain. He also asked Acosta to persuade Sánchez to change his position on the conquest of China, and Acosta's mission with regard to the bellicose Sánchez was a success. With the help of the provincial of Andalucia, Acosta persuaded the Philippine agent to drop his plan for the conquest of China, which Sánchez never mentioned to Philip II when he later had his audience with the king to discuss other Filipino affairs. During this process Acosta also wrote two memoranda to the general criticizing Sánchez's ideas about spreading Christianity in China through its armed invasion.[19]

Sánchez's dealings with Acosta at this time seemed to have been concluded amicably. However, several years later, in 1593, Aquaviva would send Sánchez as the Society's personal representative to Philip II in an attempt to get the sovereign to desist from the plan concocted by Acosta to convoke a general congregation. Among the arrows in his quiver that Sánchez would launch against Acosta at that time was the unsubstantiated charge that he came from a *converso* family; this would become the source of the allegation of his Jewish roots.

Before taking up Acosta's tumultuous life back in Europe, and by way of summarizing his fourteen years in the Americas, it would be advantageous to present a portrait of the man who was returning to Spain. The purpose is to highlight, in the light of his American years, some life experiences from this time and characteristics of his personality which will loom large during the last thirteen years of his life. The thirty-two-year-old priest of frail health who arrived in Peru in 1572 knew himself to be a promising and talented preacher and teacher, given his previous success in these ministries in Europe. These talents were recognized, confirmed, and toasted during his years in Peru. But in addition, the teacher and preacher of Alcalá, Ocaña, and Plasencia became the author, theologian, provincial, and man of confidence of Lima's ecclesiastical and civil elite. In the process, Acosta was transformed and his opinions about himself, the world, and the Society crystalized.

But these opinions crystalized in the mind not just of a Jesuit missionary but of a man who realized that his opinions were more respected than those of his contemporaries by virtue of his intellect, prudence, and experiences. Some of these American experiences would prove to be particularly formative of this "new" Acosta returning to Spain, and they would clash with the status quo he would encounter in the Society upon his return. In particular, his experience of Jesuit governance in Peru and of affairs of civil and religious import in the court of the Peruvian viceroys and the archbishop of Lima would fill him with a confidence and a sense of himself that surely explain some of the iconoclastic actions and liberties he took back in Spain.

Acosta's style of religious leadership was eclectic. At times he could be flexible, and at other times he exhibited a tenacity that verged on stubbornness. He worked tirelessly to insure that the Society did not neglect its obligation to evangelize the indigenous people; to this end he crafted innovative reinterpretations of the order's prohibitions against accepting parishes and fixed revenues and traveled hundreds of miles through inhospitable and dangerous terrain to insure it. His love for the order and his tenacity in defending its way of proceeding put him at odds with the highest power in Peru. It would be a long-lasting struggle, which he won for the Society but at the cost of paralyzing the majority of her ministries in the kingdom during the battle's duration. He governed while facing both external opposition from the viceroy and internal opposition from a visitor who remained in the province for a record four years. Yet his vision for the province prevailed over both adversaries.

In short, a more sickly Acosta set off for his homeland in 1586, but hardly the psychologically broken man that his letters petitioning his return at the end of his provincialate in 1581 painted. Rather, it was Don José de Acosta, self-assured, accustomed to playing for high stakes and winning, and living religious life by his own rules who disembarked in Andalucia in 1587. In many ways he reminds one of those legendary Jesuits of Ignatius's generation who both forged the way for the Society's success in Italy, Spain, and Portugal and who at the same time were so cantankerous and convinced of the worth of their opinions that they were also accountable for the early Society's greatest crises. Don José was very much in the league of Frs. Nicolás Bobadilla, Simão Rodrigues, and Antonio de Araoz.

CHAPTER 4

The Nadir of Acosta's Life
Spain and Rome, 1587–1600

Back in Spain: 1587–1591

If Padre José left a Castile in ascendancy in 1571, in 1587 Don José returned to a Spain, *Hispania*, at the height of its imperial prowess. Ironically, in the late 1580s Spain was also at the beginning of a long and slow process of political, military, and economic decline precisely because of the burdens that accompanied its imperial status, burdens it was ill equipped to meet. In 1580 Philip II had secured the succession to the Portuguese crown and its vast colonial empire in South America, Africa, and Asia. Spain's interests shifted from the Mediterranean to the Atlantic, where from Lisbon Philip II's concerns included protecting the bullion routes from the Americas, countering English might on the high seas, and crushing rebellion in the strategic and prosperous Low Countries.

It will be no surprise, then, that Don José, the faithful servant of the crown at Lima III and knowledgeable veteran missionary in both Peru and Mexico, armed with a glowing letter of recommendation from the viceroy of Peru, was received by Philip II in Madrid. Not once but twice, in December 1587 and January 1588, was Don José summoned before the king to report on various matters related to the king's possessions in the Americas. Acosta won the king over with the many interesting details he could provide about diverse subjects related to the New World, and he covered the gamut from ecclesiastical and civic affairs to the natural sciences. His conquest of the goodwill of Philip II was cemented when he dedicated the first printed edition of the *De Procuranda* to him on January 20, 1588.[1] In addition to his debriefing with His

Catholic Majesty, Don José had various meetings with other court personages; among them were the members of the Council of the Indies and the papal nuncio, Monseñor Cesare Speciani, who provided him with a letter of introduction to Pope Sixtus V.

Among the matters of import that Acosta dealt with at court at this time were the approbation of the decrees of Lima III and the sanction and funding of the College of St. Martin in Lima for the sons of Indian *kurakas*. In the first matter he had to do battle with Domingo de Almeida, the representative of the secular clergy of Charcas in present-day Bolivia, who opposed the reforms of Lima III before the Council of the Indies. From several other documents written by Acosta to press his agenda it is known that he also treated the matters of the episcopal visitation of doctrinas administered by religious, episcopal vacancies in the Americas, and the business affairs of clerics.[2]

After visits in January 1588 to Valladolid, where his brother Jerónimo was rector of the Jesuit professed house, and to Segovia, Acosta set off for Rome in the summer of 1588, where he arrived in September. He remained in the Eternal City for a brief two months. During this time he conferred with Sixtus V, the Roman curia, and Fr. General Aquaviva and his assistants.

With the pope and the cardinals of the Roman curia, Acosta discussed many of the same issues he discussed with Philip II and his deputies on the Council of the Indies. Again he did battle with a representative of the secular clergy from Peru, Francisco Estrada, sent to the Holy See to thwart the implementation of Lima III. Acosta's diplomatic deftness once again shone, and he managed to persuade the pope's secretary of state, Cardinal Caraffa, to change his mind and refrain from annulling the decrees of Lima III, as Estrada had nearly convinced him to do. Don José also procured a series of papal privileges for the College of St. Martin.

If the discussions at the papal court concerning Lima III were to be of tremendous significance for the Church in Peru and the Americas, the most significant discussions for the remainder of Acosta's personal life occurred at the Jesuit curia. Aquaviva commissioned Acosta to be his personal representative to Philip II. It was his hope that Don José's newly found esteem and influence with the monarch would help resolve the tensions between Philip and the Society. The king considered the Society a disloyal institution, and an order failing in religious élan and orthodoxy. In particular, Aquaviva's marching orders to Acosta were fourfold: make Philip II happy, satisfy the chief inquisitor, Cardinal Quiroga, and his deputies with regard to the Society's cooperation with the Inquisition on a number of matters, bring some tranquillity to those Jesuits who were disaffected with the general's governance, and by all means prevent the Society from being canonically visited by someone who did not belong to it, as Philip II had proposed to the pope.[3]

Upon his return to Spain Acosta met with the king and convinced him that Jesuits were better suited to carry out the visitation of the Society that he desired. Acosta himself undertook the visitations of the provinces of Andalucia and Aragon from 1589 to 1591 while Fr. Gil González Dávila visited the provinces of Toledo and Castile, and Fr. Pedro Fonseca visited the Portuguese province. But the problems in Spain went far beyond the issue of an official visitor.

Division in Jesuit Spain

It is not fair to say that the troubles that plagued the Spanish Assistancy began during the term of Claudio Aquaviva. However, the Neapolitan's tenure as superior general of the Society did unleash an intense if not completely new problematic period both internally in the Spanish houses of the Society and externally in the Society's relations with Philip II, his Inquisition, and the Holy See.

The set of problems which developed into a crisis began in March 1586, when four Jesuits, all men who had held important positions in the Castile province of the Society, were summoned to Valladolid and arrested by the Inquisition. Among them was Fr. Antonio Marcén, the provincial of the Jesuit province of Toledo. The case for which they were summoned involved the alleged sexual misconduct of a Jesuit confessor in Monterrey with several women who sought him out for confession. The charge against the Jesuit superiors imprisoned by the Inquisition at Valladolid had to do with their obstruction of the Inquisition's procedures by not handing over the Jesuit confessor accused of misconduct in the confessional.

But this case was really about a much larger problem: resentment of the Society's influence in Spain and its independence from the Inquisition. At issue was the Society's lack of cooperation with the Inquisition's proceedings, as well as certain pontifical privileges that the Society enjoyed with regards to the absolution of heretics in the sacrament of penance. In addition, the contents of the 1586 edition of the *Ratio Studiorum*, the magna carta of Jesuit education, concerning the adequacy of the Vulgate translation of the Bible and the importance of the study of Greek and Hebrew were considered dangerous.

The *Ratio* was perceived as lukewarm in its defense of the Vulgate, the official Catholic translation of the Bible, which was maligned by some Reformers;

it was also suspect in its Protestant-like enthusiastic endorsement of the study of ancient languages. And so, in addition to examining the four Jesuits it imprisoned, the Inquisition ordered the Society's Constitutions, its bulls of papal approbation and privilege, its rules, and the *Ratio Studiorum* examined for heterodoxy. The Inquisition also decreed that Jesuits could not leave the national territory without its permission lest any Jesuit guilty of heresy escape its reach. Rumors ran rampant about what would come next, and an air of malaise began to take hold among Jesuits throughout Spain.

As the Inquisition proceeded in secrecy against the four Jesuits and the Society's foundational documents, the memorialistas reappeared upon the Spanish scene. They were a relatively small group of Jesuits, no more than thirty in number from the Castile and Toledo provinces, who wrote many memoranda ("memorials"), often anonymous, to the king and to the Inquisition complaining of the chaotic state of affairs in the Society. Their writing campaign had actually begun some ten years earlier, during the tenure of Fr. General Mercurian, but at that time it had little impact. But during this atmosphere of crisis from 1586 to 1589 it was well received by the Inquisition. The movement died out by 1605.

The memorialistas were concerned about what they considered the inherent injustice of the Society's organization. In particular, they felt that the Society vested tremendous power in the office of a foreign superior general resident in Rome, who was misinformed and unfamiliar with the Society in Spain. The most significant sources of the Spaniards' discontent with Aquaviva in particular, both within and outside of the Society, were his imperious style of governance and the centralizing policies he followed in keeping with the trend initiated and expanded by his two predecessors in the office, Borja and Mercurian. Both of these characteristics of the Aquavivan generalate irked the Spanish Jesuits and Philip II's sense of nationalism and offended the long-established custom in Spain of doing things related to ecclesiastical affairs *a la española*.

Some historians have examined this turbulent period of the Society's history and have suggested that the memorialistas were really champions of democracy who battled the totalitarianism of the Jesuit way of proceeding created by St. Ignatius.[4] It would seem, though, that the memorialistas were rather motivated by a whole range of issues. Among these must be included resentment at being passed over as superiors in favor of Jesuits from a younger generation, distrust of a non-Spanish general, Hispanic political, cultural, and religious chauvinism, and fear of what was foreign and perhaps heretical. These men were unconvinced of new developments and were resistant to a more centralized, distant, and rule-driven Society of Jesus than they had entered and in which they had spent the early part of their religious life. The memorialistas were men confident in a king who prided himself on being the champion of Catholicism. They also trusted the king's ministers and instruments, i.e., the Inquisition, that would keep Spain free of the violence and disorder associated with heresy and rampant elsewhere in Europe at that time.

Toward a Solution to the Crisis: Acosta's Role

The Constitutions of the Society of Jesus provide a way to address complex issues such as those that racked Spain in the late 1500s, a general congregation of the order. A general congregation must meet after the death of a superior general in order to elect his successor; this had happened four times in the Society's history. A mechanism also exists to summon a general congregation for other matters of great importance; this was seen as a rare occurrence, and it had never happened before 1592. The movement to call a general congregation was perceived as disobedience to Fr. General Claudio Aquaviva, who did not favor it, and to the whole order that at the congregation of procurators of 1590 had voted not to convoke such a meeting at that time. José de Acosta was the man most responsible for persuading Philip II to pressure the pope to order the Jesuits to summon a general congregation. In fact, Acosta himself would attend the Fifth General Congregation as the king's personal representative.

Acosta was in breach of the spirit of the Society's vow of obedience by not informing Aquaviva of the king's request to the pope that a congregation be summoned against Aquaviva's and the Society's desire. But as Acosta suggests in his apologia, it was a rather murky judgment whether to inform Aquaviva of the king's plans before seeing the pope when the king had commanded him not to talk to anyone except Clement VIII about the matter and when Aquaviva's own conduct was at issue. To have approached Aquaviva would have risked imperiling his mission to the one whom Acosta considered the highest authority in the Society and indeed in all of Christendom, the pope. But even apart from the question of to whom he owed ultimate obeisance, Acosta may have been faced with the more pragmatic but no less torturing issue of how to proceed in the best interest of the Society in light of Philip II's distrust of Aquaviva and decision to seek the Society's visitation by an extern.

Given the latter situation, it may reasonably be argued that Acosta's disobedience to Aquaviva was the lesser of two evils and that it prevented the greater disaster of placing the Society in Spain under the authority of the king himself through his chosen visitor. Acosta's disobedience in serving as Philip's agent for the convocation of the congregation spared the Society of having its largest assistancy severed from its head. Therefore, Acosta's actions my be seen as disobedient but given the difficult circumstances in which he found himself they were not unreasonable or morally unjustifiable decisions.

Acosta was trapped between, on the one hand, his desire to serve his king and to prevent the Society from being visited by an extern and, on the other hand, his obligation as a Jesuit to be candid with a superior with whom he had less than complete trust and who had shown himself adamant against the convocation of a general congregation. This seems a more probable description of what moved Don José to try to convoke the congregation than the view that influenced by melancholia and ambition he lashed out at Aquaviva for not having named him a provincial after the visitations of 1589–91.[5]

A comprehensive treatment of this most complex and interesting period of the Society's history is beyond the scope of this book, and even Acosta's motivation for endorsing the congregation and for attending as Philip's representative is the subject of much study. Appendix one details how a different interpretation of the sources leads one to a different conclusion about Acosta's motivations in these affairs.

More generally, it seems safe to postulate that some of the motivations of the memorialistas would have appealed to Acosta's basest and to his most noble desires for himself and the well-being of his homeland, his king, and the Society. But as Acosta's actions and written statements against the memorialistas during and after his visitations of Aragon and Andalucia suggest,[6] he was in favor of the idea of convoking a general congregation only to examine the memorialistas' proposals and Aquaviva's behavior as general.[7] Acosta did not see his purpose as radically altering the Jesuit Institute, let alone bringing about its demise. His position, clearly stated in his apologia, was that the changes proposed by the memorialistas were of such a nature that they could be approved only by a general congregation. He argued that previous congregations had done the same in the past. His votes against the memorialistas' proposals in the general congregation also show that he hardly became the undiscriminating champion of their agenda.

Who can doubt that pride and resentment did play some role in Don José's deliberations in choosing to move against Aquaviva? As is seen from Peruvian reports after his provincialate, Acosta was prone to melancholia and had come to live a religious life characterized by special requirements concerning his room and board. Besides, for several months after his visitation of the Aragon province Acosta did not hear from the general, after repeated letters to him, and during this time his reputation and work on the visitations were being maligned; it is quite plausible that his respect, trust, and confidence in Aquaviva would have been sorely tried.

It is also true that Acosta's dealings with distinguished personages seemed to have reinforced his sense of self-import and *gravitas*. If any one could have thought himself suited to reform Aquaviva's shortcomings it was Don José, former missionary and provincial, author, diplomat, confidant of inquisitors, bishops, kings, and popes. He was a mere three years older than the general but, after all, was fifteen years Aquaviva's senior in religion.

In addition to the psychological factors that may have influenced Acosta, less passionate reasons and concerns made Acosta's move against Aquaviva seem justified and even heroic to a loyal subject of Philip II and son of Ignatius. Among these less passionate concerns was Aquaviva's distant, imperious, and rule-driven style of governance, for which the Fifth General Congregation itself reprimanded the Neapolitan. This style of Jesuit governance was very much at odds with the governance that Acosta and the memorialistas experienced during the less centralized days of the first generation of the Society, when Ignatius and Laínez governed in Rome and Nadal, Borja, and Araoz ruled as comisarios in Spain. It was Acosta's more collegial and personal style of governance as provincial of Peru—a style that allowed him to convoke a province congregation to decide the issue of the doctrinas and saw him log hundreds of miles on horseback to visit his subjects dispersed throughout a territory twice the size of the Iberian peninsula.

Perhaps the most important and convincing reason for Acosta's role in the convocation of the congregation is the one he cites in his apologia. Here he explains his concern that, given the continuing complaints expressed to Philip II about Aquaviva's governance and the governance of the Society's superiors in Spain even after the visitations of 1589–91, the king once again was contemplating naming a non-Jesuit to conduct another visitation of the Society in Spain. The king's distrust of Aquaviva was fueled by his confessor and his inquisitors, who, despite Aquaviva's letters professing his desire to please the king, had seen the general deftly enlist the Holy See in move and countermove to keep the Society free of the authority and jurisdiction of the Inquisition.

In 1588, Aquaviva had ordered Acosta to prevent at all costs a visitation of the Society by and extern. He had succeeded then, but now with the new threat Acosta felt that the best way to avoid this visitation was to suggest the convocation of a general congregation to address the memorialistas' complaints and the king's concerns about Aquaviva's antipathy to the Inquisition.[8]

The Fifth General Congregation: 1592–1594

There are other reasons to believe that Acosta's motivation for procuring the Fifth General Congregation was more rational than has been suggested by some historians of the period. Acosta demonstrated much integrity during the difficult two years from 1592 to 1594. While in Rome at this time he worked for the convocation of the congregation and his admittance and participation at its sessions as Philip II's representative. The reports and impressions about Acosta's actions before and during the general congregation by Philip II and Cardinal Francisco de Toledo, S.J., and the acts of the congregation itself reveal a man who was not the uncritical lap dog of Philip II. Nor, once the congregation tried to satisfy Philip II's concerns about the Society, reprimanded certain actions of the general's governance of the Society, and rejected the changes proposed by the memorialistas and expelled many of them, did Acosta become a sycophant of Claudio Aquaviva so as to win favor with the general.

At the same time Don José endured a campaign waged by Aquaviva to discredit him before the Society, Clement VIII, and Philip II. The general tried to exclude him from the congregation on the grounds that he had not been canonically elected. The campaign had mixed results. Aquaviva failed to exclude Acosta from the congregation; Acosta attended by pontifical order. Neither did the general's smear campaign undermine Philip II's and Clement VIII's opinion that Acosta was a suitable representative of the king to the congregation. Aquaviva advanced very general charges about his probity of life during his days in Peru as well as the calumny that he was of *converso* stock. The general himself brought these charges to the pope and dispatched Fr. Alonso Sánchez to do the same before Philip II.

Within the Society and especially among the Jesuits of Rome and the delegates to the congregation, Aquaviva's defamation of Acosta as the leader of the perturbatores was a success. For most of his nearly two-year stay in the Eternal City at this time, Acosta found himself marginalized both within the congregation and in the Jesuit community of the *penitenzieri*, or Jesuit confessors who ministered at the Basilica of St. Peter's. Aquaviva had exiled him from the professed house, Acosta's first residence in Rome, once his business to the see of Peter had come to light. During the congregation itself Acosta was forced to take an oath that he had neither written any of the memoranda against the Society's Institute nor sympathized with the proposals of the memorialistas to change it. From the tone of the *cri de coeur* that is his apologia, one receives the distinct impression that his isolation from the Society was an almost unbearable cross for Acosta.

It seems that as early as the beginning of 1593 Philip II had doubts about Acosta's loyalty to him.[9] The king's reticence toward Acosta raises questions about any portrait of Acosta as the uncritical servant of the crown and its design to procure the memorialistas' changes to the Institute. Before the opening of the Fifth General Congregation on November 3, 1593, Acosta wrote several letters to Philip II informing him of his negotiations with Francisco de Toledo, S.J., Clement VIII, Aquaviva, and the Duke of Sesa, the Spanish ambassador to the Holy See. These letters indicate that Acosta was aware that the fathers who would be elected to attend the congregation might not take kindly to Philip's role in its convocation. Acosta envisioned the possibility that they might confirm Aquaviva in his governance.

Acosta was also aware that he as the king's agent might be considered persona non grata by the congregation. And so he asked the king for permission not to represent him before the assembly if he saw that the congregation was ill-disposed to his intervention. He furthered advised His Catholic Majesty to prepare several memoranda for the congregation outlining his position. Depending on the mood of the congregation, one or another of the memoranda would be presented to the assembly in his name.[10] Acosta's suggestions seem to have been accepted by the king, as the events of the congregation indicate and as the notes of his ministers confirm. The king's business during the sessions of the congregation was brought to the delegates' attention by his majesty's memoranda and letters, by the speeches of the Duke of Sesa, and in the most decisive way toward the end of the congregation in February 1594 by the intervention of Cardinal Francisco de Toledo, S.J., on behalf of Clement VIII.

It is in light of this strategy that Acosta's supposed abandonment of Philip II's position during the sessions of the congregation must be seen. It was not, as some have suggested, that Acosta's actions at the congregation were two-faced because he distanced himself from the memorialistas, voted with the majority, and pledged his fidelity to Aquaviva.[11] That Acosta did not betray Philip II by voting with the majority on almost all the matters discussed is confirmed by the Duke of Sesa's letter to the king. The ambassador encouraged the king at the end of the congregation to be benevolent with Acosta, who had served him well and suffered much during the congregation's proceedings. And, indeed, upon Acosta's return to Spain in June 1594, Philip II showed himself grateful to him for all he had done on his behalf before and during the congregation.

The clearest testimony to Acosta's integrity during the proceedings of the congregation and to his characteristic independence of judgement was his negative vote on the exclusion of New Christians, or Christians with Jewish or Moorish ancestry, from being admitted to the Society. Only Acosta and one other delegate, Francisco Arias, voted on December 23, 1593, against the other sixty-two delegates of the congregation to prevent decree fifty-two from being adopted. Influenced by the erroneous impression that all but perhaps two of the memorialistas were New Christians[12] and anxious to please Philip II and the Inquisition, the congregation caved in to pressures supportive of this measure that had been pushed on, but successfully resisted by, the Society since the time of St. Ignatius. It is ironic that a congregation that was so concerned with preserving the original spirit and intention of St. Ignatius for the Society voted to adopt a policy that was so loathsome to him. And it is even more ironic that the man who was considered the delegate of the perturbatores should be one of only two delegates to resist this decree on the grounds that it violated the Society's long-established practice and the intention of its founder.

Acosta's vote on the issue of the exclusion of New Christians from the Society illustrates his integrity and independence of judgment against incredible pressures to conform to an action supported and favored by both Aquaviva and Philip II. An affirmative vote for decree fifty-two by Don José would have surely been a politically astute move for him to make. It would have curried favor for him with the delegates, Aquaviva, and Philip II without alienating any of them. Furthermore, it would have dispelled one of the rumors that Aquaviva was spreading against him, that is, that the Acostas were New Christians descended from Portuguese Jews.

By resisting the politically opportune move and voting his conscience, Don José once again behaved as we have seen him behave in the past. For example, he had the independence of mind to both support and challenge Viceroy Francisco de Toledo in his policies according to what he considered to be the more prudent. When the latter tried to implement policies that Acosta considered detrimental to the native peoples and the Society, Don José marshaled his pen against these policies, just as he supported him in his policy concerning the reductions and accepted the one at Juli for the Society. Indeed, this balance and independence of judgment was one of the defining characteristics of Acosta's thinking that, as we shall see in the next two chapters, is evident again and again in his writings.

On balance, the goals Acosta intended for the congregation were accomplished, and Philip II's interests were well served. Above all, the Society was spared an external visitation. Aquaviva was sufficiently chastised by a number of decisions taken by the congregation at the command of the Pope. Among these must be included the report from the congregation commission appointed to review his generalate and the papal order to elect new general assistants who were more sympathetic to the Spanish crown.

Philip II and the Inquisition triumphed over the general in several battles. The congregation conceded that Jesuits should be subject to the Inquisition in Spain by renouncing their privilege to absolve heretics without informing it of this act. The congregation also allowed Jesuits to serve the Inquisition without the authorization of their superiors. Finally, the congregation decreed that Jesuits should renounce all noble titles or ecclesiastical benefices at the time that they made their first vows after their noviceship.

However, the price that Acosta paid for the success of his master's proposals was not a small one. His reputation throughout the Society as the champion of the perturbatores was so sullied that, as the first modern scholar of his life and works has written, in subsequent years his other accomplishments would be disregarded. He was even expunged from certain official histories of the order.[13]

It would be inaccurate to infer that Philip II's success at the congregation meant that Fr. General Aquaviva was the vanquished party of the meeting. By the congregation's decision, New Christians finally came to be excluded from the Society. This was a confirmation of Aquaviva's decision in 1592 to prevent their admission in the provinces of Spain and Portugal, and it was perceived as a direct blow against Acosta and the memorialistas who were reputed to be New Christians. Father Aquaviva remained in power and prevented most of the changes proposed by the memorialistas from being implemented, even after they were brought to the congregation's attention by Philip II's ambassador to the Holy See. The only exceptions were the convocation of a general congregation every six years and the election of new general assistants, which the congregation saw itself forced to accept by papal command. Furthermore, Aquaviva procured the congregation's expulsion of most of the memorialistas from the Society.

The Final Years of Acosta's Life: 1594–1600

Aquaviva was not pleased with the possibility of Acosta's return to Spain, where he could continue to have access to the corridors of power. He had several Jesuits in Spain informally inquire at court about the king's disposition on the matter. But it was clear that the king felt he was in Acosta's debt and that Acosta enjoyed not only royal favor but also the protection of the Holy See. Acosta returned unhindered to Spain with the other delegates of the congregation in late April 1594. On June 27, 1594, he was received by the king at El Escorial, and he gave an account of his work in Rome; Philip II was pleased with him. In July 1594, Acosta returned to Valladolid where he assumed the rectorship of the professed house, the post he had held before he left for Rome in 1592.

That very same month Acosta wrote Aquaviva pledging his filial obedience. He finished his term as rector at Valladolid in 1595 and continue to live in the professed house, where his brother Jerónimo also resided, until the end of 1596. In November 1596, he would tell the visitor of the province of Castile, Fr. García de Alarcón, S.J., that he realized he had caused much trouble by his actions associated with the Fifth General Congregation, but he justified himself by claiming it avoided an external visitation of the Society.

His relations with Aquaviva would remain proper, if always somewhat distant. A good example of this is a letter that Aquaviva wrote him in February 1597, in response to his request to visit Madrid. The reason for the visit was to form part of a commission of theologians convoked by Philip II to examine a memorandum written by some theologians of the Roman curia against the king's involvement in the most recent papal conclaves. While in Rome Acosta had, with other Spanish theologians convoked by the Spanish ambassador, written a memorandum defending the king's actions. Now, at the ambassador's request, Philip II had ordered the matter reconsidered in Madrid, and Acosta was once again invited to participate.

He attended the meeting held in the summer of 1598 in Madrid. At its conclusion he was received by Philip II, who greeted him warmly and once again thanked him for his work both in the past and present on behalf of the crown. Aquaviva's response to the invitation was less than enthusiastic. In the letter authorizing Acosta's participation, Aquaviva wrote and underlined that of course he could treat that matter. But that matter and that matter only.

During his time in Valladolid Acosta's principal activities were the governance of the professed house, preaching, and writing. He had several writing projects going at the same time which ranged from the preparation of three volumes of sermons, which he had given during his days in Peru, to a commentary on the psalms and a six-volume work of scholastic theology and scriptural commentary. The three volumes of sermons would be published, and he died while working on the commentary on the psalms, which he completed up to Psalm 100. Aquaviva encouraged him in his writing, but in the fall of 1596 suggested to him by letter that, given the theological debates of the times, it was best that he cease work on the six volumes of scholastic theology and Scripture.

It should be remembered that the *De Auxiliis* controversy over grace and free will between Jesuit and Dominican theologians was in full swing at the time. Acosta was a staunch supporter of the open Thomism of the First School of Salamanca. He was not an enthusiast of the Jesuit theologians such as Suárez and Molina, who opposed the thinking of the Dominicans such as Báñez of the more closed Second School of Salamanca. The Jesuits proposed a much freer and eclectic interpretation of St. Thomas that Acosta and other older Jesuits, among them the memorialistas, saw as innovations unfaithful to the thought of the Angelic Doctor.[14] So sympathetic was Acosta to the Dominican position that in 1595 he was invited to preach at their church in Valladolid, St. Paul's, on the very feast of St. Thomas Aquinas himself.

At the beginning of 1597 Don José was transferred by the provincial to the Jesuit college of Salamanca, where he assumed the rectorship of that divided house. It was a move that did not please Father Aquaviva, but finally the general acquiesced and also named Acosta one of the province consultors. The rectorship that Acosta assumed in Salamanca was no sinecure. The community was plagued by divisions stemming from the *De Auxiliis* controversy.

In 1593, Fr. Miguel Marcos went to Rome for the general congregation and was replaced in his chair of theology by Fr. Francisco Suárez. Like Acosta and many other older Fathers, Marcos was a staunch Thomist who did not appreciate Suárez's interpretations of the Angelic Doctor. When Marcos returned from Rome in 1594, Suárez was happy to hand back to him his teaching responsibilities, but Marcos refused to teach while Suárez remained under the same roof with him. Marcos resumed teaching briefly during the 1594–95 term, but once again abandoned the classroom. The situation remained unsettled until January 1597, when a compromise was engineered with the good offices of Philip II himself. The king offered Suárez a chair in Coimbra, which allowed him and his supporters in the house to leave Salamanca without losing face. It also provided the way for Marcos to return to the classroom definitively. It is not clear that Acosta had a direct hand in these events, but from Marcos's history of the community it is clear that Acosta's rectorship was well received by the latter.

Apparently Marcos was not the only one pleased with Don José's manner of governing during his last years in Salamanca. To the acclaim of the community, Acosta saw to it that the college's physical plant was upgraded by the addition of a garden and more commodious refectory. Neither did he ignore the community's spiritual well-being. During his first year in office he gave a series of acclaimed and entertaining conferences to the scholastics on the nature of the Jesuit Institute. In particular, he treated the differences between the Jesuit way of proceeding and that of other religious orders. In addition to his duties as the rector of the Jesuit college in Salamanca, Acosta was engaged in a number of other ministries. He continued to write and publish, of course, and he returned to the pulpit and to his contacts with the elites of society. While in Salamanca he founded the Marian Congregation of the Annunciation for the university city's cap-and-gown set.[15]

He also led the community in practicing the corporal works on mercy. In 1599 a great famine engulfed Galicia, Asturias, and Portugal. The cities of Castile were inundated with refugees from these regions seeking sustenance and a better life. Like the other cities, Salamanca faced a precipitous rise in its vagabond population. Estimates of the number of homeless in the city at this time are as high as 4,000. At the forefront of the town's efforts to feed and lodge these indigents was Don José. He led the scholastics of his community in all types of spiritual and material assistance and service to the homeless. And he set an example for other religious leaders by lodging the homeless in the chapel of the community.[16]

Shortly thereafter, on February 15, 1600, after a brief illness, Don José died in the same city where forty-eight years before he had entered the Society of Jesus. Accounts from the time of his funeral indicate he was mourned not only by the Jesuits of his community but by many other religious and prominent men and women of the city on the Tormes. Apparently, recalling only his successes in religious life, academe, and service to the *patria*, they hailed him as a paragon of virtue, of secular and divine learning, and of service to his Catholic majesty Philip II.

— *Part Two* —

José de Acosta

HIS THOUGHT AND WRITINGS

DE PROMVLGANDO

EVANGELIO

APVD BARBAROS:

SIVE

DE PROCVRANDA

Indorum salute, Libri sex.

Authore IOSEPHO ACOSTA *Presbytero*
Societatis IESV.

EDITIO NOVISSIMA

LVGDVNI,

Sumptibus LAVRENTII ANISSON.

M. DC. LXX.

SVPERIORVM PERMISSV.

Title page of *De Procuranda Indorum Salute*
Lyons, 1570

CHAPTER 5

Jesuit Theological Humanism

Jesuit Theological Humanism

The previous four chapters have surveyed José de Acosta's varied and eventful life. Trained in the tradition of early Jesuit humanism and the Thomistic theology of the First School of Salamanca, Acosta the young priest sailed for Peru, where he assumed important positions in the Society's internal administration. Don José also played an important role in the civic and religious life of the kingdom as advisor, preacher, and theologian to the archbishop of Lima and the viceroy, as well as other colonial elites. He returned to Spain after sixteen years in the Americas very much the prototypical Renaissance man, as adept in the discourse of the academy as he was at the machinations of the royal court.

The next three chapters focus on Don José's hybrid way of doing theology, Jesuit theological humanism. The term *Jesuit theological humanism*[1] is an instrument of exploration to account for Acosta's style of doing theology. Jesuit theological humanism is marked by a highly rhetorical style that is concerned with moving an audience's heart to work on behalf of the salvation and evangelization of the Amerindians. It employs both the methods and sources of the humanists and of scholasticism, as well as a ministerial spirituality that is characteristic of Ignatius of Loyola and his followers. Above all, Acosta's Jesuit theological humanism is characterized by its eclecticism. Don José created a way of doing theology that served his ministerial concern to save and evangelize the Amerindians by integrating various theological trends of the Early Modern Period.

Jesuit theological humanism is in the tradition of Renaissance humanism[2] for several reasons. Don José's elegant and literate prose, principally in Latin, resembles the humanist concern for writing that was lucid and that emulated the literary style of the Greco-Roman classics. Acosta's concern with moral issues related to the Spanish conquest of the Americas and the salvation and evangelization of the Amerindians echoes the humanists' focus on ethical topics in their works. Acosta's frequent references to sacred and ancient history in support of his arguments is also in keeping with this cultural, literary, and educational movement that flourished in Europe from the fourteenth through the sixteenth century.

Furthermore, Acosta's Jesuit theological humanism also bears a striking resemblance to what has been called "Christian humanism,"[3] that is, the theology done by humanists and influenced by their scholarly interests in the Greco-Roman and Christian classics, philology, and elegant literary expression. Acosta's theological humanism resembles this type of theology in that it eschews the speculative concepts of the Schoolmen, favoring rather the use of the narrative found in what the humanists considered the Christian classics—the Bible and the Fathers. It also avoids scholasticism's use of the *quaestio* and commentary format and its concern to present a systematic and coherent elaboration of the Christian faith following the topics or articles contained in the creed, as was done in the great *summae*.

Acosta adopts the humanist penchant for the eclectic theological treatise.[4] These treatises were highly rhetorical and concerned with moving the heart to action. Their topics often focused on pressing moral issues. Acosta's two great American theological treatises, the *De Procuranda* and the *Historia*, like other humanist treatises were destined not for theological specialists trained in the universities but rather for a wider circle of readers. In the case of the *De Procuranda*, which was written in Latin, the audience would have been humanistically educated; but the *Historia*, which was written in Spanish, did not presuppose an audience with a professional university education or a humanistic formation. Instead, it was written for the intellectually curious who had an interest in knowing about the novelties of the New World.[5]

Yet Acosta, who was well schooled in the Thomism of the First School of Salamanca, never rejects the thought of the Angelic Doctor as did such prominent humanists as Valla[6] and Erasmus.[7] And while there were other Renaissance thinkers, such as Pico della Mirandola, Ficino, and Bandello, who were great admirers of the Dominican from Aquino,[8] Acosta is much more than an admirer. Especially in the *De Procuranda*, Don José repeatedly makes use of the theological method of the "open Thomism" of the First School of Salamanca.

Like the theologians of the First School of Salamanca, Acosta makes use of the Christian and Hebrew Scriptures, the Fathers, the Schoolmen, and the canons of the Church's ecumenical and provincial councils. In the *De Procuranda* he often employs these sources in the same way that scholastic theologians of the First School of Salamanca employed them, as proof texts. The humanist concern for philological and contextual analysis is not as evident in the *De Procuranda* as it is in some of Acosta's other works. For example, his unfinished commentary on the psalms[9] illustrates his competence in philological analysis, and, as we shall see elsewhere in this chapter, his use of history in the *Historia* resembles the way that some humanists conceived and employed it in their writings.

History, as Acosta understands and uses the term, is not the same as it is understood in the late twentieth century. History for Acosta is a well-written narrative of all sorts of true facts and events from the past, including the history, the religion, and the economic, social, and political organization of a people.[10] So history for Acosta encompasses not only today's understanding of history but also what today would be identified as the human or social sciences such as economics, sociology, anthropology, and ethnology. Furthermore, Acosta, as a good humanist, understands history to have a moral end. The events and facts from the past that he recounts are narrated for the purpose of instructing the reader in the actions one would take. In the case of the *Historia*, Acosta is concerned with actions related to the governance of the Indies and the impact of those actions on the salvation and the evangelization of the Amerindians.

The "Mystical Theology" of Jerónimo Nadal, S.J.

Acosta's theological writings bear their greatest resemblance to theological humanism insofar as they resemble Jerónimo Nadal's concept of *mystical theology*. As was seen in chapter two, Jerónimo Nadal visited Alcalá during Acosta's years there and gave a series of talks that profoundly influenced the Jesuits' way of life and studies. Among many other things, Nadal said that in studying theology the young Jesuits had to combine "the practical with the speculative" and "the spiritual life . . . with knowledge and theology."[11]

Nadal's way of doing theology attempted to combine positive theology and the theological precision of scholasticism in an elegant and rhetorical literary style and that reflected the humanist concern for piety and morality. Unlike scholastic theology, which was concerned about proving theses, Nadal wanted to move his audience to a course of action for the good of souls. In his writings, Acosta reflects this concern by marshaling the theological sources of the scholastics and humanists with urgency and passion to press home the point that the Amerindians could be evangelized and saved.

Nadal called his appropriation of positive theology "mystical theology." By *mystical theology* he did not mean the theory of mystical phenomena but rather the experience of these phenomena. Nor did Nadal's use of the term *mystical* mean what is understood by it today, that is, extraordinary spiritual experiences such as an out-of-body experience or an ecstasy. Rather, by *mystical* Nadal understood inner movements of devotion that were not thought to be uncommon experiences in the life of prayer and piety of many ordinary people.[12] He summarized the salient characteristics of Jesuit mystical theology, and indeed the whole Jesuit way of proceeding, with the phrase: *spiritu, corde, practice*, that is, in the Holy Spirit, from the heart, and pastorally useful.[13]

Nadal, who had made the Spiritual Exercises under Ignatius's direction in 1545, assumed the presupposition of Thomistic theological anthropology that Ignatius had made his own in the introductory remarks for those who give the Spiritual Exercises. Nadal believed from his personal experience of prayer and of the Exercises that one could cooperate with God's grace to discover, taste, and savor God's activity in the world and in one's own soul. Guided by the paradigms of the life of Christ and the teaching of the Church and relying on the insights garnered from Ignatius's own spiritual journey, one could scrutinize these movements of the spirits, as Ignatius called them. Through this analysis and examination of one's interior movements, called "discernment," one could come to an understanding in faith of God's will for oneself. And through this understanding one could thus make choices that help one further God's designs for the world. All this lay behind what Nadal meant by *spiritu*, in the Spirit.

Nadal insisted that this fundamental approach to spiritual life that characterized Jesuit spirituality should also inform the way young Jesuits studied theology and Jesuit theologians taught and did theology. The speculative thought of the schools that was so valued by Ignatius for the clarity and insight it could provide for an understanding of the faith had to be joined to one's feelings and to the interior movements of spirits one experienced in prayer. Nadal wanted to translate the speculative teachings of scholastic theology into a "humanistic rhetoric."

While the Schoolmen saw theology as primarily a speculative discipline that "was addressed to the head not the heart," the mystical theology of the Jesuits led to the transformation of scholastic theology because it produced new sensibilities and sensitivities. Thus the Jesuit student of theology and the Jesuit theologian could prevent the dryness to which speculative theology was prone. In this way, the will could be mobilized into action for the greater glory of God and the good of others. Hence the importance that Nadal attached to a theology that was *corde*, from the heart.

Nadal's mystical theology was not a new system of theology that competed with other schools such as those of Sts. Thomas and Bonaventure, of Duns Scotus and William of Ockham. Nadal insisted that the Society of Jesus did not have "its own particular way of talking" about theological issues; rather he wanted the Society to follow the accepted theological positions of the Church and in particular the thought of the Angelic Doctor. The novelty of his mystical theology was in its form, which Nadal did not claim to have invented. Rather, this was a return to a form of doing theology that had been prevalent in the Church during the monastic period and which "joined piety and spiritual feeling with speculation."[14]

Jerónimo Nadal wanted Jesuits to package or express the opinions of the Schoolmen in a way that was clear, simple, easy to understand, and geared to some persuasional end. In other words, Nadal insisted that Jesuit mystical theology be *practice*, that is, pastorally useful or helpful to a person's advancement in the spiritual life, especially doing spiritual and corporal works mercy. In this way Nadal tried to steer a middle course between what he considered two theological and pastoral extremes of his day. On the one hand he rejected the disdain for speculative theology and passivity in the spiritual life expressed by the Reformers and the *alumbrados*. And on the other, he fought the suspicion that certain speculative theologians, such as Melchior Cano and Tomás de Pedroche, had of the spirituality of Ignatius's Spiritual Exercises and of its adaptation to the pastoral ministry and theology of the early Jesuits. Nadal said of these theologians that they had forgotten that the Holy Spirit existed.

Acosta's Theology for the Americas

Acosta's theology, however, did not simply imitate Nadal's mystical theology. Don José was conscious that he was doing theology for a new world and that this required new approaches and solutions not easily understood by European theologians. In the *De Procuranda* he noted the need for theologians to come to the Americas:

> our theologians from Spain, no matter how famous and illustrious they are, nonetheless, fall into not a few errors when they judge matters pertaining to the Indies. Those who are in the Indies can see it with their own eyes and touch it with their own hands. And even when they are less famous theologians, they nonetheless reason more logically and hit the mark more often."[15]

Thus, although Acosta's American writings may be partially described as a hybrid of several sixteenth-century theological currents, his Jesuit theological humanism is more than any one or any combination of these currents. He went beyond these currents by incorporating some unique elements from the American context where he labored. In addition to the theological sources used by the humanists and the scholastics, Acosta employed the best findings that the Aristotelian natural philosophy of his day provided about the Americas as well as early historical and ethnographical accounts of the Aztec and Inca empires. Herein lies a clear example of the uniqueness of his theological style.

Unlike the many theologians of his day who considered the Amerindians as forsaken peoples in the clutches of the devil, Acosta had no reservations about using the history and social organization of the Inca and Aztec empires. He also incorporated scientific accounts about the geophysical and zoological uniqueness of the Americas into his theological arguments. Using these sources of the history, ethnography, and natural science of the New World, he argued that the people of the Americas had not been abandoned by God and were capable of being evangelized.

In this way, to paraphrase Acosta himself, he could reason more logically and hit the mark more often about theological and pastoral matters concerning the Indies than could more prestigious Spanish theologians who had never set foot in the New World. Such matters included whether it was expedient to hold that the Amerindians could be saved without explicit faith in

Christ and whether Jesuits in the Americas should be dispensed from their prohibition to accept *doctrinas*, or Indian parishes. As was seen in chapter three, it was at the reduction of Juli that Acosta's theological and pastoral solutions came to be applied most extensively by his Jesuit confreres and bore their greatest fruit.

Don José's awareness that the problems and situations encountered in the Indies required new theological and pastoral solutions, his optimism that the evils of the Spanish conquest could be corrected and that the Amerindian could indeed be evangelized and saved, and his curiosity about the natural and cultural novelties of the New World resemble the unique characteristics of Hispanic Renaissance humanism.[16] Hispanic Renaissance humanism had both an interest in the exotic cultures of the Indies and a faith that sixteenth-century Spaniards lived in a privileged historical moment. Reflecting the chauvinism of an international empire at its zenith, many early modern Spanish humanists believed that progress beyond the accomplishments of the past was possible and that a new and better future could actually be realized by their efforts.

The two chapters that follow examine the theological method and form of Acosta's thought. The method, described in chapter six, uses both the open Thomism of the First School of Salamanca and the humanist understanding and use of history in theological argumentation. The form, explained in chapter seven, is a highly rhetorical and elegantly literary prose similar to Jerónimo Nadal's mystical theology; chapter seven also underscores some of the most important Jesuit themes in Acosta's writings that reflect the spirituality of St. Ignatius's Spiritual Exercises.

The separation between theological method and form is, in fact, difficult to substantiate in the work of any theologian since they are inseparable and influence each other; it is particularly difficult to make such a strict separation when describing theological humanism since the humanists' concern with elegant literary expression made narrative a crucial aspect of their way of doing theology. Still, such a distinction is useful for the sake of explanation and examination of Acosta's way of doing theology. This study will be based mainly on Acosta's American works: the *De Procuranda Indorum Salute*, the *Historia Natural y Moral de las Indias*, and the *Doctrina Christiana y Catecismo para Instrucción de los Indios*.[17] For this study, a brief overview of the these three works, Acosta's American trilogy,[18] will provide useful background.

Acosta's American Trilogy: An Overview

The **De Procuranda Indorum Salute**, written in 1576, was the first book penned by a Jesuit in the Americas. It comprises six books, each book with an average of twenty-two chapters; its length is approximately 550 pages.

The first book presents Acosta's principal concern: that the Amerindians can indeed be evangelized and saved. He refutes those who argue against this position and exhorts both priests and royal administrators to collaborate with Christ in God's will for the indigenous peoples of the Americas. While never adopting Bartolomé de las Casas's jeremiads against the Spanish conquest of the Indies, Acosta makes it clear in this first book that the failure of the evangelization of the Amerindians did not lie with them but with the Spaniards. According to Acosta, it was the Spaniards' cruelty and other sins, as well as the ineffectual methods of evangelization employed by many of the missionaries, that are responsible for the paucity in the harvest of souls.

The second book of the *De Procuranda* treats a number of controversial theoretical questions associated with the evangelization of the Amerindians. Acosta addresses whether it is licit to wage war against unbelieving Amerindians because of their infidelity and rejects this position. He takes up the issue of the Amerindians' violations of the natural law and again concludes that these violations are not sufficient reasons to wage war against them. Furthermore, Don José agrees that the slaughter of innocents by tyrants is a sufficient reason to wage war but rejects that this reason applies to the Indies since the conquest of the Indies by the Spaniards has shed more innocent blood and caused more injustices than any Amerindian tyrant had caused.

He also writes about the concern that some had that the evangelization of the Indies was not favored by God. Some believed that because, unlike other missionary enterprises throughout the Church's history, the evangelization efforts of those who ministered in the Americas was not accompanied by miracles, God did not wish the salvation of the indigenous peoples of the Indies. Acosta refutes this opinion, and in what will become a recurrent theme in various of his writings he argues that God has been preparing the salvation of the Amerindians over the course of the centuries. Indeed, he sees the greatest impediments to the spread of the gospel in the Indies to be not the disposition or natural ability of the Amerindians but the rapacious and incorrigible behavior of the Spaniards, both ordained and lay, who scandalize the neophytes in the faith and raise doubts about its validity.

Books three through six address more-practical problems and suggest remedies for their resolution. In book three the problems addressed are about the civil, political, and economic administration of the Indies. Acosta makes suggestions about the type of royal functionary who should be sent to govern in the Indies and asks whether it is just that the native peoples pay tributes to the Spaniards and how these should and should not be assessed. He writes about the *encomienda* system, the obligations that the *encomenderos* have to the Amerindians in their charge, and how priests should hear the confessions of the *encomenderos*. Don José also focuses on the problem of drunkenness among the Amerindians and makes some suggestions for abetting this social problem. He concludes book three by warning that the customs of the indigenous peoples that are not against the tenets of Christianity should be conserved and that the Spaniards should be careful not to overly Hispanicize the Amerindians.

Book four is concerned with the priests who labor among the native peoples. Acosta stresses the necessity to send only the most exemplary ministers to work among the indigenous people and insists that these should learn the languages of their flocks. An interesting and visionary suggestion is made in chapter eleven of this book, where Acosta stresses that the Indies need theologians; he advocates that theologians be sent to the Americas so as to avoid European theological solutions that often miss their mark.

Finally, books five and six treat a whole series of issues dealing with the catechism and the sacraments. In book five, among other topics Acosta argues against those who hold that only implicit faith in Christ is necessary for salvation and argues that the Society of Jesus should accept Indian parishes. In book six the typical Jesuit concern to promote frequent confession and communion is evident. Acosta argues against the practice common in the Peruvian Church at the time that denied the Amerindians communion. And again he insists on the importance of learning the native languages so that a remedy could be put to the scarcity of Indian confessions.

The **Historia Natural y Moral de las Indias** was completed upon Don José's return to Spain in 1587 and first published in 1590 in Spanish. It represents the mature reflection of his American experience after his fifteen-year stint in Peru and Mexico. Originally the parts of these books that dealt with the Andean regions were published in 1589 along with the *De Procuranda* and made up a separate work called *De Natura Novi Orbis Libri Duo*.[19]

The work is made up of seven books, of which one through four deal with various natural phenomena in Peru and Mexico, the *historia natural*. Thus, books one and two deal with the earth and its relation to the cosmos, while book three examines the constitution of the world by the four primal elements of air, water, earth, and fire. Book four moves to more-particular considerations and examines the mineral, vegetable, and animal novelties found in the Americas.

Books five through seven describe the religious practices and other customs of the Aztecs and Incas, as well as their history and political and social organization; this is the *historia moral*. Books five and six bear a great resemblance to Eusebius of Caesarea's *Praeparatio Evangelica*.[20] Just as Eusebius chronicled the religion of the Greeks, Egyptians, and Hebrews with apologetic aims for Christianity, Acosta attempts something similar for the Aztecs and Incas. Of course, Acosta is not defending the Amerindian religions per se, as Eusebius was doing for Christianity. As we shall see in chapter six, Acosta maintains that the inhuman and diabolical customs of the Amerindians had parallels in the religious practices and customs of the Hebrews, Greeks, Romans, and other Mediterranean peoples. Indeed, Don José cites Eusebius and other patristic and classical authors by name to underscore this opinion.[21]

Finally, book seven devotes two chapters to the miracles worked by the Trinity in the Americas for the benefit of the faith of the Amerindians. For Acosta these "miracles" include how God disposed the religious beliefs and social practices of the Amerindians so that Christianity could be easily propogated, in addition to healings and mass conversions occasioned by the actions of Christian missionaries and laypeople and to the termination of droughts.

The **Doctrina Christiana** is a collection of catechetical books principally written by Acosta at the order of the Third Provincial Council of Lima (1582–83). In 1585 the book was published in a trilingual edition of Spanish, Quechua, and Aymara at the printing press of the Jesuit college of Lima and thus became the first book ever to be published in Peru. It comprises a long and a short catechism and the so-called third catechism, which presents the essentials of the Christian faith in a series of thirty-one sermons.

In addition, it contains some brief notes concerning the Quechua and Aymara languages that are pertinent to the translation of Christian words and concepts, a confessional manual for priests noting, by each of the ten commandments, particular sins common to the peoples of Peru, and a description of the religious errors and superstitions of the native peoples. It is a work the purpose of which is to instruct these peoples in the basics of Christianity and to inform the priests who minister among them about their pagan religious practices and other sins.

Jesuit Theological Humanism in Acosta's Other Works

The *De Procuranda*, the *Historia*, and the *Doctrina Christiana* embody the salient characteristics of Acosta's Jesuit theological humanism; they best exemplify Acosta's unique way of doing theology and are his most important works. However, Don José also produced other theological writings, and these too reflect his Jesuit theological humanism. As was seen earlier, Acosta was an accomplished orator. Throughout his life preaching was a habitual ministry for him, as indeed it was for many Jesuits of his generation. Don José's other theological writings are either examples of this important ministry or aids to it.

Two years after his return to Spain from Mexico in 1588 he published two works in one volume, the *De Christo Revelato, libri novem* and the *De Temporibus Novissimis, libri quatuor*.[22] Both works are compendiums of scriptural and patristic citations for use by preachers in sermons having a Christological or apocalyptic theme. As homiletic aids, they are organized thematically by different titles applied to Christ and topics pertaining to the last days. Under each chapter heading in these works, Acosta provides references to the life of Christ and the end times contained in the gospels, other New Testament books, and relevant passages from the Hebrew Scriptures and the Fathers. They were meant to be suitable texts that preachers could incorporate into their sermons.

The *De Temporibus Novissimis* originated from Acosta's work as a censor of books in Peru. At the request of Fr. General Aquaviva, he examined the writings on the book of the Apocalypse of Fr. Lope Delgado, S.J., of the Juli mission. Lope Delgado's writings were never published, but Acosta used his notes from his examination of them to write the *De Temporibus Novissimis*.

To the extent that the *De Christo Revelato* and the *De Temporibus Novissimis* provide the sacred orator with ample biblical and patristic sources to illustrate the Christological and apocalyptic themes of his sermons, they reflect the penchant of the Dominican theologians of the First School of Salamanca, responding to humanist criticisms leveled against scholasticism, to incorporate more scriptural and patristic sources into their argumentation. However, missing from these two works are references to classical and contemporary history and to the natural and human sciences as they were understood in Don José's day, which so punctuate his American trilogy.

Acosta's interest in homiletics was further developed in his other great theological publication that was printed in his twilight years, three volumes of sermons for Sundays and major feasts.[23] All these works date to Acosta's American period, and many of the sermons were delivered to Spanish audiences in Peru and Mexico. However, when he translated them into Latin upon returning to Spain he also edited them to make them more suitable for a wider audience. Therefore, he eliminated most references to the colonial context from which they originated.[24]

These three volumes of sermons, which Acosta published between 1596 and 1599, bear the greatest resemblance to Jerónimo Nadal's mystical theology, which is also reflected in Don José's American works. Unlike the Spanish sermons in vogue at the end of the sixteenth century, which were characterized by a highly florid Baroque style, Acosta's sermons were relatively straightforward and brief. He favored the style of classical and patristic rhetoric and was inspired by Fray Luis de Granada's *Reglas de Retórica*,[25] a highly influential text on homiletics. Meant for audiences familiar with Christian culture, they are lengthier than the sermons he penned for the *Doctrina Christiana*. They are also replete with scriptural and patristic references to make their points. As with the sermons Acosta wrote for native peoples and in keeping with the tenets of Nadal's mystical theology, they are also *spiritu*, *practice*, and *corde*. They refrain from controversial or complicated theological themes, play on their audience's emotions, and seek to move their hearts to a more lively faith that seeks to help souls.

However, as in the case with the *De Christo Revelato*, these sermons do not contain the varied natural and anthropolological references to the American context that so permeates Acosta's American trilogy. The sermons also lack the unity that characterizes Acosta's American writings and is provided by his burning concern to promote the salvation of the native peoples. Thus it may be said that while certain facets of Acosta's Jesuit theological humanism continued to inform his homiletic writings, the nature of this genre impeded the full manifestation of Don José's unique way of doing theology. It is in Acosta's American trilogy that the influence of Jesuit theological humanism is most clearly in evidence.

HISTORIA
NATVRAL Y
MORAL DE LAS
INDIAS.

EN QVE SE TRATAN LAS
cofas notables del cielo, y elementos, metales,
plantas, y animales dellas : y los ritos, y
ceremonias, leyes, y gouierno, y
guerras de los Indios.

*Compuefta por el Padre Iofeph de Acofta Religiofo
de la Compañia de Iefus.*

Dirigida al Illuftrifsimo Señor Don ENRIQVE DE
CARDONA Gouernador por fu Mageftad
en el Principado de Cathaluña.

En Barcelona, a cofta de Lelio marini, Vene-
ciano, al Carrer de la Boqueria, 1591.

Title page of *Historia Natural y Moral de las Indias*
Barcelona, 1591

CHAPTER 6

The Method of Acosta's Humanism

The three sections of this chapter examine the theological method employed by José de Acosta in his American trilogy. Before turning to this task, two *caveats* are in order. As was mentioned in the previous chapter, method and form are, in reality, closely related; while distinct, they so mutually inform each other that a strict separation between them is artificial. This chapter on Don José's theological method and the following one on the form of his theology speak as if they were two different characteristics of his Jesuit theological humanism. This is a heuristic approach used to better understand some of the facets of Acosta's way of doing theology. It would be inaccurate in the end, however, to leave the impression that Don José's method of doing theology and the way he expresses it are two separate and unrelated monads.

Acosta's theological style is a hybrid of different scholarly trends of the Early Modern Period. The way of doing theology of the Dominicans of Salamanca is preponderant and easily identifiable in Don José's writings, particularly the *De Procuranda*, but it is not the exclusive method he employs. The various ways he uses historical and ethnographic sources in his theological arguments are a good example of this. In the *De Procuranda* Acosta often uses examples from religious and profane history as prooftexts, as scholastic theologians tended to employ the *loci* they marshaled in support of the theses for which they were arguing. Don José is often unconcerned with a philological or contextual analysis of the historical sources he cites from the Bible, the Fathers, and Christian and pagan history. History is used in this case to find examples to illustrate the thesis that he is defending.

In other writings, however, Acosta's use of historical and ethnographic sources is aimed at finding the truths that could be elicited from history and applied to a contemporary dilemma. In these cases, more often seen in the *Historia* than in his other works, Acosta's use of historical sources resembles the way certain humanists, such as Petrarch and at times Erasmus, wrote and conceived of history. Don José presents in narrative form historical and ethnographic accounts of different peoples so that his reader may learn from these accounts what to do in the present concerning the salvation and evangelization of the Amerindians. He crafts a story using details from the peoples of classical antiquity, the Hebrews, and the pre-Christian peoples of Europe that underscore the parallels between how God dealt with these peoples and how God was working in his day to save the native peoples of the Americas.

It would be inaccurate, therefore, to say that the only theological method that Acosta employs in his writing is that of the First School of Salamanca. It is eclecticism that is the hallmark of Acosta's Jesuit theological humanism. Still, in this eclectic approach to doing theology, the method of the First School of Salamanca is very important.

The Open Thomism of the First School of Salamanca

The Thomism that the young José de Acosta was taught at the Jesuit house of studies in Alcalá in the mid-1560s had its origins in the thought of the great Dominican Master of the Convent of San Esteban of Salamanca, Fray Francisco de Vitoria. From 1510 to 1522 Francisco de Vitoria was trained and lectured at the Dominican *studium* of the Couvent de Saint Jacques in Paris.[1] Here he was initiated into the study of St. Thomas's *Summa Theologiae* by Fray Peter Crockaert, O.P. Eventually Vitoria returned to Spain and after 1526 ensconced himself at what became the premier Dominican *studium* in all of Spain, the Convent of San Esteban in Salamanca. Vitoria trained many of Spain's great Thomistic theologians, such as Domingo de Soto, O.P., Mancio de Corpus Christi, O.P., and Francisco de Toledo, S.J., but perhaps the greatest of these and the one who managed to systematically articulate the nature of the theological method of the Vitorian Thomists of Salamanca was Melchior Cano, O.P.

From Salamanca Vitoria and his disciples initiated the restoration of St. Thomas on the Spanish theological scene. They accomplished this by the formation of future professors and by a literary output that brought the thought of the Angelic Doctor to bear on burning issues of the day, especially the ethical problems posed by the expanding Spanish empire in the Americas. Acosta writes in his book *De Christo Revelato* that while in Spain he had the opportunity to read about the history of Peru and the Spanish wars of conquest of those lands.[2] Furthermore, his works, especially the *De Procuranda*, abound with references to the Dominican masters, among whom Domingo de Soto is the theologian he cites most often.[3]

Vitoria's Thomism is also known as the First School of Salamanca, or *open Thomism*. The term *open Thomism* is used it to distinguish the Thomism of the First School of Salamanca (1526–80), originated by Vitoria, from that of Second School of Salamanca (1580–1650), under the intellectual leadership of Frays Bartolomé de Medina, O.P., and Domingo de Báñez, O.P. The open Thomism of the First School of Salamanca was, among other things, characterized by flexibility and openness to the critiques that had been made of St. Thomas Aquinas and other scholastics by humanists such as Erasmus. On the other hand, the Second School of Salamanca was less willing than the First to entertain positions different from those held by the Angelic Doctor.[4]

The theologians of the First School of Salamanca were willing to depart from the positions taken by St. Thomas when they saw good reason to do so, as for example on the question of salvation outside the Church. Salamancan Dominicans such as Vitoria, Cano, and Soto went beyond St. Thomas's position and argued that those who had heard the gospel preached in an unconvincing way could be guiltless of their unbelief in Christ and that explicit faith in Christ was not necessary for salvation.

They also sought to incorporate more of the Christian classics, that is, the Bible and the Fathers, and accounts of Christian history into their theological argumentation. They heeded the humanist critique of the speculative language of the scholastics and avoided it by expressing themselves in a more literary style.[5] Vitoria was educated in the classics for close to eight years, first in Burgos and then in Paris. His Latin was recognized as polished, clear, and, unlike that of other scholastics, easy to understand. The famous Spanish humanist Luis Vives wrote to Erasmus of Vitoria that he had studied the classics since his childhood with outstanding results.[6]

However, the classical formation received by Vitoria and others of the First School of Salamanca and their concern to express themselves in a written Latin that was literary should not be understood as meaning that the Dominicans of Salamanca were humanist theologians. They were scholastic theologians who used the Christian classics and history as the scholastics did.[7] That is, unlike the humanists they were not interested in a philological or a contextual interpretation of the Bible, of the Fathers, or of history. Rather, they employed these sources in a nonhumanist way, and they cited passages from the Scriptures, the Fathers, and historical accounts as prooftexts to support the theses for which they were arguing.

Fray Melchior Cano, O.P., Vitoria's most accomplished student, systematically expounded the master's theological method. In his *De locis theologicis* Cano underscores the four tasks of theology: to find the revealed truths in the Sacred Scriptures and Tradition, to deduce the corresponding conclusions from these revealed truths, to defend the faith from heresy, and to illuminate and confirm the teachings of Christ and the Church with the advances of what today would be called the human and natural sciences. Incorporating the insights of Dutch humanist Rudolf Agricola about rhetorical *loci*, Cano ordered ten *loci theologici*, or common authorities, to which theologians would appeal to accept or refute a thesis under discussion.

At the apex of Cano's hierarchy of theological sources are three that contain the deposit of faith, or the content of Christian revelation and its normative interpretations by the Church's hierarchy. They include, in order of importance, Sacred Scripture, the apostolic tradition, and the teachings of the bishops of the Catholic Church. The seven other sources in descending order are the councils of the Church, especially the general councils, the magisterium of the Bishop of Rome, the Fathers, the scholastic theologians, canon law, human reason, and written human history.

As with all Christian theology, the end of this type of scholasticism was to plumb the riches of God's revelations to the human family. These revelations include God's creating and sustaining actions of the natural order and his interventions in human history, in particular in his relationship with his people, Israel, and especially in the life, death, and resurrection of his son, Jesus Christ.

There are no extant samples of Acosta's systematic treatment of such topics in Christian theology as Christology, the Trinity, the sacraments, or the Church, as there are with many scholastic theologians. Rather, in his American trilogy Acosta concerned himself with applying both his vast theological knowledge and also considerable expertise in the history, customs, and flora and fauna of the New World to what he considered to be the pressing task facing the Church in the Americas. That task was collaborating with God in the salvation of the native peoples and removing the various impediments to this enterprise.

Of all of Acosta's writings, the methodological elements of the open Thomism of the First School of Salamanca are most evident in the *De Procuranda*, which abounds in references to the masters of the First School of

Salamanca, especially Fray Domingo de Soto. As early in the *De Procuranda* as in its letter of dedication, Acosta mentions that he will appeal to the sources employed by the theologians of the First School of Salamanca.[8] In addition to Scripture and the Fathers, Acosta says, he has consulted experts on the Indies and their writings about the New World. The end of this theological enterprise is also stated lucidly by Don José: it is to argue for the salvation of the Indians against those who do not believe this to be possible.

Two Examples from the De Procuranda of Acosta's Open Thomism

Two examples from the *De Procuranda* will serve to illustrate Acosta's use of the theological method of the First School of Salamanca. The first of these is his argument for the necessity of explicit faith in Christ for salvation; the second is his typology of cultures, which has enjoyed its own level of celebrity.

The first example is found in chapter three, book five, where Acosta takes up the issue of the necessity of explicit faith in Christ for salvation. The principal interlocutor, but by no means the only scholastic, that Acosta argues against is the famous Dominican theologian at the University of Salamanca, Domingo de Soto.[9] Don José disagrees with Soto's position that implicit faith in Christ for salvation was sufficient for those who were inculpably ignorant of the gospel. Acosta's position on the matter is that unless one has explicit faith in Christ one cannot be saved, because it is only through faith that one can have knowledge of Christ, which otherwise is inaccessible to human reason.[10] Acosta refutes the authorities cited by Soto by appealing to the various theological *loci* proposed by the First School of Salamanca.

Acosta rejects Soto's position and that of other members of the First School of Salamanca. The first of the authorities used by the Dominicans of Salamanca to justify their position was St. Thomas Aquinas. They appealed to St. Thomas's position that at the time when a child reached the age of reason he could and should turn to God, and if the child did this he or she would receive the grace of justification. The First School of Salamanca teased out of this position that it was not necessary for the child to know more, for salvation, than what is naturally good, insofar as he or she can know this good at the age of reason. In support of St. Thomas's position, the Dominicans of Salamanca cited several Johannine, Marcan, and Pauline texts which underscore the necessity to believe in Christ for salvation.

Acosta rebuts Soto's position that it would be unjust for God to withhold salvation from those who through no fault of their own have not heard the gospel and therefore could not come to explicit faith in Christ. Acosta cites St. Thomas's opinion that while those who through no fault of their own do not have explicit faith in Christ cannot be charged with the sin of infidelity, nonetheless they can justly be condemned by God because of original sin or other sins which they themselves have committed. If however, these people did what was possible on their part and turned to God, then God would send a preacher as he sent Peter to Cornelius so that they would come to certain knowledge of the gospel. Don José also cites St. Augustine, who maintains in his *City of God* that even those holy men, like Job, with whom God was well pleased before the coming of Christ should not be considered to have been saved without a revelation that Christ was the only mediator between God and humanity.

Acosta makes the argument based on Thomas's proviso that God would send a messenger to preach the gospel and thus provide supernatural faith to those who did all they could to turn to him. He argues that such a means of acquiring supernatural faith is not to be considered a miracle but rather the ordinary means God uses, even in Acosta's day, for the salvation of those who follow the natural law but through no fault of their own have not heard the gospel message. To support this argument Acosta appeals to recent Christian history. Don José cites the case of fellow Jesuit Francis Xavier and his recent and spectacular missionary successes in the East Indies as an example of God sending a messenger in modern times to preach the gospel to a people who had not heard of Christ.

The arguments and authorities that Acosta cites against Soto illustrate how he appealed to many of the *loci* that the First School of Salamanca employed in its theological argumentation. But perhaps the most original use of *loci* that he employed in his theological arguments is his hierarchical classification of cultures or peoples. This is the second example chosen from the *De Pro-curanda* to illustrate Acosta's use of the theological method of the First School of Salamanca.

In the prologue of the *De Procuranda* Acosta notes that it is an error to think of all the people of the Indies as the same; he understands *Indies* to mean both the peoples of the West and East Indies, that is, the peoples of the Americas and of Asia whom the Europeans had recently come to know. He further notes that it would be a grave error for the enterprise of their evangelization to consider all these peoples as the same. (He sometimes calls these peoples "barbarians," referring to the term from Greek antiquity for those who were considered foreigners.) And so he develops a tripartite hierarchy of cultures with the aim of developing missionary strategies appropriate to each. Acosta's threefold classification of cultures or nations in the *De Procuranda* and its variation in the *Historia* have received much attention from historians of the early human sciences and have earned Don José the titles of "Pliny of the New World" and "protoethnographer" or "protoanthropologist."[11]

The first and highest level of Acosta's classification of cultures is those peoples who, he says, "do not separate themselves very much from right reason and the common customs of the human species." That is, they have organized themselves into stable republics with public laws, fortified cities, and magistrates. Most important, these peoples have a written language. Among the peoples that Acosta names as belonging to his highest category of culture are the Chinese, the Japanese, and other peoples of the East Indies.[12]

The second class of peoples is those who, although they have never developed a written language, a body of laws, or a philosophy, are organized in republics with true magistrates and stable settlements with some form of civic organization, armies, and finally some solemn form of religious cult. Among the second class of barbarians, Acosta identifies the Aztecs and Incas. He says that their empires and republics, laws and institutions are truly worthy of admiration. Though they do not express themselves in writing, Acosta continues, the Aztecs and Incas do manage to preserve their history and develop methods of accounting and a calendar through a system of signs and monuments invented by themselves. These demonstrate their great ability and creativity. Nonetheless, they do not have a government of law, nor do they follow the right use of reason.[13]

The third and final group of nations are those who Acosta says resemble wild animals because they do not have laws, king, treaties, magistrates, or republics. They are nomadic, or if they have stable settlements they tend to live in caves like animals. Among those whom he identifies as belonging to this class are the Caribs, Chunchos, Chiriguanans, Mojos, most of the peoples of Brazil and Florida, and in the East Indies many of the peoples who live in the Moluccas (present-day Indonesia).[14]

As we shall see below in our discussion of the *Historia*, Acosta makes use of this tripartite classification of peoples to argue for the capacity of the Aztecs and Incas to be evangelized. He argues that just as peoples like the Japanese and the Chinese who belong to the first class of cultures and yet possess certain religious practices that could be considered demonic are nonetheless sufficiently advanced to be evangelized, so too with the Aztecs and Incas. Despite the greater abundance of idolatrous practices among the Aztecs and

Incas and their lack of cultural and political sophistication, nonetheless they too could be first educated and then christianized. In the *De Procuranda*[15] he often reminds his readers that just as many of the Christian peoples of Europe such as the English, the Irish, and even the Spanish were thought to be no better than beasts by their first evangelizers and yet came to be civilized and converted to Christianity, so too could the peoples of the Americas come to be saved. Or, as Acosta would also put it: first make them human, and then Christians.[16]

Acosta's understanding of a hierarchy of cultures had the further implication that a people could climb that ladder of civilization.[17] This was accomplished by means of the use of right reason that followed God's natural law and the social organization into stable republics governed by public laws.[18] Thus for Don José the salvation of the Indians meant not only the preaching of the Christian gospel to them but also their humanization understood as the adoption of civilized social and religious customs similar to those found in Europe. Native customs could and should remain insofar as they were not a violation of the natural law and could be so adapted that they were not contrary to the Christian gospel.

Acosta's cultural classifications are, from the standpoint of theological method, interesting for several reasons. For one thing, he has extended the application of history as a *locus* of theological argumentation by considering the history, religion, customs, and social, political, and economic organization of the Aztecs and Incas. The use of the history of pagan peoples in theological argumentation was not new in theology. Acosta justifies his ethnographic accounts of the Aztecs and Incas, which some considered to be chronicles of the devil's actions in the Americas, by mentioning the writings of Eusebius of Caesarea, Clement of Alexandria, and other patristic theologians and some classical authors. These authors also wrote about pagan rites and customs that were considered inhuman and diabolical.[19] However, what is new about Acosta's use of peoples' history and customs is that he did it not for European pagans such as the Greeks and Romans but for American pagans, who were considered by some of Acosta's contemporaries to be subhuman.

As will be elaborated more completely in the next section, there were theologians in Acosta's time who argued that the Amerindians had been justly forsaken by God. They bolstered their argument for God's rejection of the Amerindians by pointing to the scant fruits that their evangelization had produced in Acosta's time, to Amerindian customs and practices that were idolatrous and violated the natural law, and to what seemed to them to be the inordinately long time that God took to provide preachers of the gospel for the Americas. These signs, they argued, pointed to the depravity of the Amerindians, their enslavement by the devil, and most tragically God's just condemnation for their unwillingness and incapacity to receive the gospel that the Spanish preached.

The nefarious consequence that followed from this line of reasoning, which we will see below that Acosta rejected and repeatedly rebutted in his writings, was that the Spaniards had no obligation to continue to evangelize these hard-hearted and incorrigible people. The Amerindians, Acosta's opponents argued, did indeed deserve to be abandoned by God and to be subjugated and given no special rights or protections by the Spanish crown.

Another interesting dimension of Acosta's use of ethnograhic accounts about the Amerindians in his writings is how these accounts influenced his theology and how his faith influenced these accounts. Acosta's ethnograhic observations and investigations seem to have had an impact on his faith. This is reflected in his writings in the way he incorporated the ethnographic sources at his disposal with great passion and with an unabashed pastoral end, that is, his great dream of the salvation and better evangelization of the native peoples. Acosta was one in a long line of Jesuits who personally observed and collected ethnographic data about the peoples they were sent to evangelize.[20] Many of these Jesuits appear to have been so affected by their research and what they observed that their religious conviction that God willed these peoples to be saved and their missionary impetus to find ever more effective ways to evangelize them was increased.

God's desire to save all peoples was imaginatively captured by St. Ignatius in his meditation on the Trinity's deliberations before the incarnation took place for the sake of the salvation of the human race.[21] This optimistic Jesuit soteriology appears to be reflected in the way that Acosta interpreted the history and customs of the Amerindian peoples he encountered and studied. In elaborating an early ethnology of these American natives, Acosta was able to find God at work where some of his contemporaries only saw the devil's handiwork. Thus it can be said that Acosta's writings show how theology was influenced by the findings of the forerunners of contemporary social sciences.

At the same time, the ethnographic data Acosta observed personally and collected from others appears to confirm his optimistic Christian faith that God desired to save the Amerindians. More will be said about how this characteristic Jesuit trait of finding God in the world is evident in Acosta's writings in the next chapter, which deals with Jesuit spirituality. For now Don José's own words on the matter will conclude this section:

> In my travels, ordered by obedience, throughout this entire region of Peru and other places, I consulted not a few very competent persons about questions concerning the Indies. I avidly read some of the works they wrote with painstaking care. In conclusion, with these helps and with the light and help of divine wisdom that I frequently implored, I see that not only the knowledge of the situation of the Indies, but also, after so many experiences, trust has increased not a little in me. I give infinite thanks to the most gentle providence of God for having shown me by the increase of deeds themselves how far from God's liberality were my hopes for the salvation of the Indians . . .[22]

Humanist Theological Method in Acosta's Other Works

In Acosta's other American works, the *Historia* and the *Doctrina Christiana*, one notes that the Salamancan theological method is in evidence here too but not to the extent that it is in the *De Procuranda*. More in evidence here is a humanist approach to doing theology. In the *Historia* especially, Don José weaves historical and ethnographic sources about the Aztecs and Incas and the Hebrews and other peoples of the Mediterranean to create a narrative with a clear theological end. The *Historia* seeks to rebut those who considered the Amerindians as beyond God's redemption and to move the hearts of its readers to take action on behalf of the evangelization of these native peoples.

While the First School of Salamanca did incorporate historical sources to bolster theological arguments, in the *Historia* Acosta is not using history for prooftexts. Rather the comparisons he makes between the history and religious and social organization of the Amerindians and those of the Hebrews and of the Greeks, Romans, and other European peoples he mentions reflect, as was mentioned above, the way humanists such as Petrarch[23] and Erasmus[24] conceived and incorporated history into their writings.

The past deeds, characteristics, and temperament of a people were understood by these humanists as providing positive and negative moral lessons for future generations. History was seen as "philosophy teaching by example," in which the past instructs the present.[25] In the *Historia*, Acosta argues that although the history and customs of the Hebrews and of Europeans of old indicate that they engaged in inhuman and diabolical rites, these Mediterranean peoples were not beyond the mercy of God, who in due time provided for their evangelization and salvation; he argues that the Aztecs and Incas too were capable of such divine mercy.

Acosta writes the *Historia* to report "the news of the treasures that the Lord our God has deposited and parceled out in those kingdoms [i.e., the Indies], so that their inhabitants might be aided more by those from over here [i.e., Spain] to whom divine and supreme Providence has entrusted them."[26] His audience is Spaniards who play a role in the affairs of the Indies and therefore whose decisions may either help or retard the spread of the gospel in those lands. But unlike the audience of the *De Procuranda*, these Spaniards are not New World administrators *in situ* or missionaries working among the Amerindians.

Nonetheless, in the last three books of the *Historia*, which deal with the customs and history of the Aztecs and Incas, Acosta occasionally makes references to Sacred Scripture, particularly the Hebrew Scriptures, and also the Fathers, Aristotle, and conciliar decrees from Lima III. Acosta wanted to counter the opinion held by some of his contemporaries that the native peoples were so depraved and under the sway of Satan that they could not be evangelized.[27]

As was noted above, pessimism about the salvation of the Indians and disdain for their barbarity was an opinion that Acosta encountered on several occasions during his American sojourn. Viceroy Toledo cited the tyranny and crudeness of the Incas to mount his military campaign against the Inca stronghold in Vilcabamba and to institute the reductions. And among Acosta's brother Jesuits there was the opinion, most forcefully articulated by Luis López, that the Indians were incapable of understanding the Christian faith and that the lack of miracles accompanying their evangelization was a sign of God's displeasure with the enterprise because of the native peoples' obduracy.

Behind these opinions, held by many royal administrators, was the understanding that if the native peoples could not be civilized and evangelized then the Spaniards need not treat them as brother Christians and fellow subjects of his majesty enjoying the same rights and protections as any other Spaniard. Acosta's use of these theological sources in his description of the pagan religious practices of the native peoples served to remind his readers that such idolatrous practices were not an indication of a totally depraved and demon-controlled people. They had also been practiced by the great empires of classical antiquity, Athens, and Rome, as well as by God's own people, the Hebrews.[28] Acosta's subtext is that if Israel was idolatrous and yet not rejected by God, then neither should the Spaniards reject the native peoples of the Americas on the grounds that they are depraved and idolatrous nations.

After book five, which deals with the idolatrous practices of the native peoples of Mexico and Peru, there follows a book where Acosta recounts the social organization and culture of the native peoples and where he does not employ any theological sources to excuse their barbarism. The social structures that he chronicles in book six would have seemed remarkably cultured and civilized to early modern Spaniards. Don José writes about the calendar, written language, books, educational program for their youth, accounting methods, courier system, the government, order of succession and laws, architecture, agriculture, handiworks and crafts, tax system, occupations and skills, military victories, techniques and orders, and dances and feasts of the Aztecs and Incas.[29] He even includes several chapters in book six where, following the description of similar institutions in the Indies, he describes the educational achievements of the Chinese as well as their calendar, books, and written language.[30] In book five he noted that, just like the Incas, the highly sophisticated Japanese had been duped by the devil and practiced a form of confession of their sins that mimicked the sacrament established by Christ for his Church.[31]

In so doing, Acosta is subtly underscoring the similarities between the great civilizations of the Far East that were recognized to be on par with European culture and the culture and civilization of the Indians which some Spaniards still considered to be subhuman and diabolical. Indeed, Acosta begins book six by not hiding his intention of dispelling the opinion that the Indies are populated by men devoid of reason, entitling the first chapter of this book "That the opinion that the Indians are lacking in intelligence is false." It is as if this whole book is an argument from native history and culture to convince his European readers that the Aztecs and Incas are more than capable of being evangelized.

If one considers the first four books of the *Historia*, where Acosta chronicles the novelties in flora and fauna of the Americas, alongside book six, where he presents the achievements of Aztec and Inca culture and their similarities to European culture, one can discern a similarity of purpose. That is, in both books one through four and in book six Acosta presents the natural and social order of the Americas in their spectacular novelty while also underscoring that they are in continuity with the natural order and cultural achievements of Europe and the other continents. Perhaps the most effective argument he presents from the natural order to establish that the Indians were not some kind of subhuman species is his famous hypothesis that the first Americans came to the New World over a land bridge somewhere in the northern part of the North American continent and thus had genetic links to the ancestors of the Spaniards.[32] Acosta is the first to suggest such a theory for the origins of the American native peoples.

By doing this he artfully undermines those who presented the Indies as a strange and foreign place populated by subhumans who were incapable of being evangelized and therefore did not need to be respected and accorded the same rights and protections as Spaniards. Acosta establishes that the New World, both in its physical and social organization, is not so strange and nefarious a land. He refutes the belief that the New World was a land under the domination of demons that were claimed by God only when the Spaniards discovered it and went about civilizing it and christianizing it.

No, God's providence was clearly at work in the Indies before the arrival of the Spaniards. To demonstrate this, Acosta employs the interesting metaphor of the father who wishes to marry an uncomely daughter.[33] Just as this father facilitates the marriage of his ugly daughter by giving her a sizable dowry, so too has God given the dangerous and difficult lands of the New World the dowry of abundant natural resources, especially precious metals. In this way God has ensured that the Spaniards remain interested in the Indies and bring Christianity to the Amerindians.

In the final book of the *Historia*, book seven, Acosta recounts the history of the native peoples of Mexico and advances the position that God very much wants the Indians to be saved, as demonstrated by numerous miracles and other circumstances that had occurred throughout the Indies. He employs frequent examples from Scripture yet again to make his points. Before recounting various events that warned Montezuma of the coming of the *conquistadores*, Acosta cites Sacred Scripture and the Fathers to justify the reasonableness of belief in pagan prophecies and omens.[34]

Acosta employed this pattern before, throughout book four, where he cited examples from the Hebrew Scriptures before describing the idolatrous practices of the Aztecs and Incas, thus impressing upon his reader that the idolatry of the Americas was not as depraved as some thought. In book four he also recounted that the religious practices of the Aztecs and Incas bore a great similarity to the Christian sacraments and other rituals. He accounted for this by saying that the devil has often sought to deceive humans by imitating the divine worship that God has ordained for his people, and he frequently cited examples of this from the Hebrew Scriptures. But now in the final chapter of the

Historia he states unequivocally that God allowed this state of affairs to happen so as to bring good out of evil.

Thus, in this final chapter, Acosta has recourse to recent history, the history of the spiritual and temporal conquest of the Indies, to argue for God's desire that the native peoples be saved. The long captivity that the natives endured under the repression of the Aztec and Inca empires and the diabolical rites of their idolatrous religions was precisely what made them better disposed to accept Spanish rule and the Christian faith. The political, cultural, and sociological events and circumstances leading to and during the conquest are for Acosta Christian history. Though at times tainted with cruelty and injustice on the part of the conquerors, nevertheless these events were used by God for his purposes and were providential.[35]

Not only did the cruel religious practices of the Aztecs and Incas, such as human sacrifices, prepare the soil so that the seed of gospel was received in the hearts of the native peoples as good news of liberation from oppression, but also the might and size of these empires at the time of the Spanish conquest was providential. Acosta argues that the gospel was able to be spread with ease because the Inca and Aztec empires had been able to impose a common language on the many varied peoples of the Americas that they had subjugated. This made it easier for the ministers of the gospel in the Americas, who did not seem to be blessed with the gift of tongues, to more easily communicate the good news to such a plethora of nations on the American continents. And Acosta remarks that one who would doubt this assertion should consider how difficult it was to preach the gospel in parts of the Americas such as Florida and Brazil, where it native peoples were not accustomed to the political organization of an empire.

God's hand was also at work in the divisions that riddled both the Aztec and the Inca empires at the time of their conquest by Cortés and Pizarro. One would be fooling oneself, writes Don José, if one thought that it was the military prowess of the Spaniards that won the day. The ongoing military campaigns against the Araucans of Chile, the Chichimecans of Mexico, and the Chunchans, Chiriguanans, and Pilcozonans of the Andes testify to the tenacity of the native warriors. These nations had still not been subdued in Acosta's day even with numbers and weapons that were superior to what Cortés and Pizarro had for their conquests of Mexico and Peru.

Finally, Acosta takes note of the many saintly men—Dominican, Augustinian, and Franciscan missionaries, as well as bishops and good priests—whom the Lord sent to the New World. These men, writes Acosta, not only labored heroically and selflessly in the vineyard of the Indies but also performed miracles worthy of the accounts in the Acts of the Apostles.

This final chapter, which some have considered accidental,[36] is actually highly significant for the argument of the *Historia*. In it Acosta summarizes in a crescendo what he has at times stated clearly and at other times merely hinted at throughout the work, that is, that both the natural order and the moral order of the New World were so ordained by God to facilitate his divine will for the Indies, the salvation of the Indians. Whether it was the riches that God placed in the soil of the Indies, or the political organization of the great Indian empires that allowed for the easy spread of the gospel, or the tumultuous historical moment of these empires when the Spaniards arrived that made it easy for them to be conquered and for the cross to be implanted at the same time as the sword, or the devil's work in confounding the Indians with rituals and ceremonies similar to the Christian sacraments and thus making it easier for them eventually to understand and accept the Christian faith, Divine Providence had not forgotten his children in the New World. As Scripture says, God's plan was being worked out so that at the appointed time the native peoples could be redeemed in Christ.

The *Doctrina Christiana* is a collection of catechetical books principally written by Acosta at the order of the Third Provincial Council of Lima of 1582–83. Here the theological method of the open Thomism of the First School of Salamanca is hardly in evidence. Rather, the humanist emphasis on an elegant narrative and learning from the history and customs of a people is more discernable in this work.

Acosta's aim in including these ethnographic details in the confessional manual and in some of his sermons, which form part of this work, is twofold. He uses the information to illumine the *doctrinero*, or priest assigned to minister to Indian parishes, so that he might be better acquainted with the moral diseases of his flock and the wiles that the devil employs to keep these people from the Christian faith. Second, in the thirty-one sermons on the basics of the Christian faith, he at times uses examples from Indian history and culture so as to be able to present the faith more persuasively and convince the people of its truth. Such a use of human history and culture to make the faith more convincing to the hearer bears great resemblance to the way some humanists conceived of history as containing moral lessons for the present.

IOSEPHI
À COSTA,
SOCIETATIS
IESV,

DE NATVRA NOVI ORBIS
LIBRI DVO.

ET

DE PROMVLGATIONE
EVANGELII APVD
BARBAROS,
siue,

DE PROCVRANDA INDORVM
salute, Libri sex.

Title page of *De Natura Novi Orbis*
Cologne, 1596

CHAPTER 7

The Form of Acosta's Humanism

Acosta's Rhetorical Style

José de Acosta's writing did not employ the typical genre of the treatises, commentaries, and *summae* of the scholastic philosophers and theologians. His literary style most closely resembles that of the humanist theological treatise. He employed nontechnical theological language and an elegant Latin and or Spanish prose to move the hearts of his audience to solve a pressing moral issue of his day, the salvation and evangelization of the Amerindians.

Selections from the *De Procuranda*, the *Historia*, and the *Doctrina Christiana* appear in appendixes five through seven. These three passages, addressed to priests, royal administrators, and Indians, respectively, give a taste of Don José's literary style. Acosta's advice to these three audiences is meant to move their hearts to action and win them over to a more authentic Christian life, and, in particular, to enlist them as zealous participants in his great passion while in the Americas, the enterprise of evangelizing the native peoples. His style is oratorical and resembles a sermon crafted to rouse the heart and the will to action on behalf of one's brothers and sisters. Indeed, the selection presented below from the *Doctrina Christiana* is just that, a sermon meant to present the essentials of the Christian faith to the native peoples.[1]

To this end Acosta's exhortations to his various audiences employ a wide range of rhetorical devices. At times he encourages them and comforts them by reminding them that the servant is not greater than the master and that, if Jesus suffered in preaching the gospel, they should not be surprised that the same fate accompanies their evangelizing activities in the New World.[2] At other times, he ridicules them for their unwillingness to learn the native languages or excoriates them for the bad example they have set, which he sees as the primary reason accounting for the little fruit which their apostolate has produced.[3] In both of these cases Acosta's style is that of the sacred orator, not of the scholastic theologian.

Nowhere in the *De Procuranda* does one find a more lucid picture of Acosta's humanistic rhetoric than in the final book of his work, which is on how the sacraments should be administered to the native peoples. Acosta's oratorical style is evident in the chapter devoted to what he calls the most important sacrament for the Indians, confession. His praise for this sacrament underscores his ties to the way of proceeding of the early Society of Jesus, which considered the sacrament of penance one of its most important and efficacious ministries. Worthy of note is the consolation he takes in describing the sacrament as a medicine for the sick soul.

This is a different emphasis from the way that the Council of Trent viewed the sacrament. Trent saw confession as a tribunal and underscored the priest's role as judge. Acosta, on the other hand, underscores confession as a medicine and sees the priest's role as that of a healer or physician. He emphasizes the overabundance of God's grace and clemency even for those whose repentance from sin is imperfect but who avail themselves of the sacrament nonetheless.[4]

Acosta realized that there were differences among the indigenous peoples of the Americas and advocated a rhetoric adapted to their capabilities, a rhetoric that was plain and simple yet appealed to the emotions. In this appeal to preaching that was plain and simple, Acosta's rhetorical theory for the Amerindians differed substantially from the dominant style of sacred oratory recommended in the rhetorical treatises of his day.[5] Nowhere is Don José's rhetorical theory and practice more evident than in the prologue to the third catechism of the *Doctrina Christiana* and in the thirty-one catechetical sermons that make it up.[6]

These sermons are aimed at presenting the essentials of the Christian faith to the native peoples of the Americas. By the essentials of the faith Acosta means the articles of the creed, the decalogue, the seven sacraments, instruction in prayer and other pious Christian practices and the precepts of the Church, and knowledge of the Last Things; these are the traditional elements of the catechism in the late Middle Ages. All these things, Acosta says, should be presented in such a way as to awaken faith and hope so that the believer may be more diligent and magnanimous in obeying God's law.

The prologue to the third catechism, or *sermonario*, of the *Doctrina Christiana* lays out the philosophy that guided Acosta's composition of these thirty-one catechetical sermons.[7] Quoting such apostolic, patristic, and medieval authorities as Sts. Paul, Augustine, Gregory of Nazianzen, and Gregory the Great he underscores the importance of adaptation in evangelizing the native peoples. The preacher must accommodate his preaching to the capacity of his hearer, he says. Citing Hebrews 5 and Philippians 3, Acosta stresses two features that are common in these sermons, the essentials of the faith and the need to repeat these essentials over and over again to the native audiences. In particular, he states, the peoples of the Indies tend to have little knowledge about the Trinity, Jesus Christ as God-man and savior, sin, the necessity of baptism for salvation, and the reward of good and punishment of evil. Again citing St. Augustine he insists that the best way to catechize is to narrate or tell a story about the content one wishes to get across, and so a narrative quality characterizes his sermons. This emphasis on narrative is more humanistic than it is scholastic.

In addition, Don José emphasizes that in this narration the preacher should speak to the native peoples as friends and should refrain from preaching as if he were holding forth in a theater. The preacher should explain the faith, says Acosta, but beyond this he needs to persuade. While he recognizes that this is ultimately the work of the Holy Spirit, Don José maintains that providing good reasons is very helpful. When he speaks of providing "good reasons" in the sermons, he is reflecting the first letter of Peter, which exhorts the Christian to provide reasons for one's faith, but he adds that in the case of the native peoples the preacher must use reasons that are convincing to them. This means that the arguments employed must be from their experience.

Furthermore, the preacher's arguments must take special care to expose what Acosta considers the superstitious practices and the authority of the Inca priests. As was noted at the end of the previous chapter, it is for this reason that Don José included in the *Doctrina Christiana* and as part of the manual for confessors of Indians three detailed sections describing the religious rituals and beliefs found in the Andes. Acosta had gathered these descriptions from his own observations, from the decrees of the second provincial council of Lima of 1567, and from the written works of one of Viceroy Toledo's most trusted advisors, Licenciado Polo de Ondegardo.[8]

Throughout the sermons one encounters references to the religious practices of the native peoples' ancestors. When these native customs are not in contradiction with Christian practice and belief, Acosta extolls them. For example, he praises the care that the ancestors of the Incas took in burying their dead and sees in their funerary practices an awareness of the immortality of the soul.[9] But more often than not he ridicules native customs as dangerous hoaxes and deceits by which the devil has ensnared the people.

He also exposes these customs as unscrupulous inventions of native priests whose only interest was to enrich themselves with the food and money offerings made by the native peoples to the *huacas*.[10] Acosta encourages preachers to adapt his sermons that deal with these superstitions to the local idolatrous practices in their parishes. He notes that while the same rhetorical strategy of ridicule, warning, and outrage at the opportunism of the native priests could be used, the superstition denounced should not be generic but always specific to the actual practices of the audience.

However, Acosta says, the Indians like all people are more moved by arguments that appeal to their affect than those that appeal to their reason. According to Don José the purpose of the long and short catechisms, which along with the catechetical sermons form the *Doctrina Christiana*, is to help the memory of the native peoples according to their aptitude. For the more capable, especially catechists, the long catechism is suitable, and for the typical believer the short catechism is more appropriate for learning the truths of Christianity. On the other hand, the purpose of the third catechism, the *sermonario*, is persuasion. It seeks to increase belief and above all to move the hearers to practice their faith. The sermon should instruct the audience, entertain it, please it, and move it so that it may more perfectly keep the teaching of God that is received. Thus, Don José counsels the preacher that he incorporate into his sermons apostrophes, exclamations, and other oratorical conventions that incite and awaken the affections of the hearer.

Once again citing St. Paul, this time in Galatians, and St. Augustine, he insists that as important as the rhetorical strategies that move the heart are, the "efficaciousness" of the preacher also needs to be cultivated. By this he means that the preacher needs to be convinced of his subject and convey this resoluteness to his audience. The Holy Spirit is much aided, he says, "when the emotions of the preacher are on fire." This, he says, is particularly the case in the Indies because when the native peoples speak to each other they do so with great affect.

The rhetorical use of Sacred Scripture and the Fathers that we have seen Don José employing in his American writings shows clearly that he was influenced by and used positive theology to communicate his message that the native peoples could be saved. Thus he was in step with Jesuit tradition, which, as was noted in chapter two, derived from St. Ignatius a respect for positive theology in addition to and scholastic theology as useful for the ministry.[11]

Other Jesuit Characteristics of Acosta's Humanism

José de Acosta, the young Jesuit student at Alcalá, had heard the renowned Jerónimo Nadal expound his view of the theology that should characterize the Society of Jesus when he spoke at the Jesuit house of studies in Alcalá from fall 1561 through January 1562. Nadal impressed Acosta at the time and his influence lasted. In Acosta's later literary output the concerns of Jerónimo Nadal's mystical theology are most lucidly discerned, as is illustrated from the selections of Don José's writings analyzed below and also those presented in the appendixes. The Jesuit concern with developing a theology that, while communicating the generally accepted teachings of approved Doctors of the Church, stirred the heart and moved one's listener to work for the Kingdom best explains the rhetorical features which so punctuate Don José's writings.

In addition to the rhetorical nature of Acosta's writing that fits the description of Nadal's mystical theology, there are other elements in his American trilogy that reflect the way of proceeding of the early Society of Jesus. In particular, such classic themes as finding God in all things, discernment of spirits, and certain images of Christ and the devil from St. Ignatius's Spiritual Exercises are present in these three works. Furthermore, the early Jesuit concerns with adapting the gospel message to one's audience and utilizing popular religion to convey the essentials of that gospel message are also discernable in Acosta's writings.

Finding God in All Things

In the final contemplation at the end of the Spiritual Exercises, after the self-examination and begging God's assistance to rid oneself of sin and any other impediments that keep one from following Jesus Christ more closely and after contemplating the birth, life and ministry, and death and resurrection of Christ, the retreatant is presented with what St. Ignatius calls the "contemplación para alcanzar amor,"[12] the contemplation to obtain love, also known by its Latin name, the *contemplatio ad amorem*.

The purpose of the exercise is to ask God to give the retreatant "an interior awareness of so much good received, so that I [the retreatant], fully aware, may be able to love and serve his divine majesty in everything." Ignatius wants the retreatant to contemplate how God is present in his creatures proceeding up the ladder of being from the elements or mineral realm, through the world of plants, on to the realm of animals, and culminating in the world of humans. The Master of the Spiritual Exercises instructs the retreatant to contemplate how God works for him or her in all these things and suggests that the retreatant finish the contemplation saying the famous prayer, the *Suscipe*:

> Take, Lord, receive all my liberty, my memory, my understanding, and my entire will, all I have and possess. You have given it all to me, Lord, now I return it. It is yours, dispose of it wholly according to your will. Grant me only your love and your grace, these are enough for me.[13]

Acosta imitates this structure of the *contemplatio ad amorem* by structuring the *Historia* as an ascent up the ladder of being in which he highlights the new marvels of God's creation in the Americas. For Don José, the greatest of these wonders was the work of redemption of the native peoples that he believed God was working in the Indies even as he was writing. And just as the *Suscipe* prayer has the retreatant offer oneself and all the gifts one has received from God back to God, so too in the *Historia* Acosta insists that the reason he recounts the marvels of the New World, particularly the customs and history of the native peoples, is so that the reader may put all he or she has and possesses at the disposal of the great work of redemption that God is bringing about in the Indies.[14]

It was noted in the last chapter that some have considered book seven to be simply added on. They see the first six books as following Aristotle's hierarchy or ladder of being, moving from a consideration of inanimate creation through the vegetative and animal kingdoms to the zenith of creation, the world of culture created by rational creatures.[15] But read against the background of the Spiritual Exercises, the structure of the *Historia* appears in a new perspective. This final book is in fact the culmination of the *Historia*, central to Acosta's purpose. Presenting here a theological teleology, he is demonstrating that Providence was able to prepare the way for the efficacious preaching of the gospel by using the idolatrous rituals of the Amerindians to prefigure the sacraments of the Roman Catholic Church. Thus in their own way even these base pagan beliefs and practices helped people to find God.

In reviewing the *Historia*, the great Spanish poet and theologian, Fray Luis de León, O.S.A., who served as a censor, wrote:

> I have seen this Natural and Moral History of the Indies that Father José de Acosta of the Society of Jesus writes, and what refers to the doctrine of the faith, it is Catholic. And of the rest, it is worthy of the great prudence and learning of the author, and all should read it so that they may praise God who is so marvelous in his works. At St. Philip of Madrid, on May 4, 1589.[16]

"And all should read it so that they may praise God who is so marvelous in his works": with this sentence Fray Luis neatly summarizes the Ignatian structure of the *Historia*.

The *contemplatio ad amorem* is often seen as the clearest expression of one of the most characteristic elements of Ignatian spirituality, finding God in all things. St. Ignatius's instructions to contemplate the natural and human order of creation so as to appreciate God working in and through it for our good and salvation is associated with the saint's desire to find God in all things. Nadal personified this facet of Ignatian spirituality and wrote that Jesuits should be contemplatives in action, that is, contemplatives who are able to find God in activity, in all the things they do, and in all the situations in which they find themselves. Among other things, it is a complete break with any spirituality of flight from the world.[17]

Acosta's reading of the novelties of the New World, both natural and moral, illustrate this habit of finding God in all things by means of a contemplative reading or gaze of what he encountered in his travels throughout the Americas. The narrative he weaves in the *Historia* is, to be sure, an invaluable chronicle of the zoological, botanical, meteorological, geophysical, ethnological, anthropological, and sociological marvels he encountered in his fourteen-year sojourn in the Indies. But it is also a work with a theological purpose, and this purpose is very much imbued with this Ignatian sense of being a contemplative in action who finds God no less in the natural marvels of the Americas than in what at first glance may be the demonic religion of the native peoples. Acosta's skill at finding God in all things allows him to argue in the *Historia*, that the demonic practices of the native peoples were a marvelous example of Providence that brought good out of evil.[18]

Examen and Discernment of Spirits

One of the spiritual tools that Ignatius advises the contemplative in action to utilize in the quest to find God in all things is the examination of conscience, or examen. This form of prayer is to be practiced twice daily, at midday and before retiring. It consists of five steps in which one reviews one's day in a spirit of prayer and thanking God for graces received since the last examen; asking God for the grace to know how one has sinned and been tempted since the last examen; reviewing one's thoughts, words, and deeds hour by hour since the last examen; begging God forgiveness for one's sins during this time; and resolving with God's grace to remedy one's missteps. The examen concludes with the Our Father.[19]

For the contemplative in action, the way to find God in all things is also aided by Ignatius's understanding of interior spiritual movements, which he attributes to what he calls spirits. These spirits are of two kinds, the good spirit and the evil spirit. The good spirit is from God and the evil spirit from the devil, or the enemy of our human nature, as Ignatius calls him. Depending on the moral and spiritual state of the person, the good and evil spirits employ different tactics to move the person either toward God or away from him. Ignatius codified what he learned about the movements of the spirits from his own spiritual journey in the Rules for Discernment of Spirits, which are appended to the Spiritual Exercises.[20]

These rules of Ignatius bear a remarkable similarity to Acosta's understanding of the demonic influence on native religions.[21] Don José, like St. Ignatius, speaks of the action of the devil in the world as principally being *engaño*, or trickery.[22] Acosta reminds his readers in the *Historia* that it should not shock them that so many of the idolatrous practices of the Aztecs and Incas remind one of the sacraments of the Catholic Church, since it is well known that the devil proceeds by imitating and mocking the order that God had established.[23] In the *Doctrina Christiana* Don José includes several accounts of the idolatrous religion of the Incas so that the *doctrineros* may know the specific tricks the devil has used in Peru and may tailor their evangelizing activities to effectively expose and counter these tricks.

Throughout the Spiritual Exercises, and the Rules for Discernment are no exception, Ignatius encourages the exercitant to employ the imagination and will in the course of the program of meditations and contemplations and in the spiritual combat against the wiles of the enemy of our human nature. One spiritual trap is desolation—a decrease in faith, hope, and love—caused by the trickery and temptations of the evil spirit. To counter it, Ignatius advises the retreatant to practice *agere contra*, that is, to adopt the opposite course of action to that suggested by the evil spirit.

This has been misconstrued as indicating an essentially voluntaristic nature in Ignatian spirituality. To be sure, the Ignatian way does not ignore the role of the will in the discipline of ridding oneself of sin and disordered affections and attachments which keep one apart from God's presence. However, such a view of Ignatian spirituality is myopic precisely because it fails to clearly see the broader horizon of the role that St. Ignatius assigns to God's gratuitous desire to communicate his grace to the retreatant.

Indeed, Ignatius underscores this from the beginning of the Exercises and in every meditation and contemplation that they contain by his insistence that God deals directly with his creatures, which he knew from his own experience. Therefore, he continues, the one giving the Exercises should not interfere with the relationship between God and the retreatant.[24] Furthermore, the centrality of God's gratuitous gift of grace in Ignatian spirituality is underscored by his oft-repeated phrase in the preambles to the meditations and contemplations of the Exercises: "pedir lo que quiero," to ask for the grace I desire from God in the prayer about to be undertaken.[25]

Ignatius is fully aware that prayer is possible principally because of the action of God. It is God who grants the grace we desire and beg him for, and ultimately it does not depend on us to engineer or fabricate it in any way. This is also illustrated by the preparatory prayer which Ignatius says should initiate all the prayer periods of the Exercises, where he instructs the exercitant "to ask God our Lord for the grace that all my [the exercitant's] intentions, actions, and activities be wholly ordered to the service and reverence of his divine majesty."[26]

Interestingly, Acosta too has been misrepresented and interpreted to be voluntaristic, as St. Ignatius has been. Some have insisted that the key to understanding Acosta is his insistence on the role that free will plays in his theological anthropology,[27] or even that his theology is nominalistic and that he is incapable of discerning God's activity in the world because of his strict separation of the natural realm and the supernatural realm of grace.[28] But these views fail to grasp the role that the Ignatian understanding of the superabundance of God's grace in the world plays in Acosta's thought. Acosta, following Ignatius, believed in God's great desire to communicate himself to his rational creatures. To be sure, following the general dynamism of the Spiritual Exercises, human persons have to cooperate with God's desire to communicate himself to them by ridding themselves, with God's help, of their sins and disordered attachments. But ultimately the battle with the evil spirit has been won by the resurrection of Jesus Christ, and so it is only through trickery that the devil can place roadblocks in the way of those who desire to find God.[29]

One of the roles of the evangelizer was to expose these tricks, whether they were the idolatrous practices of the native peoples or the fallacious arguments of Spaniards that conveyed the impression that the native peoples could not be saved. As Acosta reminds the *doctrineros* in the *Doctrina Christiana*, this is best accomplished through persuasion.[30] It is by moving the hearts of one's audience, Acosta reminds those who would preach to the native peoples, to dispose and open themselves to the graces God so lavishly showers down on his people and to cooperate with God's work of redemption of the whole human race. Again we are at the heart of what Nadal called mystical theology, where persuasion is a fundamental concern, seeking to convince an audience to offer themselves to labor with Christ by appealing to their emotions and enticing their hearts.

Echoing the dynamics of the Spiritual Exercises, Acosta subscribes to the pedagogy of first humanizing the indigenous peoples before christianizing them.[31] He seeks to purge what he considers disordered affections or sin from the native peoples before introducing more spiritual matters for reflection.[32] As we have seen, Don José is not a proponent of the wholesale extirpation of native culture. His method of evangelization rejects the *tabula rasa* approach to preaching the gospel that early in the colonization of Mexico was employed by the Franciscans. He advocates preserving native culture in so far as it is not a direct violation of the gospel or of natural law.[33] At the heart of his approach, as it is of the Exercises, is the Thomist maxim that grace perfects nature and heals it of the effects of sin.

Therefore, to best prepare oneself to receive what Acosta considers to be the summit of knowledge, which is Jesus Christ revealed in Sacred Scripture and the traditions of the Church,[34] one must prepare oneself by ridding oneself, with God's help, of any impediments. Acosta's understanding of salvation for the Indians as involving replacing idolatrous and demonic native customs with *Christianitas* is ultimately an exercise in persuasion, that is, striking the idols from the heart. The will plays a role in this pastoral strategy, but above all, as Acosta's sermons and writings so manifestly illustrate, it is a question of providing reasons, through preaching and education, and above all moving the heart by presenting an alluring and enticing Christ.

Images of Christ

And who is the Christ whom Acosta would have his audiences embrace? Again the influence of Ignatian spirituality may be discerned in the response to this question, for the Christ Acosta presents in his American writings has different nuances. Acosta adapts the Christ of the Scriptures and of Tradition to most effectively impact the mind and the heart of his audience and the circumstances in which they find themselves.

In the *De Procuranda* the Christ described by Acosta often, but not exclusively, bears a great resemblance to the Eternal King described in the Spiritual Exercises.[35] He is the one who bids us labor with him in the redemption of the native peoples.[36] Christ is also "milk for the child, food for the adult, alpha and omega, beginning and end of all wisdom."[37]

In the *Historia* the Christ who most often makes an appearance is the Johannine pre-existent Word. The Trinity is presented as laboring in the Americas long before the gospel was ever preached by the missionaries. Through God's providential design the idolatrous practices which the devil used to trick the native peoples, especially sacerdotal prophecies about the arrival of strangers, prepared the way for the reception of the gospel when God's ministers arrived to evangelize the New World.[38]

In the *Doctrina Christiana*, in many of his sermons, Acosta narrates the life of Jesus from the four gospels. Again, the emphasis on narrative is characteristic of the humanist way of doing theology. Acosta underscores the redemption from sin wrought by the crucifixion of Jesus Christ and reminds his audience of Christ's great love for each one of us in that act.[39]

Popular Piety

Central to the way that Acosta envisioned the indigenous peoples encountering Jesus Christ was the utilization of certain aspects of sixteenth-century popular religion. The sixth rule for thinking with the Church contained in the Spiritual Exercises advocates respect for the mainstays of devotional Christianity. Some humanists, Erasmus among them, advocated a simplification of devout practices; they saw many of these as an obfuscation of the essentials of Christianity. And many of these practices, such as scapulars, fasting, relics, pilgrimages, rosaries, indulgences, and some devotions to the saints, were even seen as superstitions. The Jesuits sympathized with the humanist concern to foster a more Christ-centered spirituality among the faithful, but by no means did they discard all elements of the more traditional devotional Christianity from their usual ministries.

Acosta's American writings reveal the early Jesuits' use of the popular religious practices and customs of sixteenth-century Catholicism. In fact, popular piety played a crucial role in Acosta's strategy of evangelization.[40] For Acosta, salvation meant not only the preaching of the teachings of Christ contained in the gospel but also the reformation and replacement of native religious customs that were against the natural law and the gospel with religious practices and customs similar to those of sixteenth-century Iberian popular Catholicism.[41]

Accommodation

Accommodation or adaptation to the circumstances was characteristic of and indeed pervasive in the Jesuit way of proceeding. The origin of the Jesuit understanding of accommodation articulated in the Society of Jesus' foundational documents, the Spiritual Exercises and the Constitutions, is St. Ignatius's own religious experience and conviction that God deals directly and uniquely with each individual.[42] The early Jesuits were not the only ones who adapted their ministries to the circumstances, of course; accommodation was a fundamental principle in the classical tradition of rhetoric, and it found objective expression in casuistry. The rhetorical nature of Jesuit theological humanism afforded Don José this adaptability.

As has been seen, Acosta placed great importance on accommodating one's message to the audience so as to efficaciously instruct, persuade, and move the heart of the hearers to action for the good of souls. This flexibility and sensitivity to one's audience is also present in Acosta's American writings, which reveal the adaptations he makes to convince various audiences of his soteriological conviction that God desires the salvation of the native peoples.

The *De Procuranda* is concerned with providing the "complete means to help the well-being of the Indians."[43] To this end, Don José addresses the six books of the work to those directly involved in the spiritual and material well-being of the Indians in the Americas. Books one and two are directed to all Spaniards involved in this enterprise regardless of their particular offices; and they present in general terms the case for the salvation of the native peoples and tell what is useful and harmful to this enterprise. The audience of book three is the Spanish officials involved in the administration and government of the Indies *in situ*. Books four through six concern themselves with what is incumbent on the ministers of the gospel to collaborate with God's salvation of the Indians.

The *Doctrina Christiana*, on the other hand, is written with the native peoples in mind; and, as we have seen above, the style of its sermons is meant to persuade, instruct, and move the Indians to embrace the Christian faith. The *Historia* concerns itself with royal officials back in the homeland who influence the life of the Americas by their policies and decrees. As Acosta writes in the dedication to the Infanta Isabel Clara Eugenia, daughter of Philip II, he hopes that if the work pleases her she may show it to the king "so that the peoples of those kingdoms [the Indies] may be more helped and favored by those [people of this kingdom, i.e., Spain] to whom his divine and supreme Providence has entrusted them."[44]

Viewed synoptically it may be said that Acosta's American trilogy of the *De Procuranda*, the *Doctrina Christiana*, and the *Historia* make up a comprehensive strategy aimed at persuading each of the major parties involved in the evangelization of the Indies that the salvation of the native peoples is desired by God and attainable by collaborating with God's will. Each of Don José's American works provides pragmatic advice and marshals specific arguments tailored for its respective audiences.

In the *De Procuranda* the primary concern to which Acosta addresses himself is the motivations and practical courses of actions that priests and royal administrators must take to spread the gospel effectively in the Indies. It is especially concerned with the vices and abuses that the Spaniards must avoid so as not to sabotage the faith of the native neophytes. The *Doctrina Christiana* has as its focus the presentation of the Christian faith in a way that is compelling for the Indians and moves them to a deeper and more efficacious belief in Jesus Christ. The *Historia* in turn aims to convince those back in Spain who determine the fate of the Indies that the salvation of the native peoples is not impossible and that indeed God has been and continues to be at work in this regard.

Despite the different audiences addressed and the varied discourses and arguments utilized by Don José in these works, all three American works are unified by one common aim: the salvation of the Indians. And it was the adaptability to different audiences that the rhetorical nature of Jesuit theological humanism afforded him that allowed Acosta to produce three works that addressed themselves in appropriate ways to the various agents and subjects of the evangelization of the Indies. These agents and subjects were a diverse if not divergent lot of natives in reductions, royal officials in provincial capitals and *encomenderos* in isolated ranches and mines, as well as grandees of Spain who formulated American policy at Philip's monastery-palace at El Escorial. Part of the genius and uniqueness of Don José's Jesuit theological humanism is that it allowed him to present his theological arguments and practical advice for the evangelization of the Indies to these very different audiences.

It was noted above that in Don José's American writings there are at times a variety of seemingly contradictory opinions expressed about the same subject. This would seem to be the case, for example, with Acosta's thought on the humanity and intelligence of the native peoples. Some have underscored the variety of positions that Acosta expresses as indicative of his ambivalence toward the Indians.[45] In the light of our description of Jesuit accommodation in Acosta's American trilogy, some might interpret the various positions he expresses about the intelligence and humanity of the Amerindians as accommodation gone bad. Some might draw the conclusion that Acosta's "ambivalence" was really Don José being jesuitical.

Acosta's differing statements about the intelligence and humanity of the native peoples are, however, really a development in his thought on this question.[46] So if in the *De Procuranda* he underscores the barbarity of the natives, in the *Historia* he praises many of the achievements of Inca and Aztec cultures. The *Historia* is quite optimistic about the possibility that through education the native societies would be able to achieve the cultural development of European nations. And let us not forget that the *Historia*, completed in 1590, was the mature fruit of Acosta's American sojourn. The *De Procuranda*, on the other hand, was finished in 1576, only four years after Don José had disembarked on Peruvian shores.

Conclusion

José de Acosta was an intelligent and pious but frail young man born in six-teenth-century Castile. His motherland, the Kingdom of Castile, where he spent most of his life until his departure for Peru in 1571, was the largest and most prosperous of several kingdoms on the Iberian peninsula. Castile was also the most important realm of Charles I's empire; an empire on which at its height the sun did not set. Castilians enjoyed the benefits of their realm's po-sition in the Hapsburg pantheon, and during José's youth the kingdom en-joyed a religious, economic, political, and intellectual revival that had been underway since the times of the Catholic Kings, Fernando and Isabel. In the intimacy of the home too, José enjoyed privilege, comfort, and security. He was born into a devout and wealthy merchant family of Medina del Campo, one of Castile's thriving commercial centers. José would reap the fruits of Castile's revival by his exposure to the reformist educational and religious way of proceeding of the Society of Jesus and by the philosophical and theological preparation he received at the reformist and humanist center of learning, the University of Alcalá.

The Society of Jesus and the University of Alcalá steeped José in the Renaissance humanist ideal of marrying a classical education with fervent Christian faith and piety. The goal of the humanistic formation of the Jesuit colleges was *eloquentia perfecta* in the spoken and written word. From the writ-ings Acosta has left us, most of the major ones in elegant Ciceronian Latin, and from the testimony to his creative genius as a playwright and sacred ora-tor, it is evident that the young José was a paragon of this ideal. The University of Alcalá, which modeled itself on the University of Paris, offered in its theol-ogy faculty the innovative method of the three ways; theology students at

Alcalá were trained in the philosophical and theological systems of St. Thomas Aquinas, Duns Scotus, and William of Ockham.

But if there was a preponderant intellectual influence in Acosta's life it was the open Thomism of the Dominicans of the First School of Salamanca, which he learned from Fr. Alonso de Deza, S.J., at Alcalá. This Thomism incorporated the critiques that the humanist theologians made of the scholastics, especially their emphasis on positive theology, but held firm to the rationality and subtleties of St. Thomas. It was a theological formation that combined the practical and the speculative, as Jerónimo Nadal, S.J., put it. It was well-suited to the Jesuits' apostolic ministries, especially their ministries of the Word, with their emphasis on preaching that moved the heart to action on behalf of the neighbor.

José, the bright, pious, but sickly young man, emerged from this religious and intellectual preparation as an outstanding preacher and teacher who was on fire with the desire to go the Indies. Though his superiors envisioned a life of lecturing and sacred oratory in Spain and even at the Jesuits' premier educational institution of the time, the Roman College, he insisted on laboring for Christ in the vineyard of the foreign missions. In 1571 Padre José set sail for the Kingdom of Peru to realize his dream of saving Amerindian souls for Christ.

The next fourteen years in Peru were a time of both remarkable accomplishments and spectacular failures and heartache for José de Acosta. During this time he left his mark on literature, theology, and the natural sciences by his many and varied writings about the New World. In the style of the Renaissance man, José was also no less influential in the arena of civic and ecclesiastical affairs. He was at times the adversary, and at other times the confidant of inquisitors, archbishops, popes, viceroys, kings, provincials, and generals of the Society of Jesus. His achievements included excellence in preaching, theology, and the natural sciences, as well as diplomacy and court intrigue.

Above all, Acosta's time in Peru marked a personal transformation in the man. He went from being Padre José, the zealous and talented preacher, teacher, and Indies missionary, to Don José de Acosta, illustruous clergyman in the mold of such controversial Jesuits of the first generation as Antonio de Araoz, Nicolás Bobadilla, and Simão Rodrigues. He embodied both the best and worst qualities of the Spanish character of the day, that is, the proud spirit of a crusading nationalistic Catholicism bent on conquering and converting the pagan, crushing the infidel and heretic, reforming the lax in morals and inflaming the tepid of piety. Don José's Hispanic chauvinism would earn him the respect and gratitude of like-minded Spaniards who saw in their king, Philip II, a divinely appointed avenger and protector from all that threatened Spain and Catholicism. But at the same time, this nationalistic Catholicism would also earn him the derision and wariness of his superior general and most non-Spanish Jesuits of his time. This was a rejection and disdain that cost Acosta dearly in psychological suffering and isolation from his brother Jesuits.

Don José took courses of action that were brilliantly salutary and tragically divisive. His tenacity in accepting and defending the Society of Jesus' involvement in the reductions initiated in Peru by Viceroy Toledo paved the way for what some consider the Jesuits' most spectacular achievement ever. As the official theologian at Lima III and then as the principal agent of the council in Spain and Rome, he procured the approbation of a council that would have a profound effect on Church life throughout the South American continent for years to come. On the other hand, his role in the convocation of the Fifth General Congregation of the Society of Jesus violated the spirit of his vow of obedience and provoked an atmosphere of insecurity and turmoil in the Society, even while it spared it an external visitation in Spain by the agents of Philip II. Yet the change that occured in Acosta was quite dramatic, and ultimately the metamorphosis was a partial but flagrant abandonment of the ideals of his Jesuit vocation.

Singularity is perhaps the best term that comes to mind to describe Don José de Acosta's person and life. His unique gifts of intelligence and practical wisdom brought him into the limelight of his day. By the same token, his own estimation of these qualities led him to perceive himself and to act in a manner that exempted him from many of the common rules and observances of his religious institute. His sense of singularity reached such heights that he came to consider himself a more suitable agent to save the Society of Jesus than its legitimate leadership. And the outcome of his actions in that regard was, debatedly, not a complete failure.

Don José's Jesuit theological humanism places him in the great tradition of the open Thomism of the First School of Salamanca and of such humanist theologians as Jerónimo Nadal. Furthermore, it provides us with a richer understanding of the contribution that the early Jesuits made to theology. The great theologians of the early Society of Jesus were not limited to the scholastics Cardinals Francisco de Toledo and Roberto Bellarmino, and Francisco Suárez.

José de Acosta was no saint, and he often showed his shadow side. At times he was duplicitous, disobedient, imperious, and given to the comforts of the aristocracy with whom he spent much time in Lima, Madrid, and Rome. Some, of course, would say that he was thus the embodiment of all that is jesuitical.

Don José de Acosta was also a highly talented and even courageous man. He may have bordered on genius, and at certain points during his tumultous life he displayed heroic virtue. He was a prolific author, an elegant writer, a creative theologian, a honey-tongued orator, a skilled administrator, a nimble diplomat, and a zealous laborer for the salvation and evangelization of the Amerindians. For better and worse, he was the kind of man who gave rise to the legendary Jesuit.

Disputed Questions Concerning
Acosta's Life and Thought

Acosta the Theologian: Erasmian, Suarezian, or Nominalist?

Acosta's accomplishments as a theologian have been studied by a variety of scholars. His conservative soteriological views on the necessity of explicit faith in Christ for salvation,[1] his method of evangelization,[2] especially the catechisms he composed at the behest of the Third Provincial Council of Lima (1582–83)[3] and his opinions concerning the sacramental life of the Amerindians,[4] his judgment about the morality of the Spanish conquest of the Americas and other colonial institutions and practices,[5] and the theological influences on his works[6] have all received attention. These studies of the content of Acosta's theology have been laudatory, but there have been others that were negative.[7]

However, whether positive or negative, these assessments of Don José's theological output have followed the lead of the great scholar of Acosta's life and works, León Lopetegui.[8] They have focused their analysis on two of Acosta's great works, the *De Procuranda Indorum Salute* and the *Historia Natural y Moral de las Indias*. The *De Procuranda*, written in Peru in 1576[9] and first published in Madrid in 1588, deals with the evangelization of the native peoples of the Andes. The *Historia*, written intermittently between 1583 and 1588 in the Americas and Europe and first published also in Madrid in 1590, concerns itself with the flora and fauna and with the peoples of the Andes and Mexico and their evangelization. Like Lopetegui, who referred to the *De Procuranda* and the *Historia* as missiological manuals,[10] most of these scholars have praised and interpreted these two great works as missiological texts.

To be sure, this is a valid and necessary approach, but, as Pedro Leturia pointed out, it has its limitations.[11] In his review of Lopetegui's book on Acosta and the missions, Leturia correctly observed that Lopetegui's laudatory appraisal of the *De Procuranda* was concerned with correlating Acosta's sixteenth-century text with orthodox theological positions of pre-Vatican II missiology. This perspective prevented Lopetegui from fully investigating Acosta's work on its own terms and within its own historical horizon.[12]

Two other scholars have attempted to describe Acosta's theology in a way that is more attentive to his historical context. Edmundo O'Gorman and María Luisa Rivara de Tuesta have interpreted Don José's theology as Christian humanism.[13] But their studies, done in 1940 and 1970, respectively, are dated in the light of the work of Paul Oskar Kristeller and others on Renaissance humanism. For example, O'Gorman makes a sharp separation between Renaissance humanism and medieval philosophy and theology.[14] In light of Kristeller's work such a sharp distinciton is no longer tenable.[15]

In the final section of chapter seven, which deals with Jesuit spirituality, I discuss how O'Gorman's dichotomy between Renaissance humanism and medieval philosophy and theology prevents him from adequately appreciating the theological themes of Acosta's *Historia*. O'Gorman has pointed out that the overall structure of the *Historia* reflects Aristotle's hierarchy or ladder of being. The various books that make up the work move from a consideration of inanimate creation through the vegetative and animal kingdoms to the zenith of creation, the world of culture created by rational creatures. While Aristotle's hierarchical conception of the universe is certainly discernible in the *Historia*, it is not a complete explanation of the entire work. O'Gorman's interpretation ignores the important book seven of the *Historia* that deals with God's providence operative in the Americas through the Inca and Aztec empires.

O'Gorman dismisses this book as an accidental addition that does not contribute to Acosta's Aristotelianism. In book seven Acosta argues that Providence was able to prepare the way for the efficacious preaching of the gospel by using the idolatrous and demonic religion of the native peoples to prefigure the sacraments of the Roman Catholic Church. If one takes into account the theological teleology that Acosta presents in this final book, then the claim that the *Historia* embodies only Aristotelianism is less of a perfect fit. However, when book seven is taken at face value as the culmination of Acosta's argument in the *Historia* and is read against the background of the final contemplation in St. Ignatius's Spiritual Exercises, then a new reading of the structure to the *Historia* is possible.

María Luisa Rivara de Tuesta's thesis that Acosta's humanism very closely mirrors that of Erasmus[16] is also dated in the light of contemporary research on Iberian humanism and early Jesuit history.[17] For example, I documented in chapter seven the high regard that Acosta had for the use of some forms of Catholic popular religiosity to evangelize the Amerindians. This was characteristically Jesuit, yet quite different from Erasmus's disdain for such pious practices, which he considered to be superstitious. But the most fundamental error in Rivara de Tuesta's study of Acosta's humanism is her conception of humanism as a philosophical movement. This understanding of Renaissance humanism has been discarded due to Kristeller's scholarship. Kristeller convincingly argued that Renaissance humanism arose from grammatical and rhetorical studies and introduced a new classicist style into a wide range of scholarly disciplines and professional fields that had already existed since medieval times. There were humanists in such wide-ranging fields and professions as theology, jurisprudence, medicine, mathematics, and philosophy, among others.[18]

Rivara de Tuesta's states that Acosta's historical predecessors are difficult to determine[19] and that his influence on his contemporaries was negligible.[20] She mentions only three colonial authors who were influenced by Don José: Bishops Luis Jerónimo de Oré, O.F.M.,[21] and Alonso de la Peña y Montenegro, O.P.,[22] and Rev. Alonso de Sandoval, S.J.[23] Yet Don José's influence on missiology and on early modern authors interested in the New World is well documented by the dean of Acosta studies of this century, León Lopetegui, S.J.[24] Indeed, Lopetegui goes so far as to state that there is hardly an author who has written on missiological or American matters who does not know and cite Acosta.[25]

More recently, Sabine MacCormack has argued that, in contrast to Fray Bartolomé de las Casas's understanding of the role that demons play on the imagination, Acosta's understanding of the imagination did not postulate demons to account for religious error. This was the case because Acosta followed his Jesuit contemporaries such as Francisco Suárez, S.J., and other Coimbra commentators on Aristotle's *De anima*. They held that the imagination as part of the intellectual or rational soul was immortal and therefore not affected by material or demonic disturbances in the environment. "It was from such work by his fellow Jesuits," MacCormack states, "that Acosta learned to evaluate the imagination without reference to demons."[26]

MacCormack's assertion that Francisco Suárez, S.J., influenced Acosta does not seem plausible for both chronological and theological reasons. While it is true that Suárez (1548–1617) is a rough chronological contemporary of Acosta (1540–1600), intellectualy they are of two different generations. Suárez commenced his teaching career at Segovia in 1571 and achieved the apex of that career in the 1580s and 1590s, when he lectured on philosophy and theology at the Roman College, Alcalá, and Coimbra. The first of the Distinguished Doctor's many works on theology and philosophy to be published was his *De Verbo Incarnato* in 1590.[27] Thus it does not seem likely that Acosta, who was formed in Alcalá in the 1560s and was in the Americas from 1571 to 1586, would have incorporated Suárez's mature thought of the 1580s and 1590s in his American writings of the 1570s and 1580s.

Suárez's original and eclectic philosophical and theological system was characterized among other things by its differences from the interpretations of the

Angelic Doctor formulated by the Second School of Salamanca. Beginning in the 1580s and lasting into the seventeenth century, Suárez, Luis de Molina, S.J., and later their disciples postulated a metaphysics and theological anthropology that differed significantly from the leaders of the Second School of Salamanca, the Dominicans Báñez and Medina. The Second School of Salamanca held a more rigid position regarding the interpretation of St. Thomas. Unlike the First School of Salamanca, the theologians of the Second School of Salamanca were less inclined to abandon the positions of the Angelic Doctor, even when the opinions of St. Thomas were not pertinent or helpful to address contemporary problems.

The new interpretations of Suárez, Vásquez, and Molina also differed from their Jesuit confreres, such as Deza and Acosta, who were formed in and were loyal to the open Thomism of the First School of Salamanca.[28] Already since the late 1560s the Jesuit superior general in Rome received letters from the older Jesuit theologians warning of dangerous innovations and novelties among the younger Jesuits who were not teaching the accepted interpretations of St. Thomas.

In 1589 Molina's *Concordia liberi arbitrii cum gratiae donis* was published in Lisbon. It would be this text that represented the more optimistic Jesuit theological anthropology vis-à-vis the rigid and more pessimistic Thomism of the Second School of Salamanca in the *De Auxiliis* controversy of the next twenty years. The presenting problem of the *De Auxiliis* controversy was the perennially disputed theological issue of how to reconcile human freedom with the universal knowledge and power of God. By and large, the Jesuits defended the freedom of the human person by emphasizing the role that the human agent had in responding to God's grace. The Dominicans, on the other hand, safeguarded the sovereignty of God by underscoring the impotence of human beings before the power of the Creator. The impotence of human beings included their inability to accept or reject God's freely bestowed and unmerited efficacious grace, or the grace that determined the soul's predestination to eternal salvation.

However, the *De Auxiliis* controversy was not merely a theological debate. It pitted two great religious families against each other and degenerated into a heated and acrimonious confrontation between two different approaches to a whole host of religious issues of the late sixteenth century. The Jesuits and the Dominicans had different approaches concerning how to engage in ministry. The differences between the Jesuits and the Dominicans were aired outside the university lecture halls and became the topic of polemical sermons preached at churches throughout Spain. Each side accused the other of heresy. Philip II and the Spanish Inquisition tried in vain to reconcile the battling orders, which were causing confusion and scandal to Spain's faithful. The popes did not do much better, and after nine years of trying to settle the dispute by means of an extensive consultation of theologians, they finally had to acknowledge their impotence in the matter. In 1607, Pope Paul V imposed silence about the matter of free will and predestination on both the Jesuits and the Dominicans and forbade both sides to denounce their opponents' positions on free will and grace as heretical.[29]

When Acosta returned to Spain from Peru in 1587, he did not play a prominent role in the *De Auxiliis* controversy; instead he devoted his energies above all to the internal governance of the Society. However, a memorandum he wrote in 1595 concerning the *De Auxiliis* controversy[30] and an incident while he was rector of the house of studies at Salamanca in 1597 indicate that he sympathized with the older generation of Jesuit theologians who favored following the open Thomism of the First School of Salamanca.[31] In other words, Acosta's position on the *De Auxiliis* controversy was to echo the Thomistic synthesis on nature and grace that was expounded by the Vitorian Thomists of the previous generation, which emphasized human freedom. Acosta chose not to deal with the disputed theological issues that had come to the fore since 1589 with the publication of Molina's book.

In 1595 Acosta was the rector of the community of professed members of the order in Valladolid. During this time he was also engaged in the ministries of writing, preaching, and serving as consultor to the Inquisition, in which he had been engaged off and on ever since he was ordained. At this time Pope Clement VIII had decided to take matters into his own hands and convoke a consultation of theologians and cardinals in Rome to settle the virulent debate among Jesuits and Dominicans concerning grace and free will. As a preliminary step to this meeting, he ordered his nuncios to solicit the opinions of individual theologians and university faculties of theology on the matter.

In Spain both the nuncio and the General and Supreme Council of the Inquisition collected documents from 1595 to 1597. Acosta submitted a brief memorandum on the subject. The text was devoid of his usual citations from the Scriptures and the Fathers. Rather than tackle the controversial texts and issues that were being debated by the specialists at the time, his presentation was not polemical and reflected the state of the question as formulated by the Vitorian Thomists of the previous generation.[32] He emphasized human freedom, as well as God's assistance, but did not deal with the question of just how much freedom the human person had to do good. And this was the state of the question during the *De Auxiliis* controversy.[33]

In early 1597 Acosta was moved from the professed house in Valladolid to the house of studies in Salamanca. At first he exercised the office of superior of the house with the title of vice-rector because he had not yet received the official appointment from Rome. This would be delayed for several months since Fr. General Aquaviva was opposed to the appointment.[34] During the early months of his rectorship Acosta had to resolve a feud between two of the professors of the house that had been going on for several years.

In the fall of 1593, Fr. Miguel Marcos, S.J., left his post as chief lecturer of St. Thomas at the Jesuit house of studies in Salamanca to attend the Fifth General Congregation. Francisco Suárez, who was then lecturing at Alcalá, was sent to take his place. Upon Marcos's return from the congregation in early 1594, Suárez remained in Salamanca but relinquished his teaching responsibilities to Marcos. Marcos, who considered Suárez's doctrine a novel and dangerous departure from the tried and true Thomism of the First School of Salamanca that he favored, refused to assume his teaching responsibilities while Suárez remained in the house, even when the latter was not teaching. Marcos returned briefly to his teaching during the 1594–95 academic year but once again refused to teach until Suárez was moved from the community. The impasse was not resolved until early in 1597, when Acosta assumed the rectorship. Suárez accepted a chair at Coimbra, and Marcos happily returned to his teaching duties well pleased with Acosta's resolution in his favor of the dispute with Suárez.[35]

In light of this incident and Acosta's memorandum concerning the *De Auxiliis* controversy, it is not reasonable to maintain that José was a sympathizer with Suárez or his thought. By the same token and given what has been documented above about Acosta's Thomistic formation at Alcalá, it is even more far fetched to hold that Acosta was an opponent of St. Thomas's concordance between nature and grace and a nominalist who held for the separation of nature and grace. Yet this is Fernando Cervantes's argument in his recent book about diabolism in New Spain.[36] Cervantes argues that Acosta is the best example of a nominalist trend in philosophy and theology that demonizes Native American culture and religion.[37] Again in the final section of the chapter seven above, I describe how Acosta's understanding of grace and the devil bears a greater resemblance to the Thomistic teaching on these matters proposed by St. Ignatius of Loyola in his Spiritual Exercises.

Acosta's Jewish Ancestry

León Lopetegui maintains that Don Antonio de Acosta's ancestors were Portuguese Jews, but he offers no documentary evidence for this assertion.[38] In my opinion, until further research is done on the Acosta's forebears, the question of their Jewish roots remains open. Lopetegui's statements on this matter are based on very weak circumstantial evidence: that Acosta was a familiar Portuguese surname and that José's actions at the court of Philip II that led to the convocation of the Fifth General Congregation were indicative of the *converso* character.

According to Lopetegui, this converso character was vain and disobedient of established lines of authority. It sought to get its own way by going over the head of one's immediate superiors out of a sense of being up against the wall.[39] While it is true that Medina del Campo—about eighty-five miles, as the crow flies, from the Portuguese border—had seen significant numbers of Portuguese immigrants during the sixteenth century,[40] this is hardly sufficient evidence, as Fermín del Pino Díaz has pointed out,[41] to declare the Acostas to have been originally Portuguese. Lopetegui's statements about José's insubordinate actions during the events that led to the Fifth General Congregation being typical of the converso propensity for political intrigue are even less credible than his assertions about the Acostas' Portuguese origins.

The information that most clearly suggests the Acostas' Jewish ancestry stems from the charges made by Fr. Alonso Sánchez, S.J., envoy of Fr. General Aquaviva to Philip II between 1592 and 1593, of José's lack of *limpieza de sangre*, or purity of blood.[42] Sánchez had been sent to the court by Aquaviva to undermine Acosta's influence there and to derail the latter's suggestion that a general congregation be convoked to resolve the king's complaints about the general's governance of the Society, particularly in Spain and her possessions. However, as Lopetegui has pointed out, there is reason to suspect Sánchez's allegations. In 1586 Fr. General Aquaviva had appointed Acosta Sánchez's personal superior in Mexico so as to prevent what was judged to be the latter's imprudent lobbying before the crown for the armed conquest of China in order to establish Christianity there. During the time Acosta was Sánchez's personal superior, he wrote several memoranda to Aquaviva criticizing Sánchez's reasons for the armed implantation of Christianity in China.

In 1980 Lopetegui changed his opinion about Acosta's ethnic background. He wrote that in 1942 he was prevented from publishing his belief that Acosta was of Jewish ancestry because it was too sensitive a topic to broach in the anti-Semitic climate that reigned in Fascist Italy.[43] Be that as it may, the fact remains that even in 1980 Lopetegui failed to provide any solid evidence that substantiated his opinion that Acosta had Jewish ancestry.

Acosta at the Fifth General Congregation: Ambitious Melancholic Machiavelli?

Modern scholarship about this period of the Society's history and Acosta's involvement in it has followed the reconstruction and interpretation of events of the third volume of Antonio Astrain's multivolume history of the Spanish Assistancy. Acosta's biographers have been no different, and they like Astrain have portrayed the memorialistas as a minority of malcontents. While it is true that the actual number of Jesuits who wrote memoranda was no more than thirty, support for their ideas was not as insignificant as Astrain would have us believe. In 1587, the Jesuit provinces held congregations, a part of regular Jesuit governance. Such a congregation was to send a representative, a procurator, to a procurators' congregation in Rome to vote on whether a general congregation of the order should be convoked. The provincial congregation of Castile, the largest Jesuit province in Spain, with over six hundred members, voted unanimously to instruct their representative to Rome to vote for convocation. Furthermore, they gave the procurator specific instructions to press for the changes that the memorialistas were writing about.[44]

Astrain portrays the memorialistas as bent on undermining the legitimate authority of Fr. General Claudio Aquaviva. He sees the changes they advocated as designed to disfigure the essential characteristics of the Jesuit Constitutions and to placate Philip II's desire for strict control of all religious affairs within his domains. Astrain argues that the changes proposed by the memorialistas would have provided the Jesuits in Spain with a certain autonomy from Rome which would allow them to continue to do things *a la española*.

Among the changes proposed by the memorialistas were provincial congregations with authority to treat substantial matters of the province, a simplification and reform of the criteria and structure of grades in the Society, frequent visits by the superior general to his subjects outside of Rome, and a national superior, or *comisario*. This is hardly the cataclysmic undermining of the essential characteristics of the Jesuit Institute that Astrain saw in their proposals. And, ironically, many of the changes to the Jesuit Constitutions that these men advocated have been adopted by the Society's general congregations during the past thirty years. The criteria for final profession have been re-evaluated and expanded and are today more in keeping with what they were like at the time of St. Ignatius. The superior general now frequently visits Jesuits all over the globe. And Spain and several other countries now have superprovincials in addition to the various regional provincials that govern each Jesuit province.

Astrain presents Acosta as an ambitious and melancholic Machiavellian figure who was motivated by righteous indignation at not having been made provincial by Aquaviva after he discharged the general's mission to the court of Philip II and at the king's behest visited the Jesuit provinces of Andalucia and Aragon. According to Astrain, Acosta enlisted Philip II to pressure the Holy See to convoke a general congregation that would undermine Aquaviva's authority and make the general more pliable to the royal will.[45] Astrain disregards the account that Acosta narrates in his *apologia* of the events leading up to his commission by the king to procure a general congregation.[46] In this memorandum written to Clement VIII, Acosta defends himself against those who accused him of being the leader of the memorialistas and intent on undermining the true Ignatian spirit of the Society of Jesus. Neither does Astrain take into account Acosta's 1592 diary of what he did in Rome on behalf of the king.[47] Pertinent information from these and other documents is presented below to provide another reading to Astrain's reconstruction and interpretation of Acosta's role in the convocation of the Fifth General Congregation.

Astrain bases his version of events on a letter by Fr. Gil González Dávila, S.J., that describes Acosta as melancholic because Aquaviva had not written him since the visitation nor let him know what was to become of him.[48] González Dávila was one of the most distinguished members of the order at the time. He had served as provincial of various provinces and had lived with Acosta in Madrid after the latter finished his visitation of the province of Aragon. He had also been Don José's teacher at Alcalá and served as co-visitor with him of the provinces of the assistancy. Presumably he knew Acosta well.

It would seem that Astrain was justified in accepting González Dávila's testimony about Acosta's interior state. However, there are two other letters written by Acosta to Aquaviva dating from January and February 1592, at the same time as González Dávila's letter, which reveal other events that better account for Acosta's depression. Curiously, Astrain is aware of these letters, but in an uncharacteristic move by the great historian he cites them only sparsely. Astrain maintains that these letters manifest Acosta's growing pride. And it was this pride, Astrain holds, that eventually led Acosta to turn on Aquaviva for not rewarding him with a provincialate for his services at the court of Philip II and for the visitations of 1589–91.[49]

My reading of these two letters differs from that of Astrain. I do not think that they reveal Acosta's pride and resentment. Rather, they manifest his anger and distress at the attacks that were being hurled at him by both the memorialistas and those who were loyal to Aquaviva. In the first letter, Acosta asks the general not to believe the charge being leveled against him by the notorious former Jesuit and memorialista, Dr. Francisco de Abreo. The charge was that Acosta's visitations were merely pro forma and did not redress the problems that plagued the provinces of Andalucia and Aragon.[50] Acosta tells the general that he went to great lengths to track down this calumny and confronted Abreo, who denied he had said such a thing. At this time Abreo still lived in a Jesuit house as a guest, even though he had been dismissed from the Society in 1591; Abreo's influence with the king and the Inquisition was very much feared by the Society.[51] Acosta believed him, and speculated that the source of the rumor was another Jesuit, Father Lugo, who he said was known for the fabrication of incredible novelas.

The second letter that reveals a more plausible reason for Acosta's melancholia than vile ambition was written a month after the first and again directed to Aquaviva.[52] Acosta expresses his distress that in the latest package of letters received from Rome he is the only member of the community not to receive any correspondence from the general, this even after he, Acosta, had written His Paternity on various occasions concerning important matters. Furthermore, he is concerned that in the letter the general wrote to Father González Dávila, who showed it to Acosta, the general has been left with the impression that Acosta had maligned Fr. Antonio Marcén, S.J., whom the general had recently chosen as provincial of Toledo. Marcén was one of the four Jesuits imprisoned by the Inquisition in Valladolid in 1586 but eventually cleared and released two years later. Marcén was a supporter of Aquaviva, and Acosta was concerned that the general not have the impression that he thought ill of him or that the he considered the decision to make him provincial to be inopportune. Again Acosta fingers Father Lugo as the origin of the rumors against him.

The letters of January 8 and February 7, 1592, reveal a more probable reason for Acosta's distraught state than the alleged resentment and pride that Astrain attributes to him. The visitations of Andalucia and Aragon finished in the late summer of 1591, and for over six months Acosta received no word from Aquaviva. Acosta was aware that in the fall of 1591 the king, pressured by the Inquisition, was once again considering naming an extern to visit the Society.[53] He was also aware that he was maligned in letters to the general by memorialistas, who considered his visitations of Andalucia and Aragon a sham, and also by supporters of Aquaviva, who saw him as undermining the general's authority by second-guessing his decisions. Is it any wonder that Acosta was beleaguered and melancholic? Despite his best efforts of the past two years, his beloved Society was once again in danger of being humiliated by an external visitation, and, as if this was not enough, his own superior general seemed to doubt his fidelity and gave credence to the deleterious rumors that circulated about him.

Neither does Astrain accept Acosta's statement that the reason he proposed that the king procure a general congregation from the pope was to save the Society from a visitation by a non-Jesuit. Philip's leanings in this direction are corroborated by the statements of one of his ministers, the Count of Chinchón, to Father González Dávila.[54] Furthermore, there exists correspondence between the king and his ambassador in Rome suggesting that the monarch did not consider Acosta to be a person of complete confidence. Thus, Acosta was hardly a man bent on ingratiating himself with the king at all costs to strike back at Aquaviva.[55] This letter was written in early 1593, several months before Alonso Sánchez, Aquaviva's representative to the king, was able to meet with Philip II on March 22, 1593, and attempt to discredit Acosta before his majesty.[56]

There is yet another reason to question Astrain's reconstruction of Acosta's motivations and actions in the events that led to the convocation of the Fifth General Congregation of the Society. Astrain disputes Acosta's description of events concerning how exactly he was ordered to go to Rome to procure from Clement VIII the convocation of a general congregation. Acosta's version is that he did so at the behest of the king and with the approval of his provincial. Acosta was at this time rector of the professed house at Valladolid, a post he assumed in mid-April 1592. After a visit by Philip II to the city in August 1592, during which he also visited the houses of the Society, one of his ministers, the Duke of Chinchón, asked the provincial of Castile to order Acosta to undertake the king's commission. Acosta accepted, set off for Rome immediately, and arrived in the Eternal City in early December 1592.

Astrain's chronology is different, and he cites the correspondence of a less than impartial Alonso Sánchez, who reproduces the testimony of Fr. Lorenzo Villegas, S.J., to support his reconstruction of events.[57] Villegas claims to have been comissioned by Acosta to go to the king and speak on his behalf so that he, Acosta, could be named the king's agent in the convocation of the general congregation. I have mentioned above Sánchez's animus against Acosta. Acosta had been named Sánchez's personal superior in Mexico by Aquaviva and had written against his plans to persuade the king to invade China and Japan so as to more effectively spread Christianity in those lands. But it turns out that Villegas's account of events was not trustworthy, since according to his recollection of events Acosta's commission would have occurred in the late summer or early fall of 1591. This meant that it occurred before Acosta had presented the king with his report of the visitation of the Jesuit province of Aragon. As Astrain himself observes, it was rather unlikely that Acosta would have approached the king to obtain the commission of being his agent until he first presented the results of the Aragon visitation.[58]

My reading of the memorialista crisis is that it was more indicative of a generational shift in the early Society. The memorialistas, like Acosta, were older Jesuits who had been formed during the first generation of the Society, unlike Aquaviva who entered the Society in 1567 during the generalate of Francisco de Borja. The Society into which Acosta and the memorialistas had been socialized was smaller, and its way of proceeding was more flexible and personal than the government that began to emerge under Borja and subsequent generals. Beginning with Borja, the generals issue more and more rules in the hope of maintaining discipline and uniformity throughout an organization that was experiencing phenomenal growth in membership, as well as tremendous geographical expansion throughout the world.

Table of Contents of
the *De Procuranda Indorum Salute*

BOOK TWO: ON THE JUSTICE AND INJUSTICE OF WAR.

BOOK SIX:
THE ADMINISTRATION OF THE SACRAMENTS TO THE INDIANS.

Table of Contents of
the *Historia Natural y Moral de las Indias*

BOOK TWO: ABOUT THE BURNING ZONE AND ITS QUALITIES.

BOOK FIVE: THE MORAL HISTORY, ABOUT THE RELIGION, RITES, IDOLATRIES, AND SACRIFICES OF THE INDIANS.

BOOK SIX: ABOUT THE POLITICS, GOVERNMENT, LAWS, CUSTOMS AND EVENTS OF THE INDIANS.

BOOK SEVEN: ABOUT THE ORIGINS, SUCCESSION, PRIVILEGES, AND OTHER NOTABLE THINGS OF THE MEXICANS.

Table of Contents of the *Doctrina Christiana*

PART ONE: CATECHISM.

Christian Doctrine and Catechism for the Instruction of the Indians.
What is contained in the first part.
Royal Mandate.
Letter of the Third Provincial Council of Lima.
Decree of the Third Provincial Council of Lima about the catechism.
Letter about the translation.
Decree about the translation.
Errata.

Christian Doctrine.
A Summary of the Catholic Faith.

Brief Catechism for the *Rudi* and the Busy.
A brief talk containing a summary of what should be known by one who becomes a Christian.

Major Catechism for those who are more capable.
  First Part: Introduction to Christian doctrine.
  Second Part: About the creed.
  Third Part: About the sacraments.
  Fourth Part: About the commandments.
  Fifth Part: About praying the Our Father.

Annotations about the translation of the Christian doctrine and catechism into Quechua and Aymara. With a declaration of phrases and words that are difficult in alphabetical order.
  Difficult Words.
  General Annotations about the Aymara language.
  Brief vocabulary of the words found in this catechism in alphabetical order.

PART TWO: CONFESSIONAL MANUAL.

Confessional Manual for the Priests of the Indians.
Royal Decree.
Errata.
Letter of St. Toribio de Mogrovejo.
Decree of the Council about the Confessional Manual.

Prologue.

Confessional Manual.
    Exhortation before confession.
    First Commandment.
    Second Commandment.
    Third Commandment.
    Fourth Commandment.
    Fifth Commandment.
    Sixth Commandment.
    Seventh Commandment.
    Eighth Commandment.
    Ninth Commandment.
    Tenth Commandment.

Questions.
    Questions for native Indian leaders.
    Questions for Indian leaders appointed by the Spaniards.
    Questions for Indian sorcerers and confessors.

Exhortations after confession.
    General exhortation after confession.
    Reprimand for idolaters and the superstitious.
    Reprimand for those living in sin and the dishonest.
    Reprimand for those who do not make restitution.

Instructions against the rites and ceremonies of the Indians.
    Chapter 1. About idolatry.
    Chapter 2. About sacrifices and offerings.
    Chapter 3. About the deceased.
    Chapter 4. About sorcerers and their spells.
    Chapter 5. About omens and superstitions.
    Chapter 6. Errors against the Catholic faith into which some Indians fall.

Indian Superstitions taken from the Second Provincial Council of Lima
    of 1567.

The Errors and Superstitions of the Indians taken from Master Polo's treatise.

Chapter 1. About the *huacas* and idols.

Chapter 2. About spirits and the deceased.

Chapter 3. About the statues of the Inca.

Chapter 4. About omens.

Chapter 5. About the confession and penance they did for their sins.

Chapter 6. About the way they made sacrifice.

Chapter 7. About the order of the year and seasons.

Chapter 8. About the feasts of each month of the year.

Chapter 9. About the extraordinary feasts.

Chapter 10. About spells.

Chapter 11. About sorcery and fortune telling.

Chapter 12. About the ministers of the sacrifices.

Chapter 13. About the priests and doctors.

Chapter 14. About the sacrifices and what was sacrificed.

Chapter 15. How the Inca gave his *huacas* to all his kingdoms in the fashion of Cuzco.

Decree of the Provincial Council about the Exhortation to prepare for a good death.

Brief Exhortation for Indians about to die so that a priest or someone else will help them die well.

Another longer Exhortation for Indians who are not about to die but have the need to prepare their souls.

Litany.

Summary of some of the faculties and privileges granted for the Indies by several Pontiffs.

The form to be followed in publishing the impediments to marriage.

Common form of the Marriage Banns.

PART THREE: SERMON MANUAL.

Third Catechism and exposition of the Christian doctrine by sermons.

Errata of the sermons.

Royal Mandate.

Table of Contents of the Sermons.

Letter of St. Toribio de Mogrovejo.

Prologue.

Sermons
1. The presuppositions of the faith.
2. Sin and how much God deplores it.
3. Jesus Christ, the only cure for sin.
4. What we must do to be saved.
5. What is God?
6. God's creation of the angels.
7. God's creation of the earth and of man.
8. Jesus Christ's foundation of the Church.
9. Faith is not enough for salvation, repentance of sins is necessary.
10. What is a sacrament and on baptism.
11. Sin after baptism may be pardoned only by the sacrament of confession.
12. An examination of conscience is necessary for a good confession.
13. About the Most Holy Sacrament of the Altar.
14. About the Sacrament of Confirmation.
15. How chastity is the more perfect state, but not obligatory.
16. Impediments that annul marriage.
17. The Sacrament of Extreme Unction.
18. The whole law of God is contained in ten words.
19. Against sorcerers and their superstitions.
20. About oaths and swearing.
21. About the third commandment.
22. About the fourth and fifth commandments.
23. Against drunkenness.
24. About the sixth commandment.
25. About the seventh commandment.
26. About the eighth, ninth, and tenth commandments.
27. About charity and alms-giving.
28. About prayer.
29. About the Our Father, the Hail Mary, the Sign of the Cross, blessing one-self with holy water, and other things the faithful use.
30. About the Last Things.
31. About the Final Judgement.

APPENDIX 5

Acosta on Jesus' Hardships as Encouragement for Those Who Minister in the Indies, *De Procuranda*, Book I, Chapter 3

. . . Moved by the sight of the few who followed Jesus Christ, John the Baptist said to his disciples: "He who comes from heaven is above all. He bears witness to what has been heard, yet no one receives his testimony." It seemed to the Baptist that, given the dignity of such a teacher, to have so few disciples was to have none. But let us listen to the very captain and apostle of our confession, who addressed his prayer and complaint to the Eternal Father: "I have labored in vain, I have spent my strength for nothing and vanity." Wouldn't you call these many and great tasks of preaching, vigils, traveling to places and castles, clamoring, sailing, curing the sick, performing marvels vain and almost sterile if you take into account the small number of disciples Christ had and the multitude and hardness of heart of his enemies? Wouldn't you say that so much strength was wasted and so much fortitude consumed, when you contemplate him crucified and abandoned in part by his own and in part betrayed and tormented by the insatiable cruelty of his enemies, wounded and put on the cross? But how does the wisest of teachers reason? How does he encourage and comfort himself? "My judgment," he says, "is before the Lord, and my reward is from my God." It is as if he said: "I do not guard myself against men, I do not look for their favor, rather I look only to God; I know the righteousness of his judgment; I consecrate my work to him, I place my hope in him, because of his grace I do all things and suffer joyfully, judging my losses as triumphs." This is the spirit, the mind of the Savior. All who engage in the work of God and wish to be considered his faithful and true laborers should think about these things. We do not take care of our own business, but rather the Lord's; let us quickly look after the work, and leave the fruit to God . . .

Acosta on the Usefulness of Knowing the "Superstitions" of the Amerindians, *Historia*, Book V, Chapter 31

. . . For Spaniards over there [in the Indies] and anywhere, this account [of the Indians' superstitions] may be helpful so as to be grateful to God, our Lord, and thus give him infinite thanks for so great a good as having given us his holy law, which is entirely just, clean, and useful. And this is easily known by comparing it with the laws of Satan under which so many unfortunates have lived. It may also be useful to know the pride, envy, wiles, and cunning of the devil with those whom he holds captive, because on the one hand he wishes to imitate and compete with God and his holy law and on the other hand he mixes so much vanity, filth, and even cruelty just as one whose work is spoiling all that is good and corrupting it.

Finally, one who would see the blindness and gloom that for such a long time provinces and great kingdoms have lived under, and many people and a great part of the world still live similarly deceived, will not be able, if he has a Christian bosom, but to give thanks to the Most High God for those whom he has called from such darkness to the admirable light of his gospel and to beg the immense charity of the Creator that he increase and conserve them in their understanding and obedience. And while at the same time grieving for those who are still on the road to perdition, let him ask the Father of Mercy that he show them the treasures and riches of Jesus Christ, who with the Father and the Holy Spirit reigns forever and ever. Amen.

Acosta's Catechetical Sermon on Charity and Alms-giving, *Doctrina Christiana*, "Tercero Cathecismo y Exposición de la Doctrina Christiana por Sermones," Sermon 27

In many sermons I have told you what the commandments of God contain, declaring each one in turn. In this sermon I would like to teach you how you have the law of God in one word. And if you keep it you will fulfill all the commandments.

Jesus Christ our Lord said that all the law of God and the commandments were contained in these two: love God above all things, and your neighbor as yourself. And the Apostle Paul says that the fulfillment of the law consists in loving, and he says that the one who loves one's neighbor as one should fulfills everything that God demands. So, my dearly beloved brothers and sisters, if we wish to know that we are fulfilling the law of our God we ought to look and see if we love God and our neighbors as we should. Because it is clear that the one who loves the devil, and the mountains, and the *huacas*, and who does injury to God's holy name bearing false witness, and who does not go to mass on a feast day, does not love God.

And it is also very clear that one does not love the neighbor who does not respect him, nor looks after the well being of one's father or mother, and more so the one who takes human life or another's wife or property or raises false witness against one's neighbor. But the one who has faith, hope, and love of God, serves and adores only him as his Lord and God, and the one who loves his neighbor as himself does not do him any harm nor speak ill of him, nor his wife, nor his property, nor his reputation. Do you want to know what it means to love one's neighbor as oneself? Look at how you want others to treat you, and do that to your neighbor, and then realize that you love him as you love yourself.

Tell me, what would you say if someone told you that they loved you very much, and yet this person didn't stop slapping you, and cursing you, and stole your property, and seeing you in need, this person told you to go fishing without giving you anything? Tell me, what would you say about this person who did these things to you? Wouldn't you say that this person was making fun of you? And that this person was your enemy and wished you evil? Who could doubt it? Well, my brothers, this is what God says through the words of Saint John his apostle, that we love not with words but in deeds and truth, and elsewhere he says that perfect love of God is fulfillment of his commandments.

Those who say that they keep God's law and honor themselves by saying they are Christians and yet mistreat their brothers or steal from them, or trample upon them, or take their property, or make them work and do not pay them, or take their wives or daughters, or place curses upon them, these people lie and are enemies of Jesus Christ because they dishonor his law.

When you see *viracochas* [Spaniards] who beat up Indians, or pull their hair, or curse them to the devil, and take their food, and make them work and don't pay them, and call them dogs, and are angry, prideful, these *viracochas* are enemies of Jesus Christ and are evil; and despite the fact that they say they are Christian, they do not do the deeds of Christians; rather they do those of the devil. Jesus Christ abhors them because they are like evil children who turn against their father.

This is how these baptized Christians who know the law of God behave, but they do not serve God, rather they offend him and break his laws. Because God orders them to love you as they love themselves and do you no harm, and rather treat you well. When you see other *viracochas* who do not mistreat you, but rather treat you as their children, and protect you from evil people, and aid you in your needs, understand that these are good Christians who keep the law of Jesus Christ and are his children and have learned from him, because he orders that we love one another and that no one mistreat another, but rather treat all people well. This is the complete law of Jesus Christ, and by this we know who has been taught by Jesus Christ.

What he taught by word and deed—loving us miserable people unto death and shedding his blood on the cross for us—anyone who loves his neighbor in this way, that one is a disciple of Christ, and one who doesn't, isn't, and if he says he is, he lies as the evil man that he is. So said Jesus Christ himself: people will know that you are my disciples if you love one another. This is the true sign of the good Christian: don't think that you will enter paradise if you arrive wearing a long habit or a crown on your head; rather do what is good and do what God commands. Even if one is a priest, or even a bishop, if he does not treat his neighbor well but rather treats him badly, hurting him, stealing from him, he is not a good Christian, nor a disciple, nor a friend of Jesus Christ; instead he is his enemy.

Jesus Christ, who is your God and your creator, loves you very much as his children, even if you are poor and violent, and demands that all treat you well and do good to you. The one who mistreats you so angers Jesus Christ your God, that the one who lays a hand on you hurts him. Look how you are the apple of his eyes, and what a good God you have and how much he loves you. And if you find yourself persecuted and afflicted by evil men, raise your eyes to the heavens, because the one who will vindicate you is there, and he will return for you, and though at times he pretends not to hear, at the appointed moment he will so punish the world that it will tremble. For he neither wants nor suffers that the ones for whom he gave his precious blood should be mistreated.

Those who are real disciples of Christ imitate him by giving their neighbor not only their property but also their very lives. This is what Saints Peter, Paul, Stephen, and the other saints did. This is also what you should do because you are baptized Christians: you should love one another and do all that you can for each other. Not as in the past, nor as many of you evil ones do today, who do not look after the sick, nor the aged, nor the poor; rather you get rid of them and hold them in low esteem, you value and serve only the rich and those who rule you and take care of you. This is how your ancestors behaved. This is not the law of Christ, nor are those who do this good Christians. Perhaps, men should be dogs because the skinny and wasted ones are bitten by the others. No, my brothers and sisters, not like this, if you are baptized Christians it should show in your good works. Note that Christ says that this is how we know his disciples.

The Indian who looks after the poor, the sick, and the elderly and shares with them what he has, that one is a disciple of Christ and a good Christian. Christianity consists in loving one another and doing good to each other, just as God himself says. When you are sick, how would you like to be taken care of? When you are naked, how do you wish to be clothed? When you are hungry, how would you like to be fed? When you are traveling and have no home or lodging, how would you like to be welcomed? Well then, do the same to your neighbor and you will be blessed. O blessed are those who do good, because that is the work of God, and that is what it means to be a son of God.

Don't think, brothers and sisters, that you should do good only to your kinsmen, but also do good to those from another clan and to the stranger from another town, and to all men who are in need. You should do good to all because they are all your neighbors, and all have the same God and Lord and Father in heaven. If you do good only to your relative or friend, you will not be received into heaven, because you do not do that for Jesus Christ, rather you do it because of your friendship or relation; but charity embraces all.

So, brothers and sisters, from today forward let there not be so much hardness of heart among you, but let all be love and charity. Try to outdo one another in doing good, because there is great glory in this. This is what it means to be a Christian and children of God. And know my brothers and sisters that what you give your neighbor out of love for Jesus Christ, God himself writes it down in his book and repays it twice. First here on the earth, making your affairs, children, and home prosper, and then in heaven, granting you eternal rest. What a great reward to give out of love of God, and God repays us much better than man.

If you give silver or your lambs to win over other men, wouldn't it be better to win favor with God? God himself tells us so: blessed are the merciful because mercy will be shown them. And if you want to know how and what good you should do, this is shown by the works of mercy of the catechism. They are to give food to the hungry, drink to the thirsty, and invite the poor to your table and give him to drink, and give him of your *chuuno* or maize, dress the naked; some of you have two or three shirts and blankets and your neighbor doesn't have any, and he goes around in tatters with his body exposed. Give him clothing and you shall be children of God.

Visit the sick and the imprisoned; often you leave your friends by the side of the road because you don't want to take care of them and help them. Beware, because this is like killing them, and God will demand an accounting of this. The one who knows how to heal without superstition should heal the poor for love of God, and he will have his recompense in heaven. Welcome the pilgrim and don't mistreat the stranger or be cruel to him; rather help them and offer your house to those who don't have a place to stay. Be pious men and be compassionate with those experiencing bad fortune, console the grieving, give counsel and instruct those who are ignorant, be humble and loving like children of God and not hard and cruel like the children of the devil.

I now turn to tell you that the whole law of Jesus Christ consists in loving your neighbor, love him with your heart and in deeds, and you will be loved by God, and you will win the prize of glory. In the holy gospel Jesus Christ says that on the day of judgment the King of Glory will return in great majesty with all his angels, and they will gather all the peoples in front of them, and sitting on his throne he will order set apart those who are good and those who are bad just as the shepherd separates the sheep from the goats. The good he will place on his right hand and the bad on his left hand. Then the King will say to those on his right hand, "Come blest ones of my Father, take possession the kingdom that was prepared for you since the beginning of the world, because I was hungry and you gave me to eat, I was thirsty and you gave me to drink, I was a guest and you welcomed me, I was naked and you clothed me, I was sick and you visited me, I was in prison and you came to me." Then the just will respond, saying: "When did we see you hungry and fed you? When did we see you thirsty and gave you drink? When did we see you as a stranger and gave you lodging? When did we see you naked and clothed you? When did we see you infirm and in prison and visited you?" The King of Heaven will respond, "Truly I say to you that the good that you did to the least of my brothers you did unto me."

In the same fashion the King will say to the bad ones on his left: "Leave me you evil ones, to the eternal fire that is prepared for the devil and his evil angels. Because I was hungry and you did not feed me, I was thirsty and you did not give me to drink, I was a guest and you did not welcome me, I was naked and you did not cover my nakedness, I was sick and in prison and you did not visit me." Then the evil ones will also say: "Lord, when did we see you hungry? or thirsty, or a pilgrim, or naked, or sick, or imprisoned, and we didn't attend to you and give you what you needed?" Then the King will respond: "Truly I say to you that the good that you left undone to one of these little ones you left it undone to me." And so these evil ones will go to eternal torment, but the just will go to eternal life.

All these words are Our Lord Jesus Christ's in his holy gospel. This is why, my beloved brothers and sisters, the one who wants to be a saint the day of the final judgement ought to do the good that one is able to one's neighbors during this life, complying with the works of mercy, the corporal ones and when he could the spiritual ones also, and remember that the poor represent Jesus Christ and that Jesus Christ receives the good and the alms that you do and give to the poor. How wonderful it is to do good to Christ, who has done and continues to do so much for us. This would satisfy a thousand times over all that one could give for love of God, but he does not ask you for it. Rather, God asks you to give what you can easily give so that you are not left without what you need, and this he repays with the prize of Heaven that he gives you forever and ever. Amen.

ENDNOTES

Introduction

1. José de Acosta, *De Procuranda Indorum Salute*, 2 vols., ed. Luciano Pereña Vicente, CHP vols. 23–24 (Madrid: CSIC, 1984, 1987).

2. Idem, *Historia Natural y Moral de Indias*, in *Obras del P. José de Acosta de la Compañía de Jesús*, ed. Francisco Mateos, 3–250, BAE vol. 73 (Madrid: Editorial Atlas, 1954).

3. Idem, *Doctrina Christiana y Catecismo para Instrucción de los Indios, Facsímil del texto trilingüe*, ed. Luciano Pereña Vicente, CHP vol. 26-2 (Madrid: CSIC, 1985).

4. P. Fray Benito Jerónimo Feijóo y Montenegro, "Glorias de España," in *Obras Escogidas del P. Fray Benito Jerónimo Feijóo y Montenegro*, Biblioteca de Ribadeneira, vol. 56 (Madrid: Ribadeneira, 1883), 215, quoted in Francisco Mateos, "Introducción: Personalidad y Escritos del P. José de Acosta," xxxviii, n. 96.

5. Miguel de la Pinta Llorente, *Actividades diplomáticas del P. José de Acosta; en torna a una política, y a un sentimiento religioso* (Madrid: CSIC, 1952).

6. Ricardo Narvaez Tossi, *Aportes del Padre José de Acosta, S.J., en la historia del pensamiento económico peruano* (Lima: Universidad de Lima, Facultad de Economía, 1989).

7. Agustín Udías, "José de Acosta (1539–1600): A pioneer of geophysics," *Eos* 67 (1986): 461–62.

8. José Alcina Franch, "Introducción," in *Historia natural y moral de las Indias*, ed. José Alcina Franch, 7–39, Colección Crónicas de América 34 (Madrid: Historia 16, 1987); Daniel Basauri, "El P. José de Acosta y la implantación del método científico en las ciencias físico-naturales," *Estudios Centro-Americanos* 1/1,3 (1946): 13–18, 22–27; Nicole Bensimon, "Le Père Acosta naturaliste: humanisme et expérience" (Doct. diss., Institute of Hispanic Studies, University of Paris, 1957); Manuel Moreyra, "El Padre José de Acosta y su

labor intelectual," *Mercurio Peruano* 22 (1940): 546–53; Mariano Picón-Salas, "La extrañeza americana. La obra del P. Acosta," in *De la conquista a la independencia*, 125–28, 2d ed., Colección Tierra Firme 4 (México-Buenos Aires: Fondo de Cultura Económica, 1950).

9. Enrique Alvarez López, "La filosofía natural en el Padre José de Acosta," *Revista de Indias* 4 (1943): 305–22.

10. E. Aguirre, "Una hipótesis evolucionista en el siglo XVI. El P. José de Acosta, S.J., y el origen de las especies americanas," *Arbor* 36 (1957): 176–87; Daniel Basauri, "El P. José de Acosta y los orígenes del hombre americano," *Estudios Centro-Americanos* 1/6 (1946): 19–26; Fermín del Pino Díaz, "Contribución del P. Acosta a la constitución de la etnología: su evolucionismo," *Revista de Indias* 38 (1978): 507–46.

11. Millán Arroyo Simón, "El P. José de Acosta, S.J., (1540–1600) y la educación de los indios en América," *Theológica Xaveriana* 43/4 (1993): 353–72; Elmer Robles Ortíz, *Educación y ciencias sociales en el pensamiento de José de Acosta* (Trujillo: Editorial Libertad, 1990).

12. Antonio Gómez Robledo, "Las ideas jurídicas del P. José de Acosta," *Revista de la Escuela Nacional de Jurisprudencia* 2 (1940): 297–313; Joaquín López de Prado, "Fundamentos del Derecho Misional en José de Acosta, S.J.," *Missionalia Hispánica* 22 (1965): 339–66.

13. Elvira Gangutia Elícegui, "El P. Acosta y las teorías lingüísticas de la Ilustración," in *América y la España del siglo XVI*, ed. Francisco de Solano and Fermín del Pino Díaz, vol. 1, 363–72 (Madrid: CSIC, 1982); José María Enguita Utrilla, "El americanismo léxico en la *Peregrinación de Bartolomé Lorenzo*," *Anuario de Lingüística Hispánica* 4 (1988): 127–44; idem, "Las lenguas indígenas en la evangelización del Perú a través de la obra del Padre Acosta," in *Actas del II Congreso Internacional de la Lengua Española*, ed. Manuel Ariza, vol. 2, 343–61 (Madrid: Pabellón de España, 1992); Pedro Marín Agreda, *Estudio de los indigenismos en la "Historia natural y moral de las Indias" del P. José de Acosta*, 2 vols., Colección Tesis doctorales n. 161/93 (Madrid: Editorial de la Universidad Complutense, 1993).

14. José Juan Arrom, "Precursores coloniales de la narrativa hispanoamericana: José de Acosta o la ficción como biografía," *Revista Iberoamericana* 44 (1978): 369–83; Martin Lienhard, "Una novela hispanoamericana en 1586. (J. Acosta, *La peregrinación de Bartolomé Lorenzo*)," in *Miscelánea de Estudios Hispánicos. Homenaje de los hispanistas suizos a Ramón Sugranyes de Franch*, ed. Luis López Molina, 175–87 (Montserrat: L'abadia de Montserrat, 1982).

15. Herman J. Muller, "British Travel Writers and the Jesuits," *Mid-America* 35 (1953): 91–116.

16. Armando Nieto Vélez, *El Padre José de Acosta y su comprensión del mundo indígena* (Lima: Ediciones Vida y Espiritualidad, 1988); idem, "Reflexiones de un

teólogo del siglo XVI sobre las religiones nativas," *Revista de la Universidad Católica*, no. 2 (Dec. 1977): 133–48.

17. Pino Díaz, "Contribución del P. Acosta," 507–46; idem, "Culturas clásicas y americanas en la obra del P. Acosta," in *América y la España del siglo XVI*, ed. Francisco de Solano and Fermín del Pino Díaz, vol. 1, 327–62 (Madrid: CSIC, 1982); idem, "Edición de crónicas de Indias e Historia intelectual, o la distancia entre José de Acosta y José Alcina," *Revista de Indias* 50 (1990): 861–78; idem, "Humanismo Renacentista y Orígenes de la Etnología: A Próposito del P. Acosta, Paradigma del Humanismo Antropológico Jesuita," in *Humanismo y visión del otro en la España moderna: cuatro estudios*, 379–429, ed. Berta Ares et al. (Madrid: CSIC, 1992); idem, "Los Reinos de Méjico y Cusco en la obra del P. Acosta," *Revista de la Universidad Complutense* 28 (1979): 13–40.

18. Luciano Pereña Vicente, "Estudio Preliminar. Proyecto de sociedad colonial; pacificación y colonización," in *De Procuranda Indorum Salute*, ed. Luciano Pereña Vicente, CHP vol. 23, 3–46 (Madrid: CSIC, 1984).

19. The following are the best biographical studies available to date: José Alcina Franch, "Introducción," in *Historia natural y moral de las Indias*, ed. José Alcina Franch, 7–39, Colección Crónicas de América 34 (Madrid: Historia 16, 1987); León Lopetegui, *El Padre José de Acosta, S.J., y las misiones* (Madrid: CSIC, 1942); Francisco Mateos, "Introducción: Personalidad y Escritos del P. José de Acosta," in *Obras del P. José de Acosta de la Compañía de Jesús*, ed. Francisco Mateos, BAE vol. 73, vii–xlix (Madrid: Editorial Atlas, 1954).

20. José de Acosta, *De Christo revelato libri novem, simulque De Temporibus Novissimis libri quatuor* (Rome: Iacobum Tornerium, 1590).

21. Ana de Porres to Laínez, May 30, 1564, ARSI, Hisp. 101, f. 184; Ana de Porres to Borja, October 22, 1567, ARSI, Hisp. 107, f. 111; Antonio de Acosta to Borja, October 2, 1569, ARSI, Hisp. 112, f. 2.

22. Acosta to Laínez, October 17, 1559, ARSI, Hisp. 96.

23. Ibid., all at ARSI, March 1, 1560, Hisp. 97, ff. 59–60; April 5, 1560, Hisp. 97, f. 101; June 12, 1560, Hisp. 97, f. 186; October 5, 1560, Hisp. 97, f. 379; January 3, 1561, Hisp. 98, f. 11; May 1, 1561, Hisp. 98, ff. 166–68; September 3, 1561, Hisp. 98, ff. 323–25; January 1, 1562, Hisp. 99, ff. 1–6; May 12, 1562, Hisp. 99, ff. 205–9; September 1, 1562, Hisp. 99, ff. 307–9; January 3, 1563, Hisp. 100, ff. 46–50; May 31, 1563, Hisp. 100, ff. 221–22; January 7, 1564, Hisp. 101, ff. 31–33; May 28, 1564, Hisp. 101, ff. 175–77; September 30, 1564, Hisp. 101, f. 304.

24. Acosta to Aquaviva, January 8, 1592, ARSI, Hisp. 134, f. 147; ibid., February 7, 1592, Hisp. 134, f. 169.

25. Acosta, *Conciones in Quadrigesimam* (Salamancae: Ioannem et Andream Renaut, fratres, 1596); idem, *Conciones de Adventu* (Salamancae: Ioannem

et Andream Renaut, fratres, 1597); idem, *Tomus Tertius Concionum* (Salamancae: Ioannem et Andream Renaut, fratres, 1599).

26. Idem, "In Psalmos Davidis commentarii…[1598–1600]," MS. 659, Biblioteca General de la Universidad de Salamanca, Salamanca, Spain.

27. José Simón Díaz, "P. José de Acosta," in *Bibliografía de la Literatura Hispánica*, vol. 4 (Madrid: CSIC, 1955), 412–23; idem, *Jesuitas de los Siglos XVI y XVII: Escritos Localizados* (Madrid: Universidad Pontificia de Salamanca and Fundación Universitaria Española, 1975); José de Uriarte and Mariano Lecina, *Biblioteca de escritores de la Compañía de Jesús pertenecientes a la antigua Asistencia de España desde sus orígenes hasta el año 1773*, vol. 1, pt. 1, (Madrid: Sucesores de Rivadeneyra, 1925), 24–33.

28. Acosta, *De Procuranda*; idem, *Doctrina Christiana*.

Chapter 1: The Genesis of Acosta's Jesuit Vocation: 1540–1552

1. My reconstruction of Medina del Campo in the sixteenth century is derived from the following sources: Bartolomé Bennassar, "Medina del Campo: un exemple des structures urbaines de l'Espagne au XVIe siècle," *Revue d'Histoire Economique et Sociale* 4 (1961): 474–95; José Escudero Solano, "Medina del Campo, estudio de un pequeño núcleo urbano de Castilla la Vieja," *Estudios Geográficos* 101 (1965): 439–506; Cristóbal Espejo and Julián Paz, *Las antiguas ferias de Medina del Campo* (Valladolid: Tipografía del Colegio de Santiago, 1908); Eufemio Lorenzo Sanz, *Historia de Medina del Campo y su tierra*, 3 vols. (Valladolid: Ayuntamiento de Medina del Campo, Consejería de Educación y Cultura de la Junta de Castilla y León, 1986); Alberto Marcos Martín, *Auge y Declive de un Núcleo Mercantíl y Financiero de Castilla la Vieja: Evolución demográfica de Medina del Campo durante los siglos XVI y XVII* (Valladolid: Universidad de Valladolid, Secretariado de Publicaciones, 1978); Gerardo Moraleja Pinilla, *Historia de Medina del Campo* (Medina del Campo: Ayuntamiento de Medina del Campo, 1971); Antonio Sánchez del Barrio, *Estructura urbana de Medina del Campo* (Valladolid: Junta de Castilla y León, Consejería de Cultura y Bienestar, 1991).

2. Luis Fernández Martín, "El Colegio de los Jesuitas de Medina del Campo en tiempo de Juan de Yepes," in *Juan de la Cruz, Espíritu de Llama: Estudios con ocasión del cuarto centenario de su muerte (1591–1991)*, ed. Otger Steggink (Rome: Institutum Carmelitanum, 1991), 41.

3. Unless otherwise noted, the description of the geopolitical, socioeconomic, and religious-cultural situation of sixteenth-century Castile is drawn from Henry Kamen, *Spain 1469–1714: A Society of Conflict*, 2d ed. (New York: Longman, 1991), 62–257.

4. Charles I to the pope and cardinals in Rome, 1536, quoted in ibid., 66.

5. Acosta, "Respuestas del P. José de Acosta al cuestionario del P. Nadal . . ." reproduced in Lopetegui, *Acosta y las misiones*, app. 1, 613.

6. For an English biography of Nadal see William V. Bangert, *Jerome Nadal, S.J. (1507–1580): Tracking the First Generation of Jesuits*, ed. and completed by Thomas M. McCoog (Chicago: Loyola University Press, 1992).

7. On Nadal's questionnaire, see Thomas Vance Cohen, "The Social Origins of the Jesuits, 1540–1600," 2 vols., Ph.D. diss., Harvard University, 1973; idem, "Why the Jesuits Joined, 1540–1600," in *Historical Papers*, 237–58 (Ottawa: The Canadian Historical Association, 1974).

8. Fernández Martín, "El Colegio de los Jesuitas," 43–44.

9. For a detailed discussion of the scholarly debate about the Acostas' Jewish heritage see the section with the same title in appendix 1.

10. Antonio de Acosta to Borja, October 2, 1569, ARSI, Hisp. 112, f. 2. No evidence has been found to verify that Antonio de Acosta ever in fact entered the Society or that his wife entered a convent.

11. Ana de Porres to Laínez, May 30, 1564, ARSI, Hisp. 101, f. 184.

12. Ibid.

13. Idem to Borja, October 22, 1567, ARSI, Hisp. 107, f. 111.

14. Luis de Valdivia, "Colegios de la Provincia de Castilla, 1641(?)," TMS [carbon copy], IHSI Library, Rome, Italy, 17.

15. The particulars about the Jesuit foundation at Medina del Campo are derived from Fernández Martín, "El Colegio de los Jesuitas," 41–61.

16. Acosta, "Respuestas al cuestionario," 613–14.

17. John W. O'Malley, *The First Jesuits* (Cambridge: Harvard University Press, 1993), 55.

18. Acosta, "Respuestas al cuestionario," 615.

19. O'Malley, *The First Jesuits*, 55.

20. Acosta to Loyola, December 29, 1554, quoted in Fernández Martín, "El Colegio de los Jesuitas," 46.

Chapter 2: Acosta's Formation as a Jesuit: 1553–1571

1. Valdivia, "Colegios de Castilla," 124v.

2. Pino Díaz, "Acosta y la Evangelización de las Indias Orientales," 277–78.

3. Acosta to Borja, April 23, 1569, in Mateos, *Obras*, 251–52.

4. León Lopetegui, "Vocación de Indias del P. José de Acosta, S.J.," *Revista de Indias* 1 (1940): 88–89; idem, *Acosta y las misiones*, 43–44.

5. Unless otherwise noted, the information on Alcalá and its university is taken from Ramón González Navarro, "El Colegio Mayor de San Ildefonso y la

Universidad de Alcalá," in *Historia de la Educación en España y América*, ed. Buenaventura Delgado Criado, vol. 2: *La Educación en la España Moderna (Siglos XVI–XVIII)* (Madrid: Ediciones SM and Morata, S.L., 1993), 258–75.

6. José García Oro, "La reforma de las órdenes religiosas en los siglos XV y XVI," in *La Iglesia en la España de los siglos XV y XVI*, ed. José Luis González Novalín et al., vol. 3, pt. 1 of *Historia de la Iglesia en España*, ed. Ricardo García-Villoslada et al., 268–69. BAC Maior 18; Madrid: La Editorial Católica, 1980.

7. Vicente de Beltrán de Hereida, "La facultad de teología en la Universidad de Alcalá," in *Miscelánea Beltrán de Hereida. Colección de Artículos sobre Historia de la Teología Española*, vol. 4, Biblioteca de Teólogos Españoles, vol. 28 (Salamanca: Editorial OPE, 1973), 124–25.

8. Melquíades Andrés Martín, *La teología española en el siglo XVI* (Madrid: Editorial Católica, 1976), vol. 1, 33–36, 51–53.

9. Ibid., 56.

10. Jordán Gallego Salvadores, "La enseñanza de la metafísica en la Universidad de Alcalá durante el Siglo XVI," in *Analecta Sacra Tarraconensia* 46 (1973): 345–86.

11. Juan Urriza, *La Preclara Facultad de Artes y Filosofía de la Universidad de Alcalá de Henares en el Siglo de Oro. 1509–1621* (Madrid: CSIC, 1942), 461–62.

12. Vicente de Beltrán de Hereida, "La Preclara Facultad de Artes de la Universidad de Alcalá," in *Miscelánea Beltrán de Hereida*, vol. 4, 181–82.

13. Beltrán de Hereida, "La facultad de teología," 129–47, 154–55.

14. Ibid., 126.

15. Antonio Astrain, *Historia de la Compañía de Jesús en la Asistencia de España* (Madrid: Administración de Razón y Fe, 1912), vol. 2, 61.

16. Beltrán de Hereida, "La facultad de teología," 129.

17. Urriza, *La Preclara Facultad de Artes*, 248.

18. Cristóbal de Castro, "Historia del Colegio de la Compañía de Jesús de Alcalá de Henares, 1600(?)" MS., vol. 2, pt. II, bk. IX, ch. V, p. 14, IHSI Library, Rome, Italy.

19. Urriza, *La Preclara Facultad de Artes*, 248.

20. Castro, "Historia del Colegio," MS., vol. 2, pt. II, bk. IX, ch. V, p. 14.

21. Deza to Aquaviva, 1582, quoted in Vicente de Beltrán de Hereida, "La enseñanza de Santo Tomás en la Compañía de Jesús en el primer siglo de su existencia," in *Miscelánea Beltrán de Hereida*, vol. 2, 333–34.

22. Castro, "Historia del Colegio," MS., vol. 2, pt. II, bk. IX, ch. V, p. 15.

23. Andrés Martín, *La teología española*, vol. 1, 178, 179 n. 13. I have not been able to determine that in José's time there were special lectures in positive theology at the Jesuit college. Andrés Martín's references to the private lectures in positive theology at the Jesuit college at Alcalá do not substantiate

this point. Nonetheless, it is indisputable that Acosta's theological writings evidence the influence of positive theology even if it cannot be documented that he attended lectures in this subject while he studied theology at Alcalá.

24. James K. Farge, "The University of Paris in the Time of Ignatius of Loyola," in *Ignacio de Loyola y su tiempo*, ed. Juan Plazaola (Bilbao: Ediciones Mensajero, 1991), 221–43.

25. Ignacio de Loyola, Spiritual Exercises #363, in *Obras Completas*, ed. Ignacio Iparraguirre and Cándido Dalmases, 4th ed., BAC 86 (Madrid: La Editorial Católica, S.A., 1982), 288.

26. Idem., Constitutions, pt. IV, ch. 5, #351, in ibid., 522.

27. Idem., Constitutions, pt. IV, chs. 12, 14, ## 446, 464, in ibid., 539, 543.

28. Andrés Martín, *La teología española*, vol. 1, 185–86.

29. Acosta to Laínez, January 1, 1562, ARSI, Hisp. 99, f. 5.

30. Manuel Ruiz Jurado, "Cronología de la vida del P. Jerónimo Nadal, S.J. (1507–1580)," *AHSI* 48 (1979): 248–76.

31. Jerónimo Nadal, "Exhortationes Complutenses (Alcalá, 1561), Twelfth exhortation, #230," in *Commentarii de Instituto Societatis Iesu. MHSI, vol. 90. Epistolae et Monumenta P. Hieronymi Nadal Tomus V Commentarii de Instituto S.I.*, ed. Miguel Nicolau (Rome: MHSI, 1962), 450.

32. My descriptions of these apostolates or ministries are taken from O'Malley, *The First Jesuits*, 91–104, 126–29, 137–52, 168–74.

33. Acosta to Laínez, March 1, 1560, ARSI, Hisp. 97, ff. 59–60; April 5, 1560, ARSI, Hisp. 97, f. 101; June 12, 1560, ARSI, Hisp. 97, f. 186; October 5, 1560, ARSI, Hisp. 97, f. 379; January 3, 1561, ARSI, Hisp. 98, f. 11; May 1, 1561, ARSI, Hisp. 98, ff. 166–68; September 3, 1561, ARSI, Hisp. 98, ff. 323–25; January 1, 1562, ARSI, Hisp. 99, ff. 1–6; May 12, 1562, ARSI, Hisp. 99, ff. 205–9; September 1, 1562, ARSI, Hisp. 99, ff, 307–9; January 3, 1563, ARSI, Hisp. 100, ff. 46–50; May 31, 1563, ARSI, Hisp. 100, ff. 221–22; January 7, 1564, ARSI, Hisp. 101, ff. 31–33; May 28, 1564, ARSI, Hisp. 101, ff. 175–77; September 30, 1564, ARSI, Hisp. 101, f. 304.

34. Acosta to Laínez, January 3, 1561, ARSI, Hisp. 98, f. 11.

35. Astrain, *Historia*, vol. 1, 397.

36. Acosta, "Respuestas al cuestionario," 614.

37. Acosta to Laínez, September 30, 1564, ARSI, Hisp. 101, f. 304.

38. Acosta to Laínez, October 5, 1560, ARSI, Hisp. 97, f. 379; May 1, 1561, ARSI, Hisp. 98, ff. 166–68; January 7, 1564, ARSI, Hisp. 101, ff. 31–33; May 28, 1564, ARSI, Hisp. 101, ff. 175–77.

39. Quarterly letter of Acosta to Laínez, May 1, 1561, ARSI, Hisp. 98, ff. 166–68; September 3, 1561, ARSI, Hisp. 98, ff. 323–25; May 12, 1562, ARSI, Hisp. 99, ff. 205–9; January 3, 1563, ARSI, Hisp. 100, ff. 46–50; May 28, 1564, ARSI, Hisp. 101, ff. 175–77.

40. Astrain, *Historia*, vol. 2, 507.
41. Acosta to Laínez, May 28, 1564, ARSI, Hisp. 101, ff. 175–77.
42. Quarterly letter of Acosta to Laínez, May 12, 1562, ARSI, Hisp. 99, ff. 307–9; January 3, 1563, ARSI, Hisp. 100, ff. 46–50.
43. Acosta to Laínez, May 12, 1562, ARSI, Hisp. 99, ff. 205–9.
44. Acosta to Laínez, January 3, 1563, ARSI, Hisp. 100, ff. 46–50.
45. Acosta to Laínez, September 3, 1561, ARSI, Hisp. 98, ff. 323–25.
46. Quarterly letter of Acosta to Laínez, May 1, 1561, ARSI, Hisp. 98, ff. 166–68; September 1, 1562, ARSI, Hisp. 99, ff. 307–9; January 3, 1563, ARSI, Hisp. 100, ff. 46–50.
47. Acosta to Laínez, October 5, 1560, ARSI, Hisp. 97, f. 379.
48. Acosta to Laínez, May 1, 1561, ARSI, Hisp. 98, ff. 166–68.
49. Acosta to Laínez, October 5, 1560, ARSI, Hisp. 97, f. 379; January 1, 1562, ARSI, Hisp. 99, ff. 1–6.
50. Lopetegui, *Acosta y las misiones*, 33–34.
51. Acosta, "Respuestas al cuestionario," 613.
52. Ibid., 615.
53. Andrés Martín, *La teología española*, vol. 1, 52.
54. Ibid.
55. Nigel Griffin, "A curious document: Baltasar Loarte, S.J., and the years 1554–1570," *AHSI* 45 (1976): 66–94.
56. Acosta, "Lo que al Padre José de Acosta le pasó con el Reverendísimo Arzobispo de Santo Domingo sobre cosas de la Compañía," in Mateos, *Obras*, 254–60.

Chapter 3: The Apogee of Acosta's Life: Peru, 1572–1586

1. Unless otherwise noted, my reconstruction of the Kingdom of Peru at the time of Acosta's arrival relies on the following: Clarence H. Haring, *The Spanish Empire in America* (New York: Harcourt Brace Jovanovich, 1975); James Lockhart, *Spanish Peru 1532–1560: A Colonial Society* (Madison: The University of Wisconsin Press, 1968); Daniel E. Shea, "A Defense of Small Population Estimates for the Central Andes in 1520," in *The Native Population of the Americas in 1492*, 2d ed., ed. William M. Denevan (Madison: The University of Wisconsin Press, 1992), 166.
2. Unless otherwise noted, the information on the tenure of Viceroy Toledo is drawn from Steven J. Stern, *Peru's Indian Peoples and the Challenge of Spanish Conquest: Huamanga to 1640*, 2d ed. (Madison: The University of Wisconsin Press, 1993), 76–79, 102–3, 115–19, 123–27.
3. Unless otherwise noted, the portrait of the Jesuits in Peru at the time of Acosta's arrival relies on the following: Antonio de Egaña, "El Virrey don

Francisco de Toledo y los jesuitas del Perú (1569–1581)," *Estudios de Deusto* 4 (1956): 127–36; Angel Santos Hernández, *Los Jesuitas en América*, Colección Iglesia Católica en el Nuevo Mundo (Madrid: Editorial MAPFRE, 1992); Rubén Vargas Ugarte, *Historia de la Iglesia en el Perú*, vol. 2: 1570–1640 (Burgos: Imprenta de Aldecoa, 1959); idem, *Historia de la Compañía de Jesús en el Perú*, vol. 1: 1568–1618 (Burgos: Imprenta de Aldecoa, 1963).

4. Vargas Ugarte, *Historia de la Compañía*, vol. 1, 84. Both Lopetegui, *Acosta y las misiones*, 131, and Mateos, "Introducción," in *Obras*, xii, maintain that he was fluent in Quechua.

5. Acosta, *De Procuranda*, bk. V, ch. 4; bk. VI, chs. 16, 21.

6. Idem, *De Temporibus Novissimis*, bk. II, ch. 2.

7. For the inquisitorial process against Cruz see Vidal Abril Castelló, ed., *Francisco de la Cruz, Inquisición, Actas I. Anatomía y biopsia del Dios y del derecho Judeo-cristiano-musulmán de la conquista de América*, CHP vol. 29 (Madrid: CSIC, 1992); idem, "Fray Francisco de la Cruz, el lascasismo peruano y la prevaricación del Santo Oficio limeño, 1572–1578," in *Los Dominicos y el Nuevo Mundo: Actas del II Congreso Internacional, Salamanca, 28 de marzo–1 de abril de 1989*, 157–225, ed. José Barrado (Salamanca: Editorial San Esteban, 1990). In both of these works Abril Castelló maintains, without giving any evidence, that Acosta, motivated by self-hatred of his own Jewish background, unjustly condemned Cruz, who was also of *converso* background.

8. Acosta, *De Procuranda*, bk. III, chs. 2–3.

9. Acosta to Philip II, March 7, 1577, in *Organización de la Iglesia y las Ordenes Religiosas en el Virreynato del Perú en el siglo XVI: Documentos del Archivo de Indias*, vol. 1, ed. Roberto Levillier (Madrid: Sucesores de Rivadeneyra, 1919), 114–16.

10. Provincials of the Religious Orders of Peru to Philip II, November 28, 1579, in Levillier, *Organización*, vol. 1, 119–25.

11. In light of both Acosta's confrontations with Viceroy Toledo and, as we shall see, the criticism of the Spanish conquest, colonization, and evangelization of the Americas expressed in the *De Procuranda* and censored by the Inquisition before its publication, it is remarkable that David Brading has described him as a political opportunist. To Brading, Acosta was ultimately concerned with justifying Spanish dominion over the New World and the indigenous peoples. This prevented him from taking his reformist concerns to their logical conclusion and, like Las Casas, denouncing Spanish hegemony in the Americas. See David A. Brading, *The First America: The Spanish Monarchy, Creole Patriots, and the Liberal State 1492–1867* (Cambridge: Cambridge University Press, 1991), 184–85.

12. Acosta, "Memorial de Apología o Descargo Dirigido al Papa Clemente VIII," in Mateos, *Obras*, 372–73.

13. Unless otherwise noted, the portrait of the Juli reduction that follows relies on the following: Xavier Albó, "Jesuitas y culturas indígenas. Perú 1568–1606. Su actitud, métodos y criterios de aculturación," *América Indígena* 26 (1966): 249–308, 395–445; Norman Meiklejohn, *La Iglesia y los Lupaqas de Chucuito durante la Colonia*, Colección Archivo de Historia Andina 7 (Cuzco: Centro de Estudios Rurales Andinos "Bartolomé de Las Casas" and Instituto de Estudios Aymaras, 1988); Rubén Vargas Ugarte, "Método de la Compañía de Jesús en la educación del indígena. (La doctrina de Juli)," *Mercurio Peruano* 22 (1940): 554–66.

14. For the influence of the Juli reduction on the Paraguayan reductions, see Rafael Carbonell De Masy, "Las Reducciones de Paraguay; Opción por los pobres y obediencia religiosa," *CIS* 24 (1993/2): 9–30; Alfonso Echánove, "Origen y evolución de la idea jesuítica de 'Reducciones' en las misiones del Virreinato del Perú: Introducción," *Missionalia Hispánica* 12 (1955): 95–144; idem, "Origen y evolución de la idea jesuítica de 'Reducciones' en las misiones del Virreinato del Perú: La Residencia de Juli, patrón y esquema de reducciones," *Missionalia Hispánica* 13 (1956): 497–540; Arthur Rabuske, "A Doutrina de Juli, do Peru, como modelo inicial das reduções do antigo Paraguai," in *A Experiência Reducional No Sul Do Brasil: Anais I Simpósio Nacional de Estudos Missioneiros, Santa Rosa, 23 a 26 de outubro de 1975*, ed. Erneldo Schallenberger (Canoas, RS, Brasil: Editora La Salle, 1982), 10–32; Guillermo Randle, "España y Roma en el orígen urbano de las misiones jesuitas guaraníes (1610–1767)," in *La Compañía de Jesús en América: Evangelización y Justicia*, 275–305.

15. Unless otherwise noted, the account of Lima III and Acosta's role in the council relies on Francesco Leonardo Lisi, *El Tercer Concilio Limense y la Aculturación de los Indígenas Sudamericanos*, 43–55, 79–83.

16. How much of the written work of the council was directly authored by Acosta is a disputed point among students of the documents of Lima III. See Antonio García y García, "La Reforma del Concilio Tercero de Lima," in *Doctrina Christiana y Catecismo para Instrucción de los Indios: Introducción. Del Genocidio a la Promoción del Indio*, ed. Luciano Pereña Vicente, CHP vol. 26-1 (Madrid: CSIC, 1986), 206–9.

17. González Dávila to Aquaviva, October 9, 1587, cited by Lopetegui, *Acosta y las misiones*, 582.

18. The information on Alonso Sánchez, S.J., and his relationship with Acosta is derived from Horacio de la Costa, *The Jesuits in the Philippines 1581–1768* (Cambridge: Harvard University Press, 1961), 84–88; John M. Headley,

"Spain's Asian Presence, 1565–1590: Structures and Aspirations," *Hispanic American Historical Review* 75/4 (1995): 623–46.

19. Acosta, "Parecer sobre la Guerra de la China, Mexico, 15 de marzo de 1587," and "Respuesta a los Fundamentos que Justifican la Guerra contra la China," in Mateos, *Obras*, 331–45.

Chapter 4: The Nadir of Acosta's Life: Spain and Rome, 1587–1600

1. The original 1576 manuscript of the *De Procuranda* had been dedicated to Fr. General Everard Mercurian, S.J.

2. Lopetegui, "Tres memoriales inéditos presentados al Papa Clemente VIII por el P. José de Acosta, sobre temas americanos," *Studia Missionalia* 5 (1949), 73–91.

3. Unless otherwise noted, the reconstruction of events leading to the convocation of and during the Fifth General Congregation relies on Astrain, *Historia*, vol. 3, 357–447, 492, 589, 607–11, 621–25.

4. Guenter Lewy, "The Struggle for Constitutional Government in the Early Years of the Society of Jesus," *Church History* 29 (1960), 141–60.

5. Astrain, *Historia*, vol. 3, 491–622.

6. See José de Acosta, "Relación de la Visita a la Provincia de Andalucía, Dirigida a Su Majestad. Cádiz, 24 de Febrero de 1590," and "Carta al Rey Felipe II de Presentación para la Visita de Aragón. Dada al Rey el 16 de Septiembre de 1590," in Mateos, *Obras*, 346–51.

7. José de Acosta, "Memorial de Apología o Descargo . . . ," in Mateos, *Obras*, 381–86.

8. Ibid., 378. For some reason, as I detail in appendix one, not much credence has been given to this motivation of Acosta's, even when the testimony of one of Philip's ministers indicates that he, Philip II, was contemplating this move.

9. See Miguel de la Pinta Llorente, "El P. José de Acosta, agente de Felipe II en la corte romana: Un capítulo de la historia de la Compañía," in *Crítica y Humanismo*, ed. Miguel de la Pinta Llorente (Madrid: Archivo Agustiniano, 1966), 123–24.

10. Ibid., 127–33.

11. See Mateos, "Introducción," in *Obras*, xxxi.

12. Concerning the ethnic background of the memorialistas see James W. Reites, "St. Ignatius of Loyola and the Jews," *Studies in the Spirituality of Jesuits* 13/4 (1981), 31–32.

13. José Rodríguez Carracido, *El P. José de Acosta, S.J., y su importancia en la literatura científica española* (Madrid: Sucesores de Rivadeneyra, 1899), 14–18.

14. Monique Mustapha, "Sur un texte retrouvé: Le Père José de Acosta et la querelle 'De Auxiliis,'" *Annales de la Faculté des Lettres et Sciences Humaines de Nice* 23 (1982): 209–16.

15. Valdivia, "Colegios de Castilla," 77–78.

16. Ibid., 79–80.

Chapter 5: Jesuit Theological Humanism

1. *Jesuit theological humanism* is a term of my own creation.

2. Paul Oskar Kristeller, "The Humanist Movement," in *Renaissance Thought and Its Sources*, ed. Michael Mooney (New York: Columbia University Press, 1979), 22–23.

3. Idem, "Paganism and Christianity," in Mooney, *Renaissance Thought*, 72, 78.

4. Idem, "The Humanist Movement," in Mooney, *Renaissance Thought*, 28–29, 31.

5. Idem, "The Scholar and His Public in the Late Middle Ages and the Renaissance," in *Medieval Aspects of Renaissance Learning: Three Essays by Paul Oskar Kristeller*, ed. and trans. Edward P. Mahoney (Durham: Duke University Press, 1974), 24–25.

6. Idem, *Le Thomisme et la Pensée Italienne de la Renaissance* (Montreal: L'Institut d'Études Médiévales, 1967), 75–90.

7. Idem, "Paganism and Christianity," in Mooney, *Renaissance Thought*, 72.

8. Idem, *Le Thomisme*, 90–123.

9. Acosta, "In Psalmos Davidis," MS. 659, Biblioteca General de la Universidad de Salamanca, Salamanca, Spain.

10. Edmundo O'Gorman, "La 'Historia natural y moral de las Indias' del P. Joseph de Acosta," in *Cuatro historiadores de Indias, siglo XVI: Pedro Mártir de Anglería, Gónzalo Fernández de Oviedo y Valdes, Fray Bartolomé de las Casas, Joseph de Acosta* (Mexico: Sep/Setentas, 1972), 222–30.

11. Nadal, "Exhortationes Complutenses," 450.

12. Miguel Nicolau, *Jerónimo Nadal, S.J. (1507–1580): Sus obras y doctrinas espirituales* (Madrid: CSIC, 1949), 250–80.

13. O'Malley, *The First Jesuits*, 250–52.

14. Nicolau, *Jerónimo Nadal*, 290–95.15. Acosta, *De Procuranda*, bk. IV, ch. XI, #2, 95.

16. José Antonio Maravall, "La fórmula del Renacimiento español," in *Estudios de Historia del Pensamiento Español. Serie Segunda. La Epoca del Renacimiento* (Madrid: Ediciones Cultura Hispánica, 1984), 92–105.

17. The English translations of the passages from these works cited in the following chapters are mine. The Spanish editions used are the following: José de Acosta, *De Procuranda Indorum Salute*, 2 vols., ed. Luciano Pereña Vicente, CHP vols. 23–24 (Madrid: CSIC, 1984, 1987); idem, *Historia Natural y*

Moral de las Indias, in *Obras del P. José de Acosta*, ed. Francisco Mateos, 3–250, BAE vol. 73 (Madrid: Ediciones Atlas, 1954); idem, *Doctrina Christiana y Catecismo para Instrucción de los Indios, Facsímil del texto trilingüe*, ed. Luciano Pereña Vicente, CHP vol. 26-2 (Madrid: CSIC, 1985).

18. See appendices two through four for the tables of contents of these works.
19. Uriarte and Lecina, "José de Acosta," in *Biblioteca de escritores*, vol. 1, pt. 1, 25, #3.
20. Eusebius of Caesarea, *Preparation for the Gospel*, 2 vols., trans. Edwin Hamilton Gifford (Grand Rapids: Baker Book House, 1981).
21. Acosta, *Historia*, bk. V, "Prologue to the books which follow," cited in Pino Díaz, "Humanismo Clasicista Mediterráneo y Concepción Antropológica del Mundo: El Caso de los Jesuitas," *Hispania* 56 (1996): 47.
22. Acosta, *De Christo revelato libri novem, simulque De Temporibus Novissimis libri quatuor* (Rome: Iacobum Tornerium, 1590).
23. Acosta, *Conciones de Adventu* (Salamancae: Ioannem et Andream Renaut, fratres, 1597); idem, *Conciones in Quadragesimam* (Salamancae: Ioannem et Andream Renaut, fratres, 1596); idem, *Tomus Tertius Concionum* (Salamancae: Ioannem et Andream Renaut, fratres, 1599).
24. Acosta, *Conciones in Quadragesimam*, "Prologus ad lectorem."
25. Rubén Vargas Ugarte, *La Elocuencia Sagrada en el Perú en los Siglos XVII y XVIII. Discurso de Recepción del R. P. Rubén Vargas Ugarte, S.J. Contestación del Director de la Academia D. José de la Riva-Agüero y Osma* (Lima: Impresores Gil, S.A., 1942), 15–20.

Chapter 6: The Method of Acosta's Humanism

1. Vicente de Beltrán de Hereida, "La formación humanística y escolástica de Fray Francisco de Vitoria," in *Miscelánea Beltrán de Hereida. Colección de Artículos sobre Historia de la Teología Española*, vol. 2, Biblioteca de Teólogos Españoles, vol. 26 (Salamanca: Editorial OPE, 1972), 55–72.
2. José de Acosta, *De Christo revelato libri novem, simulque De Temporibus Novissimis libri quatuor* (Rome: Iacobum Tornerium, 1590), bk. 2, ch. 9, 60.
3. León Lopetegui, "Influjos de Fr. Domingo de Soto, O.P., en el pensamiento misional del P. José de Acosta," *Estudios Eclesiásticos* 36 (1961): 57–72.
4. Melquíades Andrés Martín, "Pensamiento Teológico y Vivencia Religiosa en la Reforma Española (1400–1600)," in *La Iglesia en la España de los siglos XV y XVI*, ed. José Luis González Novalín et al., vol. 3, pt. 2, of *Historia de la Iglesia en España*, ed. Ricardo García-Villoslada et al. (Madrid: Editorial Católica, 1980), 284–89. It is from Andrés Martín that I take the terms *open Thomism* and *First* and *Second School of Salamanca*.
5. Ibid.

6. Vicente de Beltrán de Hereida, "La formación humanística y escolástica de Fray Francisco de Vitoria," in *Miscelánea Beltrán de Hereida*, vol. 2, 52–72.

7. Idem, "Orientación humanística de la teología vitoriana," in *Miscelánea Beltrán de Hereida*, vol. 2, 37–54.

8. Letter of dedication of the *De Procuranda* to Fr. General Everard Mercurian, S.J., by Acosta, February 24, 1577, cited in Acosta, *De Procuranda*, CHP vol. 23, 50–53.

9. While Acosta does not identify his theological adversaries by name, León Lopetegui has conclusively established the identity of Soto (1524–60) and other scholastics with whom Acosta at times agrees and disagrees. See Lopetegui, "Influjos de Soto en Acosta."

10. Acosta, *De Procuranda*, bk. V, ch. 3, CHP vol. 24, 190–207, ##4, 6–8, 12, 16–18.

11. No one has written more extensively and lucidly about Acosta's contributions to modern ethnography and anthropology than Fermín del Pino Díaz. My understanding of this aspect of Acosta's writings owes much to his research. See Fermín del Pino Díaz, "La civilización indiana como criterio de diferenciación misional para el P. Acosta," in *La Compañía de Jesús en América: Evangelización y Justicia. Siglos XVII y XVIII. Actas del Congreso Internacional de Historia*, ed. Feliciano Delgado, 251–60 (Córdoba: Imprenta San Pablo, S.L., 1993); idem, "Contribución del P. Acosta a la constitución de la etnología: su evolucionismo," *Revista de Indias* 38 (1978): 507–46; idem, "Culturas clásicas y americanas en la obra del P. Acosta," in *América y la España del siglo XVI*, vol. 1, ed. Francisco de Solano and Fermín del Pino Díaz, 327–62 (Madrid: CSIC, 1982); idem, "Edición de crónicas de Indias e Historia intelectual, o la distancia entre José de Acosta y José Alcina," *Revista de Indias* 50 (1990): 861–78; idem, "Humanismo Clasicista Mediterráneo y Concepción Antropológica del Mundo: El Caso de los Jesuitas," *Hispania* 56 (1996): 29–50; idem, "Humanismo Renacentista y Orígenes de la Etnología: A Próposito del P. Acosta, Paradigma del Humanismo Antropológico Jesuita," in *Humanismo y visión del otro en la España moderna: cuatro estudios*, ed. Berta Ares et al., 379–429 (Madrid: CSIC, 1992); idem, "El misionero español José de Acosta y la evangelización de las Indias Orientales," *Missionalia Hispánica* 42 (1985): 275–98; idem, "Los Reinos de Méjico y Cusco en la obra del P. Acosta," *Revista de la Universidad Complutense* 28 (1979): 13–40.

12. Acosta, *De Procuranda*, Proemio, CHP vol. 23, 62–63.

13. Ibid., 62–67.

14. Ibid., 66–69.

15. Ibid., bk. I, chs. 5, 8, 17; CHP vol. 23, 40–41, #2; 150–1, #1; 154–55, #2; 224–25, #3.

16. Ibid., bk. III, ch. 19; CHP vol. 23, 538–39, #1.

17. Ernesto Cavassa Canessa, "La 'Salvación de los Indios' en el *De Procuranda Indorum Salute*: Ensayo de lectura interdisciplinar," Doct. diss., Faculty of Theology, Universidad Pontificia de Comillas, 1992, especially chapter eight.

18. Acosta, *De Procuranda*, bk. V, ch. 12; CHP vol. 24, 282–85, ##6–7.

19. Idem, *Historia*, bk. V, "Prologue to the books which follow," cited in Pino Díaz, "Humanismo Clasicista Mediterráneo," 47.

20. Ibid., 47–50.

21. Ignacio de Loyola, Spiritual Exercises ##101–9, in Iparraguirre and Dalmases, *Obras Completas*.

22. Letter of dedication of the *De Procuranda* to Fr. General Everard Mercurian, S.J., by Acosta, February 24, 1577, cited in Acosta, *De Procuranda*, CHP vol. 23, 50–53.

23. Gilmore, "The Renaissance Conception of the Lessons of History," 18.

24. Idem, "*Fides et Eruditio*: Erasmus and the Study of History," 108.

25. Gilmore, "The Renaissance Conception of the Lessons of History," 18.

26. Letter of dedication of the *Historia* to the Infanta Doña Isabel Clara Eugenia of Austria by Acosta, March 1, 1590, cited in Mateos, *Obras*, 3.

27. Acosta, *Historia*, bk. V, "Prologue to the books which follow," 139.

28. Examples of Acosta's use of biblical, patristic, and conciliar citations to explain the pagan religious practices of the natives of the Indies in the *Historia* include the following: bk. V, chs. 1–7, 9, 12, 15–20, 22, pp. 140–66.

29. Acosta, *Historia*, bk. VI, 182–207.

30. Ibid., ch. 5, pp. 185–87.

31. Ibid., bk. IV, ch. 25, 119.

32. Ibid., bk. I, chs. 21–22, pp. 33–36.

33. Ibid., bk. IV, ch. 2, p. 90.

34. Ibid., bk. VII, ch. 23, pp. 235–38.

35. Ibid., bk. VII, ch. 28, pp. 244–47.

36. O'Gorman, "La 'Historia natural y moral,'" 184. For a summary of O'Gorman's interpretation see appendix one, section entitled "Acosta the Theologian: Erasmian, Suarezian, or Nominalist?"

Chapter 7: The Form of Acosta's Humanism

1. Acosta, *Doctrina Christiana*, "Tercero Catecismo y Exposición de la Doctrina Christiana por Sermones," Sermon 27, About charity and alms-giving. See appendix seven.

2. Idem, *De Procuranda*, bk. I, ch. 3; CHP vol. 23, 100–3, #3. See appendix five.

3. Ibid., bk. I, ch. 11; CHP vol. 23, 168–85, ##1–3; bk. III, chs. 11–12, 468–73, ##6, 1–2.

4. Ibid., bk. VI, ch. 11; CHP vol. 24, 420–25, ##1–2.

5. Don Paul Abbott, *Rhetoric in the New World: Rhetorical Theory and Practice in Colonial Spanish America* (Columbia: University of South Carolina Press, 1996), 71–73.

6. Acosta, *Doctrina Christiana*, "Tercero Catecismo," 351–777.

7. Ibid., 351–62.

8. Ibid., "Instrucción contra las ceremonias y ritos que usan los indios conforme al tiempo de su infidelidad"; "Supersticiones de los indios, sacadas del segundo Concilio Provincial de Lima, que se celebró el año sesenta y siete . . ."; "Los errores y supersticiones de los indios, sacadas del Tratado y averiguación que hizo el Licenciado Polo."

9. Ibid., Sermon 1.

10. Ibid., Sermon 4.

11. Loyola, Spiritual Exercises #363.

12. Ibid., ##230–237.

13. Ibid., #234.

14. Acosta states that this is the end of the *Historia* in several places. See Letter of Dedication to the Infanta Doña Isabel Clara Eugenia of Austria, 3; Prologue to the Reader, 4; bk. V, Prologue to the books that follow, 139; bk. VII, chs. 1, 28, pp. 208, 247.

15. See appendix one for a fuller treatment of my objections to O'Gorman's interpretation of book VII.

16. Luis de León, O.S.A., "Aprobación," in José de Acosta, S.J., *Historia natural y moral de las Indias, en que se tratan las cosas notables del cielo, y elementos, metales, plantas, animales dellas: y los ritos, y ceremonias, leyes, y govierno, y guerras de los Indios* (Sevilla: Juan de León, 1590), 6.

17. For a thorough analysis of the phrase "contemplative in action" see Bangert, *Jerome Nadal*, 214–15.

18. Acosta, *Historia*, bk. VII, ch. 28, p. 246.

19. Loyola, Spiritual Exercises, #43.

20. Ibid., ##313–344.

21. For the similarity of Acosta's presentation of the devil to that of St. Ignatius, see Xavier Albó, "Jesuitas y culturas indígenas. Perú 1568–1606. Su actitud, métodos y criterios de aculturación," *América Indígena* 26 (1966): 425; Cavassa Canessa, "La 'Salvación de los Indios' en el *De Procuranda*," ch. 6.

22. Loyola, Spiritual Exercises, ##314, 326, 329, 332.

23. Acosta, *Historia*, bk. V, ch. 11, p. 152.

24. Loyola, Spiritual Exercises, #15.

25. Ibid., ##48–49.

26. Ibid., #46.

27. O'Gorman, "La 'Historia natural y moral de las Indias' del P. Joseph de Acosta," 191–93.

28. Fernando Cervantes, *The Devil in the New World: The Impact of Diabolism in New Spain*, (New Haven: Yale University Press, 1994), 27–34.

29. Acosta, *Historia*, bk. V, ch. 1, p. 140; ch. 11, p. 152; ch. 24, p. 168; ch. 31, p. 182; idem, *De Procuranda*, bk. I, ch. 18; CHP vol. 23, 370–71, #1.

30. Idem, *Doctrina Christiana*, "Tercero Catecismo," Proemio, 355–58.

31. Idem, *De Procuranda*, bk. III, ch. 19; CHP vol. 23, 414–15, # 1.

32. Ibid., bk. I, ch. 8; CHP vol. 23, 154–55, #2; bk. II, ch. 18; CHP vol. 23, 370–71, 374–77, ##1–3.

33. Ibid., bk. III, ch. 24; CHP vol. 23, 586–89, ##1–2.

34. Ibid., bk. V, chs. 1–2; CHP vol. 24, 176–77, #1, 182–83, #3.

35. Loyola, Spiritual Exercises, #91–98.

36. Acosta, *De Procuranda*, bk. I, ch. 3; CHP vol. 23, 102–5, #3.

37. Ibid., bk. V, ch. 1; CHP vol. 24, 178–79, #4.

38. Acosta, *Historia*, bk. VII, chs. 23–24, 27–28, pp. 235–47.

39. Idem, *Doctrina Christiana*, "Tercero Catecismo," Sermons 3, 4, 7, 13, pp. 382–401, 424–35, 489–501.

40. Ibid., Sermon 28, About prayer, 709, 712–13.

41. Cavassa Canessa, "La 'Salvación de los Indios' en el *De Procuranda*," especially ch. 8.

42. O'Malley, "The Ministries of the Early Jesuits: Social Disciplining or Discerning Accommodation?" *CIS* 27 (1996), 31.

43. Acosta, *De Procuranda*, "Dedication of the *De Procuranda*," CHP vol. 23, 48–51.

44. Idem, "Dedication of the *Historia*," in Mateos, *Obras*, 3.

45. Abbott, *Rhetoric in the New World*, 74.

46. See Alcina Franch, "Introducción," in *Historia natural y moral*, 7–39; Carlos Baciero, "Acosta y el Catecismo Limense: una nueva pedagogía," in *Inculturación del Indio*, ed. Luciano Pereña Vicente et al. (Salamanca: Universidad Pontificia de Salamanca, 1988), 201–62; idem, "La promoción y evangelización del indio en el plan de José de Acosta," in Pereña Vicente, *Doctrina Christiana*, 117–62; Luis Martín, "The Peruvian Indian through Jesuit Eyes: The Case of José de Acosta and Pablo José de Arriaga," in *The Jesuit Tradition in Education and Missions: A 450-Year Perspective*, ed. Christopher Chapple (Scranton: University of Scranton Press, 1993), 205–14; Pino Díaz, "Los Reinos," 13–40.

Appendix 1: Disputed Questions Concerning Acosta's Life and Thought

1. Pedro S. de Achútegui, *La Universalidad del Conocimiento de Dios en los Paganos. Según los Primeros Teólogos de la Compañía de Jesús 1534–1648*,

Appendix B (Madrid: CSIC, 1951); Ernesto Cavassa Canessa, "Una metáfora teológica inculturada. La 'salvación de los indios' en José de Acosta," *Miscelánea Comillas* 51 (1993): 89–123; idem, "La 'Salvación de los Indios' en el *De Procuranda*; Rodrigo Sánchez-Arjona, "El problema de la incorporación a la Iglesia y de la fe explícita en la teología de la colonia," *Allpanchis Phuturinqa* 4 (1972): 157–81.

2. Carlos Baciero, "Presencia del P. José de Acosta en la evangelización de América," *Miscelánea Comillas* 52 (1994): 331–52; idem, "La promoción," 117–62; José Manuel Paniagua Pascual, "La evangelización de América en las obras del Padre José de Acosta" (Doct. diss., Faculty of Theology, Universidad de Navarra, 1989), partially published in *Excerpta e dissertationibus in Sacra Theologia* 16/6 (1989): 397–480; Pino Díaz, "La civilización indiana," 251–60; idem, "Acosta y la evangelización de las Indias Orientales," 275–98; Anton Pott, "Die Missionslehre des P. Joseph de Acosta, S.J." (Doct. diss., Rome: Pontifical Gregorian University, 1934); Armido Rizzi, "José de Acosta. De Procuranda Indorum Salute. L'evangelizzazione degli indios: problemi e metodi," *Futuro dell'uomo* 19/2 (1992): 69–88; Juan Villegas, "El indio y su evangelización de acuerdo a los lineamientos del P. José de Acosta, S.J.," in *La Compañía de Jesús en América: Evangelización y Justicia. Siglos XVII y XVIII. Actas del Congreso Internacional de Historia*, ed. Feliciano Delgado, 331–76 (Córdoba: Imprenta San Pablo, S.L., 1993); idem, "El Tiempo como categoría misional en el P .José de Acosta, S.J.," in *Misiones Jesuíticas en la Orinoquia (1625–1767)*, ed. José del Rey Fajardo, vol. 2: 779–99 (San Cristóbal: Universidad Católica del Táchira, 1992).

3. Carlos Baciero, "Acosta y el Catecismo Limense: una nueva pedagogía," in *Inculturación del Indio*, ed. Luciano Pereña Vicente et al., 201–62 (Salamanca: Universidad Pontificia de Salamanca, 1988); Enrique Bartra, "Introducción," in *Tercer Concilio Limense 1582–1583: Versión castellana original de los decretos con el sumario del segundo Concilio Limense*, ed. Enrique Bartra, 19–40 (Lima: Editorial ETB, 1982); Javier Castillo Arroyo, "Catecismos peruanos del siglo XVI," in *Evangelización y teología en el Perú: luces y sombras en el siglo XVI*, ed. Pablo Nguyen Thai Hop, 261–94 (Lima: Centro de Estudios y Publicaciones (CEP), 1991); Juan Guillermo Durán Jáuregui, *El catecismo del III Concilio provincial de Lima y sus complementos pastorales (1584–1585) Estudio Preliminar Textos Notas* (Buenos Aires: Publicaciones de la Facultad de Teología de la Pontificia Universidad Católica de Argentina, 1982); idem, *Monumenta catechetica hispano-americana (siglos XVI XVII)*, vol. 2 (Buenos Aires: Ediciones de la Facultad de Teología de la Universidad Católica de Argentina, 1984); idem, "El 'Tercero Catecismo' como medio de transmisión de la fe," in Pereña Vicente *Inculturación del Indio*, 83–119; J. Guerra Campos, "El catecismo trilingüe de América del Sur," *Boletín Oficial del Obispado de Cuenca* (Dec. 1977):

157–95; Lisi, *El Tercer Concilio*, 233; Luis Resines Llorente, "Catecismos Americanos de Jesuitas," in *La Compañía de Jesús en América*, 315–21; idem, "El Catecismo Limense," in *Inculturación del Indio*, 191–200; Raimundo Romero Ferrer, "La eclesiología de los catecismos limenses (1584–1585)," in *Evangelización y teología en América siglo XVI: Simpoio internacional de teología de la Universidad de Navarre*, ed. Josep-Ignasi Saranyana, vol. 2: 1277–92 (Pamplona: Universidad de Navarra, 1990).

4. F. R. Aznar Gil, "La capacidad e idoneidad canónica de los indios para recibir los sacramentos en las fuentes canónicas indianas del s. XVI," in *Evangelización en América*, ed. Dionosio Borobio García et al., Serie Salamanca en el descubrimiento de América, n. 2, 167–240 (Salamanca: Caja de Ahorros y Monte de Piedad de Salamanca, 1988); Martine Azoulai, "Les Manuels de confession espagnols à l'usage de l'Amérique. Les Indiens et leurs confesseurs chrétiens aux XVI et XVII siècles" (Doct. diss., Institute of Hispanic Studies, University of Paris, 1983).

5. Carlos Baciero, "La ética en la conquista de América y los primeros jesuitas del Perú," *Miscelánea Comillas* 46 (1988): 129–64; García y García, "La reforma del Concilio tercero," 182–89; Anthony Pagden, "The Forbidden Food: Francisco de Vitoria and José de Acosta on Cannibalism," *Terræ Incognitæ* 13 (1981): 17–29.

6. Lopetegui, "Influjos," 57–72; Mustapha, "Sur un texte retrouvé," 209–16; Josep-Ignasi Saranyana, "Teología académica y teología profética americanas (S. XVI)," in *Evangelización y teología en América siglo XVI: Simposio internacional de teología de la Universidad de Navarra*. ed. Josep-Ignasi Saranyana, vol. 2, 1035–78 (Pamplona: Universidad de Navarra, 1990).

7. Abril Castelló, "Cuestión incidental," 108–10; Brading, *The First America*, 184–95; Cervantes, *The Devil*, 25–34; Luis N. Rivera, *A Violent Evangelism: The Political and Religious Conquest of the Americas*, 133–36, 150–52, 158–59, 164–65, 206–7, 220–23, 264–65 (Louisville: Westminster/John Knox Press, 1992); Pedro Trigo, "Evangelización en la colonia. *De Procuranda Indorum Salute*: una teología patética," *Revista Latinoamericana de Teología* 20 (1990): 163–188; Noé Zevallos, "El Padre José de Acosta," in *Evangelización y teología en el Perú: luces y sombras del siglo XVI*, ed. Pablo Nguyen Thai Hop, 179–98 (Lima: CEP, 1991).

8. León Lopetegui, "¿Cómo debe entenderse la labor misional del P. José de Acosta, S.J.," *Studia Missionalia* 1 (1943): 115–36; idem, "Labor del Padre José de Acosta, S.J., en el Concilio III de Lima. 1582–1583," *Revista de Indias* 3 (1942): 63–84; idem, "Notas sobre la actividad teológica del P. José de Acosta, S.J.," *Gregorianum* 21 (1940): 527–63; idem, "Notas sobre la edición del tercer concilio provincial Limense," *Gregorianum* 22 (1944): 252–72; idem, *Acosta y las misiones*; idem, "Tres memoriales," 78–91.

9. Composition and publication dates for Acosta's works are derived from Lopetegui, *Acosta y las misiones*, and Mateos, "Introducción," in *Obras*.

10. Lopetegui, *Acosta y las misiones*, xiv, 447.

11. Pedro Leturia, review of Lopetegui, *Acosta y las misiones*, in *AHSI* 13 (1944): 117–20.

12. For a similar critique see also Cavassa Canessa, "La 'Salvación de los Indios' en el *De Procuranda*," 47–50.

13. O'Gorman, "Prólogo," in Acosta, *Historia*, i–lxxxviii; reproduced in "La 'Historia natural y moral de las Indias' del P. Joseph de Acosta," in *Cuatro historiadores*, 165–248; María Luisa Rivara de Tuesta, *José de Acosta, un humanista reformista* (Lima: Editorial Universo, 1970).

14. O'Gorman, "La 'Historia,'" 198.

15. Kristeller, "Renaissance Philosophy," in Mooney, *Renaissance Thought*, 106–34.

16. Rivara de Tuesta, *José de Acosta*, 87–93.

17. Miguel Batllori, "Las Obras de Luis Vives en los Colegios Jesuíticos Europeos del Siglo XVI," in *Humanismo y Renacimiento: Estudios hispanos-europeos*, ed. Miguel Batllori (Barcelona: Editorial Ariel, 1987), 125–49; Pascual Cebollada, "Loyola y Erasmo: Aportación al estudio de la relación entre ambos," *Manresa* 62 (1990), 49–60.

18. Kristeller, "Humanism and Scholasticism," in Mooney, *Renaissance Thought*, 90–93.

19. Rivara de Tuesta, *José de Acosta*, 119.

20. Ibid., 147.

21. Ibid., 131–32.

22. Ibid., 141–43.

23. Ibid., 132–36.

24. Lopetegui, *Acosta y las misiones*, 434–44.

25. Ibid., 434.

26. Sabine MacCormack, *Religion in the Andes: Vision and Imagination in Early Colonial Peru* (Princeton: Princeton University Press, 1991), 277–78.

27. Amalio Bayón, "La escuela jesuítica desde Suárez y Molina hasta la Guerra de Sucesión," in *Historia de la teología española*, vol. 2, ed. Melquíades Andrés Martín (Madrid: Fundación Universitaria Española, 1987), 52–53.

28. For the differences between the older generation of Jesuit Thomists and the newer one, see Beltrán de Hereida, "La enseñanza de Santo Tomás," 332–42.

29. On the *De Auxiliis* controversy see Astrain, *Historia*, vol. 4, 115–386; William V. Bangert, *A History of the Society of Jesus* (St. Louis: Institute of Jesuit Sources, 1972), 115–16; Bartolomé Parera, "La Escuela Tomista Española en el Siglo XVII," in Andrés Martín, *Historia*, vol. 2., 9–20.

30. Mustapha, "Sur un texte retrouvé," 209–16.

31. León Lopetegui, "Notas sobre la actividad teológica del P. José de Acosta, S.J.," *Gregorianum* 21 (1940), 552–57.

32. Mustapha, "Sur un texte retrouvé," 214.

33. Parera, "La Escuela," 12–13.

34. Lopetegui, "Notas," 556.

35. Ibid., 553–59.

36. Cervantes, *The Devil*, 25–34.

37. Ibid., 25–34.

38. León Lopetegui, *Acosta y las misiones*, 12; idem, "La Iglesia Española y la Hispanoamericana de 1493 a 1810," in *Historia de la Iglesia en España*, vol. 3, pt. 2, ed. Ricardo García-Villoslada et al.; *La Iglesia en la España de los siglos XV y XVI*, ed. José Luis González Novalín et al. (Madrid: La Editorial Católica, S.A., 1980), 399, n. 73.

39. Idem, "La Iglesia Española," 399, n. 73.

40. Marcos Martín, "Auge y Declive," 274.

41. Pino Díaz, "Acosta y la Evangelización de las Indias Orientales," 276.

42. Lopetegui, *Acosta y las misiones*, 11, 479–81.

43. Lopetegui, "La Iglesia Española," vol. 3, pt. 2, 399, n. 73.

44. Astrain, *Historia*, vol. 3, 435–47.

45. Ibid., 491–622.

46. Acosta, "Memorial de Apología o Descargo dirigido al Papa Clemente VIII," in Mateos, *Obras*, 368–86.

47. Idem, "Diario de la Embajada a Roma (1592)," Mateos, *Obras*, 353–68.

48. González Dávila to Aquaviva, February 9, 1592, cited in Astrain, *Historia*, vol. 3, 536.

49. Ibid., 533–34.

50. Acosta to Aquaviva, January 8, 1592, ARSI, Hisp. 134, f. 147.

51. Astrain, *Historia*, vol. 3, 364–67; 554–56.

52. Acosta to Aquaviva, February 7, 1592, ARSI, Hisp. 134, f. 169.

53. Astrain, *Historia*, vol. 3, 534–35.

54. Ibid., 625.

55. Pinta Llorente, "José de Acosta Agente de Felipe II," 123–24.

56. Astrain, *Historia*, vol. 3, 558.

57. Sánchez to Aquaviva, February 27, 1593, cited in ibid., 537.

58. Ibid., n. 1, 537.

WORKS CITED

Primary Sources

Acosta, Antonio de. Letter to Fr. General Francisco de Borja, October 2, 1569. ARSI, Hisp. 112, f. 2.

Acosta, José de. *De Christo revelato libri novem, simulque De Temporibus Novissimis libri quatuor*. Rome: Iacobum Tornerium, 1590.

_____. *Conciones de Adventu*. Salamancæ: Ioannem et Andream Renaut, fratres, 1597.

_____. *Conciones in Quadragesimam*. Salamancæ: Ioannem et Andream Renaut, fratres, 1596.

_____. *Doctrina Christiana y Catecismo para Instrucción de los Indios, Facsímil del texto trilingüe*. Ed. Luciano Pereña Vicente, CHP vol. 26–2; Madrid: CSIC, 1985.

_____. *Historia Natural y Moral de las Indias*. Ed. José Alcina Franch; Madrid: Historia 16, 1986.

_____. Letters to Fr. General Claudio Acquaviva, S.J., ARSI, January 8, 1592, Hisp. 134, f. 147; February 7, 1592, Hisp. 134, f. 169.

_____. Letters to Fr. General Diego Laínez, S.J., ARSI, October 17, 1559, Hisp. 96; March 1, 1560, Hisp. 97, ff. 59–60; April 5, 1560, Hisp. 97, f. 101; June 12, 1560, Hisp. 97, f. 186; October 5, 1560, Hisp. 97, f. 379; January 3, 1561, Hisp. 98, f. 11; May 1, 1561, Hisp. 98, ff. 166–68; September 3, 1561, Hisp. 98, ff. 323–25; January 1, 1562, Hisp. 99, ff. 1–6; May 12, 1562, Hisp. 99, ff. 205–9; September 1, 1562, Hisp. 99, ff. 307–9; January 3, 1563, Hisp. 100, ff. 46–50; May 31, 1563, Hisp. 100, ff. 221–22; January 7, 1564, Hisp. 101, ff. 31–33; May 28, 1564, Hisp. 101, ff. 175–77; September 30, 1564, Hisp. 101, f. 304.

_____. *Obras del P. José de Acosta de la Compañía de Jesús*. Ed. Francisco Mateos. BAE vol. 73; Madrid: Ediciones Atlas, 1954.

_____. *De Procuranda Indorum Salute*, 2 vols. Ed. Luciano Pereña Vicente. CHP vols. 23, 24; Madrid: CSIC, 1984, 1987.

_____. "In Psalmos Davidis commentarii . . . [1598–1600]." MS. 659, Biblioteca General de la Universidad de Salamanca, Salamanca, Spain.

_____. *Tomus Tertius Concionum*. Salamancæ: Ioannem et Andream Renaut, fratres, 1599.

Castro, Cristóbal de. "Historia del Colegio de la Compañía de Jesús de Alcalá de Henares, 1600(?)," 2 vols. MS., IHSI Library, Rome, Italy.

Eusebius of Caesarea. *Preparation for the Gospel*, 2 vols. Trans. Edwin Hamilton Gifford; Grand Rapids: Baker Book House, 1981.

León, Luis de, O.S.A. "Aprobación." In José de Acosta, S.J., *Historia natural y moral de las Indias, en que se tratan las cosas notables del cielo, y elementos, metales, plantas, animales dellas: y los ritos, y ceremonias, leyes, y govierno, y guerras de los Indios*; Sevilla: Juan de León, 1590.

Levillier, Roberto, ed. *Organización de la Iglesia y Ordenes Religiosas en el Virreinato del Perú en el Siglo XVI: Documentos del Archivo de Indias*, 2 vols. Madrid: Sucesores de Rivadeneyra, 1919.

Loyola, Ignacio de. *Obras Completas*. Ed. Ignacio Iparraguirre and Cándido Dalmases, 4th ed., BAC 86; Madrid: La Editorial Católica, S.A., 1982.

Nadal, Jerónimo. *Commentarii de Instituto Societatis Iesu. Monumenta Historica Societatis Iesu. Vol. 90. Epistolae et Monumenta P. Hieronymi Nadal Tomus V Commentarii de Instituto S.I.* Ed. Miguel Nicolau; Rome: MHSI, 1962.

Porres, Ana de. Letter to Fr. General Diego Laínez, S.J. May 30, 1564. ARSI, Hisp. 101, f. 184.

_____. Letter to Fr. General Francisco de Borja, S.J., October 22, 1567. ARSI, Hisp. 107, f. 111.

Valdivia, Luis de. "Colegios de la Provincia de Castilla, 1641(?)." TMS. [carbon copy], IHSI Library, Rome, Italy.

Secondary Sources

Abbott, Don Paul. *Rhetoric in the New World: Rhetorical Theory and Practice in Colonial Spanish America*. Columbia: University of South Carolina Press, 1996.

Abril Castelló, Vidal. "Cuestión incidental: ¿Fue lascasista José de Acosta?" In *Francisco de la Cruz, Inquisición, Actas I. Anatomía y biopsia del Dios y del derecho Judeo-cristiano-musulmán de la conquista de América*, ed. Vidal Abril Castelló; CHP vol. 29, 108–10; Madrid: CSIC, 1992.

_____. "Fray Francisco de la Cruz, el lascasismo peruano y la prevaricación del Santo Oficio limeño, 1572–1578." In *Los Dominicos y el Nuevo Mundo: Actas del II Congreso Internacional, Salamanca, 28 de marzo–1 de abril de 1989*, ed. José Barrado, 157–225; Salamanca: Editorial San Esteban, 1990.

Achútegui, Pedro S. de. *La Universalidad del Conocimiento de Dios en los Paganos. Según los Primeros Teólogos de la Compañía de Jesús 1534–1648*. Madrid: CSIC, 1951.

Aguirre, E. "Una hipótesis evolucionista en el siglo XVI. El P. José de Acosta, S.J., y el origen de las especies americanas." *Arbor* 36 (1957): 176–87.

Akkerman, F., and A. J. Vanderjagt, eds. *Rodolphus Agricola Phrisius 1444–1485: Proceedings of the International Conference at the University of Groningen, 28–30 October, 1985*. Leiden: E. J. Brill, 1988.

Albó, Xavier. "Jesuitas y culturas indígenas. Perú 1568–1606. Su actitud, métodos y criterios de aculturación." *América Indígena* 26 (1966): 249–308, 395–445.

Alcina Franch, José. "Introducción." In *Historia natural y moral de las Indias*, ed. José Alcina Franch, 7–39; Colección Crónicas de América 34; Madrid: Historia 16, 1987.

Alvarez López, Enrique. "La filosofía natural en el Padre José de Acosta." *Revista de Indias* 4 (1943): 305–22.

Andrés Martín, Melquíades. "Pensamiento Teológico y Vivencia Religiosa en la Reforma Española (1400–1600)." In *Historia de la Iglesia en España*, vol. 3, pt. 2, ed. Ricardo García-Villoslada et al.; *La Iglesia en la España de los siglos XV y XVI*, ed. José Luis González Novalín et al., 269–362; BAC Maior vol. 21; Madrid: La Editorial Católica, 1980.

_____. *La teología española en el siglo XVI*, 2 vols. BAC Maior vols. 13–14; Madrid: La Editorial Católica, 1976.

_____, ed. *Historia de la teología española*, 2 vols. Madrid: Fundación Universitaria Española, 1983, 1987.

Arrom, José Juan. "Precursores coloniales de la narrativa hispanoamericana: José de Acosta o la ficción como biografía." *Revista Iberoamericana* 44 (1978): 369–83.

Arroyo Simón, Millán. "El P. José de Acosta, S.J., (1540–1600) y la educación de los indios en América." *Theológica Xaveriana* 43/4 (1993): 353–72.

Astrain, Antonio. *Historia de la Compañía de Jesús en la Asistencia de España*, 7 vols. Madrid: Administración de Razón y Fe, 1912–1925.

Aznar Gil, F. R. "La capacidad e idoneidad canónica de los indios para recibir los sacramentos en las fuentes canónicas indianas del s. XVI." In *Evangelización en América*, ed. Donosio Borborio García et al., 167–240; Serie Salamanca en el Descubrimiento de América, n. 2; Salamanca: Caja de Ahorros y Monte de Piedad de Salamanca, 1988.

Azoulai, Martine. "Les Manuels de confession espagnols à l'usage de l'Amérique. Les Indiens et leurs confesseurs chrétiens au XVI et XVII siècles." Doct. diss., Institute of Hispanic Studies, University of Paris, 1983.

Baciero, Carlos. "Acosta y el Catecismo Limense: una nueva pedagogía." In *Inculturación del Indio*, ed. Luciano Pereña Vicente et al., 201–62; Salamanca: Universidad Pontificia de Salamanca, 1988.

_____. "La ética en la conquista de América y los primeros jesuitas del Perú." *Miscelánea Comillas* 46 (1988): 129–64.

_____. "Presencia del P. José de Acosta en la evangelización de América." *Miscelánea Comillas* 52 (1994): 331–52.

_____. "La promoción y evangelización del indio en el plan de José de Acosta." In *Doctrina Christiana y Catecismo para Instrucción de Indios: Introducción. Del Genocidio a la Promoción del Indio*, ed. Luciano Pereña Vicente, 117–62; CHP vol. 26-1; Madrid: CSIC, 1986.

Bangert, William V. *A History of the Society of Jesus*. St. Louis: Institute of Jesuit Sources, 1972.

_____. *Jerome Nadal, S.J. (1507–1580): Tracking the First Generation of Jesuits*. Edited and completed by Thomas M. McCoog; Chicago: Loyola University Press, 1992.

Bartra, Enrique, ed. "Introducción." In *Tercer Concilio Limense 1582–1583: Versión castellana original de los decretos con el sumario del segundo Concilio Limense*, 19–40; Lima: Editorial ETB, 1982.

Basauri, Daniel. "El P. José de Acosta y la implantación del método científico en las ciencias físico-naturales." *Estudios Centro-Americanos* 1 (1946): n. 1, 13–18; n. 3, 22–27.

_____. "El P. José de Acosta y los orígenes del hombre americano." *Estudios Centro-Americanos* 1 (1946): n. 6, 19–26.

Batllori, Miguel, ed. *Humanismo y Renacimiento: Estudios hispano-europeos*. Barcelona: Editorial Ariel, 1987.

Bayón, Amalio. "La escuela jesuítica desde Suárez y Molina hasta la Guerra de Sucesión." In *Historia de la teología española*, vol. 2, ed. Melquíades Andrés Martín, 39–74; Madrid: Fundación Universitaria Española, 1987.

Beltrán de Hereida, Vicente de. "La enseñanza de Santo Tomás en la Compañía de Jesús en el primer siglo de su existencia." In *Miscelánea Beltrán de Hereida. Colección de Artículos sobre Historia de la Teología Española*, vol. 2, 309–42; Biblioteca de Teólogos Españoles, vol. 26; Salamanca: Editorial OPE, 1972.

_____. "La facultad de teología en la Universidad de Alcalá." In *Miscelánea Beltrán de Hereida. Colección de Artículos sobre Historia de la Teología Española*, vol. 4, 61–157; Biblioteca de Teólogos Españoles, vol. 28; Salamanca: Editorial OPE, 1973.

_____. "La formación humanística y escolástica de Fray Francisco de Vitoria." In *Miscelánea Beltrán de Hereida. Colección de Artículos sobre Historia de la Teología Española*, vol. 2, 55–72; Biblioteca de Teólogos Españoles, vol. 26; Salamanca: Editorial OPE, 1972.

_____. *Miscelánea Beltrán de Hereida. Colección de Artículos sobre Historia de la Teología Española*, 4 vols. Biblioteca de Teólogos Españoles, vols. 25–28; Salamanca: Editorial OPE, 1971–1973.

_____. "La preclara Facultad de Artes de la Universidad de Alcalá." In *Miscelánea Beltrán de Hereida. Colección de Artículos sobre Historia de la Teología Española*, vol. 4, 175–90; Biblioteca de Teólogos Españoles, vol. 28; Salamanca: Editorial OPE, 1973.

Bennassar, Bartolomé. "Medina del Campo: un exemple des structures urbaines de l'Espagne au XVIe siècle." *Revue d'Histoire Economique et Sociale* 4 (1961): 474–95.

Bensimon, Nicole. "Le Père Acosta naturaliste: humanisme et expérience." Doct. diss., Institute of Hispanic Studies, University of Paris, 1957.

Biondi, Albano. "La *Bibliotheca selecta* di Antonio Possevino: Un progetto di egemonia culturale." In *La "Ratio studiorum": Modelli culturali e pratiche educative dei Gesuiti in Italia tra Cinque e Seicento*, ed. Gian Paolo Brizzi, 43–75; Roma: Bulzoni Editore, 1981.

Borges Morán, Pedro. *Historia de la Iglesia en Hispanoamérica y Filipinas (Siglos XV–XIX)*, 2 vols. BAC Maior vols. 37, 42; Madrid: La Editorial Católica, S.A., 1992.

_____. *Religiosos en Hispanoamérica*. Colección Iglesia Católica en el Nuevo Mundo; Madrid: MAPFRE, 1992.

Brading, David A. *The First America: The Spanish Monarchy, Creole Patriots, and the Liberal State 1492–1867*. Cambridge: Cambridge University Press, 1991.

Carbonell De Masy, Rafael. "Las Reducciones de Paraguay; Opción por los pobres y obediencia religiosa." *CIS* 24 (1993/2): 9–30.

Castillo Arroyo, Javier. "Catecismos peruanos del siglo XVI." In *Evangelización y teología en el Perú: luces y sombras en el siglo XVI*, ed. Pablo Nguyen Thai Hop, 261–94; Lima: Centro de Estudios y Publicaciones (CEP), 1991.

Cavassa Canessa, Ernesto. "Una metáfora teológica inculturada. La 'salvación de los indios' en José de Acosta." *Miscelánea Comillas* 51 (1993): 89–123.

_____. "La 'Salvación de los Indios' en el *De Procuranda Indorum Salute*: Ensayo de lectura interdisciplinar." Doct. diss., Faculty of Theology, Universidad Pontificia de Comillas, 1992.

Cebollada, Pascual, "Loyola y Erasmo: Aportación al estudio de la relación entre ambos." *Manresa* 62 (1990): 49–60.

Cervantes, Fernando. *The Devil in the New World: The Impact of Diabolism in New Spain*. New Haven: Yale University Press, 1994.

Codina Mir, Gabriel. *Aux Sources de la Pédagogie des Jésuites: Le "Modus Parisiensis."* Bibliotheca Instituti Historici S. J., vol. 28; Rome: IHSI, 1968.

_____. "La ordenación y el doctorado en teología de Jerónimo Nadal en Aviñón (1537–1538). *AHSI* 36 (1967): 247–51.

CEHILA. *Historia General de la Iglesia en América Latina*, vol. 8: Perú, Bolivia y Ecuador. Salamanca: Ediciones Sígueme, 1987.

Cohen, Thomas Vance. "The Social Origins of the Jesuits, 1540–1600," 2 vols. Ph.D. diss., Harvard University, 1973.

_____, "Why the Jesuits Joined, 1540–1600." In *Historical Papers*, 237–58; Ottawa: The Canadian Historical Association, 1974.

Conwell, Joseph F. *Contemplation in Action; a Study in Ignatian Prayer*. Spokane: Gonzaga University, 1957.

Costa, Horacio de la. *The Jesuits in the Philippines 1581–1768*. Cambridge: Harvard University Press, 1961.

Delgado, Feliciano, ed. *La Compañía de Jesús en América: Evangelización y Justicia. Siglos XVII y XVIII. Actas del Congreso Internacional de Historia*. Córdoba: Imprenta San Pablo, S.L., 1993.

Delgado Criado, Buenaventura, ed. *Historia de la Educación en España y América*, 3 vols. Madrid: Ediciones SM and Morata, S.L., 1992–1994.

Durán Jáuregui, Juan Guillermo. *El catecismo del III Concilio provincial de Lima y sus complementos pastorales (1584–1585) Estudio Preliminar Textos Notas*. Buenos Aires: Publicaciones de la Facultad de Teología de la Pontificia Universidad Católica de Argentina, 1982.

_____. *Monumenta catechetica hispano-americana (siglos XVI–XVII)*, 2 vols. Buenos Aires: Ediciones de la Facultad de Teología de la Universidad Católica de Argentina, 1984.

_____. "El 'Tercero Catecismo' como medio de transmisión de la fe." In *Inculturación del Indio*, ed. Luciano Pereña Vicente, 83–119; Salamanca: Universidad Pontificia de Salamanca, 1988.

Dussel, Enrique D. *Historia de la Iglesia en América Latina: Coloniaje y Liberación 1492–1973*. Barcelona: Editorial Nova Terra, 1974.

_____. "Hipótesis para una historia de la teología en América Latina (1492–1980)." In *Materiales para una Historia de la Teología en América Latina, VIII Encuentro Latinoamericano de CEHILA, Lima (1980)*, ed. Pablo Richard, 401–52; San José, Costa Rica: CEHILA y DEI, 1981.

Echánove, Alfonso. "Origen y evolución de la idea jesuítica de 'Reducciones' en las misiones del Virreinato del Perú: Introducción." *Missionalia Hispánica* 12 (1955): 95–144.

_____. "Origen y evolución de la idea jesuítica de 'Reducciones' en las misiones del Virreinato del Perú: La Residencia de Juli, patrón y esquema de reducciones." *Missionalia Hispánica* 13 (1956): 497–540.

Egaña, Antonio de. "El Virrey don Francisco de Toledo y los jesuitas del Perú (1569–1581)." *Estudios de Deusto* 4 (1956): 115–86.

Enguita Utrilla, José María. "El americanismo léxico en la *Peregrinación de Bartolomé Lorenzo*." *Anuario de Lingüística Hispánica* 4 (1988): 127–44.

_____. "Las lenguas indígenas en la evangelización del Perú a través de la obra del Padre Acosta." In *Actas del II Congreso Internacional de la Lengua Española*, vol. 2, ed. Manuel Ariza, 343–61; Madrid: Pabellón de España, 1992.

Escudero Solano, José. "Medina del Campo, estudio de un pequeño núcleo urbano de Castilla la Vieja." *Estudios Geográficos* 101 (1965): 439–506.

Espejo, Cristóbal, and Julián Paz. *Las antiguas ferias de Medina del Campo.* Valladolid: Tipografía del Colegio de Santiago, 1908.

Farge, James K. "The University of Paris in the Time of Ignatius of Loyola." In *Ignacio de Loyola y su tiempo*, ed. Juan Plazaola, 221–43; Bilbao: Ediciones Mensajero, 1991.

Fernández Martín, Luis. "El Colegio de los Jesuitas de Medina del Campo en tiempo de Juan de Yepes." In *Juan de la Cruz, Espíritu de Llama: Estudios con ocasión del cuarto centenario de su muerte (1591–1991)*, ed. Otger Steggink, 41–61; Rome: Institutum Carmelitanum, 1991.

Gallego Salvadores, Jordán. "La enseñanza de la metafísica en la Universidad de Alcalá durante el Siglo XVI." In *Analecta Sacra Tarraconensia* 46 (1973): 345–86.

Gangutia Elícegui, Elvira. "El P. Acosta y las teorías lingüísticas de la Ilustración." In *América y la España del siglo XVI*, vol. 1, ed. Francisco de Solano and Fermín del Pino Díaz, 363–72; Madrid: CSIC, 1982.

García Oro, José. "La reforma de las órdenes religiosas en los siglos XV y XVI." In *Historia de la Iglesia en España*, vol. 3, pt. 1, ed. Ricardo García-Villoslada et al.; *La Iglesia en la España de los siglos XV y XVI*, ed. José Luis González Novalín et al., 211–349; BAC Maior 18; Madrid: La Editorial Católica, 1980.

García y García, Antonio. "La reforma del Concilio tercero de Lima." In *Doctrina Christiana y Catecismo para Instrucción de Indios. Introducción. Del Genocidio a la Promoción del Indio*, ed. Luciano Pereña Vicente, 182–89; CHP vol. 26-2; Madrid: CSIC, 1986.

García-Villoslada, Ricardo et al., eds. *Historia de la Iglesia en España*, vol. 3, pts. 1–2. *La Iglesia en la España de los siglos XV y XVI*. ed. José Luis González Novalín et al.; BAC Maior 18, 21; Madrid: Editorial Católica, 1980.

Gilmore, Myron P. *Humanists and Jurists: Six Studies in the Renaissance*. Cambridge: The Belknap Press of Harvard University Press, 1963.

Gómez Robledo, Antonio. "Las ideas jurídicas del P. José de Acosta." *Revista de la Escuela Nacional de Jurisprudencia* 2 (1940): 297–313.

Griffin, Nigel. "A curious document: Baltasar Loarte, S.J., and the years 1554–1570." *AHSI* 45 (1976): 66–94.

Guerra Campos, J. "El catecismo trilingüe de América del Sur." *Boletín Oficial del Obispado de Cuenca* (Dec. 1977): 157–95.

Haring, Clarence H. *The Spanish Empire in America*. New York: Harcourt, Brace, 1947; reprint, New York: Harcourt Brace Jovanovich, 1975.

Headley, John M. "Spain's Asian Presence, 1565–1590: Structures and Aspirations." *Hispanic American Historical Review* 75/4 (1995): 623–46.

Kamen, Henry. *Spain 1469–1714: A Society Of Conflict*, 2d ed. New York: Longman, 1991.

Kristeller, Paul Oskar. *Medieval Aspects of Renaissance Learning: Three Essays by Paul Oskar Kristeller*. Ed. and trans. by Edward P. Mahoney; Durham: Duke University Press, 1974.

_____. *Renaissance Thought and Its Sources*. Ed. Michael Mooney; New York: Columbia University Press, 1979.

_____. *Le Thomisme et la Pensée Italienne de la Renaissance*. Montreal: L'Institut d'Études Médiévales, 1967.

Kuhlmann, Wilhelm, ed. *Rudolf Agricola 1444–1485: Protagonist des nordeuropäischen Humanismus zum 550. Geburtstag*. Bern: P. Lang, 1994.

Leturia, Pedro de. Review of *El Padre José de Acosta, S.J., y las misiones*, by León Lopetegui. In *AHSI* 13 (1944): 117–20.

Lewy, Guenter. "The Struggle for Constitutional Government in the Early Years of the Society of Jesus." *Church History* 29 (1960): 141–60.

Lienhard, Martin. "Una novela hispanoamericana en 1586. (J. Acosta, *La peregrinación de Bartolomé Lorenzo*)." In *Miscelánea de Estudios Hispánicos. Homenaje de los hispanistas suizos a Ramón Sugranyes de Franch*, ed. Luis López Molina, 175–87; Montserrat: L'abadia de Montserrat, 1982.

Lisi, Francesco Leonardo. *El Tercer Concilio Limense y la Aculturación de los Indígenas Sudamericanos: Estudio crítico con edición, traducción y comentario de las actas del concilio provincial celebrado en Lima entre 1582 y 1583*. Acta Salmanticensia, Estudios Filológicos 233; Salamanca: Ediciones Universidad de Salamanca, 1990.

Lockhart, James. *Spanish Peru 1532–1560: A Colonial Society*. Madison: The University of Wisconsin Press, 1968.

Lopetegui, León. "¿Cómo debe entenderse la labor misional del P. José de Acosta, S.J." *Studia Missionalia* 1 (1943): 115–36.

_____. "La Iglesia Española y la Hispanoamericana de 1493 a 1810." In *Historia de la Iglesia en España*, vol. 3, pt. 2, ed. Ricardo García-Villoslada et al.; *La Iglesia en la España de los siglos XV y XVI*, ed. José Luis González Novalín et al., 363–442; Madrid: La Editorial Católica, S.A., 1980.

_____. "Influjos de Fr. Domingo de Soto, O.P., en el pensamiento misional del P. José de Acosta." *Estudios Eclesiásticos* 36 (1961): 57–72.

_____. "Labor del Padre José de Acosta, S.J., en el Concilio III de Lima. 1582–1583." *Revista de Indias* 3 (1942): 63–84.

_____. "Notas sobre la actividad teológica del P. José de Acosta, S.J." *Gregorianum* 21 (1940): 527–63.

_____. "Notas sobre la edición del tercer concilio provincial Limense." *Gregorianum* 22 (1944): 252–72.

_____. "Padre José de Acosta (1540–1600). Datos cronológicos." *AHSI* 9 (1940): 121–31.

_____. *El Padre José de Acosta, S.J., y las misiones*. Madrid: CSIC, 1942.

_____. "Tres memoriales inéditos presentados al Papa Clemente VIII por el P. José de Acosta, sobre temas americanos." *Studia Missionalia* 5 (1949): 78–91.

_____. "Vocación de Indias del P. José de Acosta, S.J." *Revista de Indias* 1 (1940): 83–102.

López de Prado, Joaquín. "Fundamentos del Derecho Misional en José de Acosta, S.J." *Missionalia Hispánica* 22 (1965): 339–66.

Lorenzo Sanz, Eufemio. *Historia de Medina del Campo y su tierra*, 3 vols. Valladolid: Ayuntamiento de Medina del Campo, Consejería de Educación y Cultura de la Junta de Castilla y León, 1986.

MacCormack, Sabine. *Religion in the Andes: Vision and Imagination in Early Colonial Peru*. Princeton: Princeton University Press, 1991.

Maravall, José Antonio. *Estudios de Historia del Pensamiento Español. Serie Segunda. La Epoca del Renacimiento*. Madrid: Ediciones Cultura Hispánica, 1984.

Marcos Martín, Alberto. *Auge y Declive de un Núcleo Mercantíl y Financiero de Castilla la Vieja: Evolución demográfica de Medina del Campo durante los Siglos XVI y XVII*. Valladolid: Universidad de Valladolid, Secretariado de Publicaciones, 1978.

Marín Agreda, Pedro. *Estudio de los indigenismos en la "Historia natural y moral de las Indias" del P. José de Acosta*, 2 vols. Colección Tesis Doctorales n. 161/93; Madrid: Editorial de la Universidad Complutense, 1993.

Martín, Luis. "The Peruvian Indian through Jesuit Eyes: The Case of José de Acosta and Pablo José de Arriaga." In *The Jesuit Tradition in Education and Missions: A 450-Year Perspective*, ed. Christopher Chapple, 205–14; Scranton: University of Scranton Press, 1993.

Mateos, Francisco. "Introducción: Personalidad y Escritos del P. José de Acosta." In *Obras del P. José de Acosta de la Compañía de Jesús*, ed. Francisco Mateos, vii–xlix; BAE vol. 73; Madrid: Editorial Atlas, 1954.

Meiklejohn, Norman. *La Iglesia y los Lupaqas de Chucuito durante la Colonia*. Colección Archivo de Historia Andina 7; Cusco: Centro de Estudios Rurales Andinos "Bartolomé de Las Casas" and Instituto de Estudios Aymaras, 1988.

Moraleja Pinilla, Gerardo. *Historia de Medina del Campo*. Medina del Campo: Ayuntamiento de Medina del Campo, 1971.

Moreyra, Manuel. "El Padre José de Acosta y su labor intelectual." *Mercurio Peruano* 22 (1940): 546–53.

Muller, Herman J. "British Travel Writers and the Jesuits." *Mid-America* 35 (1953): 91–116.

Mustapha, Monique. "Sur un texte retrouvé: Le Père José de Acosta et la querelle 'De Auxiliis.'" *Annales de la Faculté des Lettres et Sciences Humaines de Nice* 23 (1982): 209–16.

Narvaez Tossi, Ricardo. *Aportes del Padre José de Acosta, S.J., en la historia del pensamiento económico peruano.* Lima: Universidad de Lima, Facultad de Economía, 1989.

The New Encyclopaedia Britannica, 15th ed. S.v. "Alcalá de Henares."

Nguyen Thai Hop, Pablo, ed. *Evangelización y teología en el Perú: luces y sombras en el siglo XVI.* Lima: CEP, 1991.

Nicolau, Miguel. *Jerónimo Nadal, S.J. (1507–1580): Sus obras y doctrinas espirituales.* Madrid: CSIC, 1949.

Nieto Vélez, Armando. *El Padre José de Acosta y su comprensión del mundo indígena.* Lima: Ediciones Vida y Espiritualidad, 1988.

_____. "Reflexiones de un teólogo del siglo XVI sobre las religiones nativas." *Revista de la Universidad Católica,* no. 2 (Dec. 1977): 133–48.

O'Gorman, Edmundo. "La 'Historia natural y moral de las Indias' del P. Joseph de Acosta." In *Cuatro historiadores de Indias, siglo XVI: Pedro Mártir de Anglería, Gónzalo Fernández de Oviedo y Valdes, Fray Bartolomé de las Casas, Joseph de Acosta,* 165–248; Mexico: Sep/Setentas, 1972.

O'Malley, John W. *The First Jesuits.* Cambridge: Harvard University Press, 1993.

_____. "The Ministries of the Early Jesuits: Social Disciplining or Discerning Accommodation?" *CIS* 27 (1996): 21–36.

Pagden, Anthony. *The Fall of Natural Man. The American Indian and the Origins of Comparative Ethnology,* 2d ed. Cambridge: Cambridge University Press, 1986.

_____. "The Forbidden Food: Francisco de Vitoria and José de Acosta on Cannibalism." *Terræ Incognitæ* 13 (1981): 17–29.

Paniagua Pascual, José Manuel. "La evangelización de América en las obras del Padre José de Acosta." Doct. diss., Faculty of Theology, University of Navarre, 1989.

_____. "La evangelización de América en las obras del Padre José de Acosta." *Excerpta e dissertationibus in Sacra Theologia* 16/6 (1989): 397–480.

Parera, Bartolomé. "La Escuela Tomista Española en el Siglo XVII." In *Historia de la teología española,* vol. 2., ed. Melquíades Andrés Martín, 9–34; Madrid: Fundación Universitaria Española, 1987.

Pereña Vicente, Luciano, ed. *Doctrina Christiana y Catecismo para Instrucción de los Indios: Introducción. Del Genocidio a la Promoción del Indio.* CHP vol. 26-1. Madrid: CSIC, 1986.

_____. *Inculturación del Indio.* Salamanca: Universidad Pontificia de Salamanca, 1988.

Picón-Salas, Mariano. "La extrañeza americana. La obra del P. Acosta." In *De la conquista a la independencia,* 2d ed., 125–28; Colección Tierra Firme 4; México-Buenos Aires: Fondo de Cultura Económica, 1950.

Pino Díaz, Fermín del. "La civilización indiana como criterio de diferenciación misional para el P. Acosta." In *La Compañía de Jesús en América: Evangelización y Justicia. Siglos XVII y XVIII. Actas del Congreso Internacional de Historia*, ed. Feliciano Delgado, 251–60; Córdoba: Imprenta San Pablo, S.L., 1993.

_____. "Contribución del P. Acosta a la constitución de la etnología: su evolucionismo." *Revista de Indias* 38 (1978): 507–46.

_____. "Culturas clásicas y americanas en la obra del P. Acosta." In *América y la España del siglo XVI*, vol. 1, ed. Francisco de Solano and Fermín del Pino Díaz, 327–62; Madrid: CSIC, 1982.

_____. "Edición de crónicas de Indias e Historia intelectual, o la distancia entre José de Acosta y José Alcina." *Revista de Indias* 50 (1990): 861–78.

_____. "Humanismo Clasicista Mediterráneo y Concepción Antropológica del Mundo: El Caso de los Jesuitas." *Hispania* 56 (1996): 29–50.

_____. "Humanismo Renacentista y Orígenes de la Etnología: A Propósito del P. Acosta, Paradigma del Humanismo Antropológico Jesuita." In *Humanismo y visión del otro en la España moderna: cuatro estudios*, ed. Berta Ares et al., 379–429; Madrid: CSIC, 1992.

_____. "El misionero español José de Acosta y la evangelización de las Indias Orientales." *Missionalia Hispánica* 42 (1985): 275–98.

_____. "Los Reinos de Méjico y Cusco en la obra del P. Acosta." *Revista de la Universidad Complutense* 28 (1979): 13–40.

Pinta Llorente, Miguel de la. *Actividades diplomáticas del P. José de Acosta; en torna a una política, y a un sentimiento religioso*. Madrid: CSIC, 1952.

_____. "El P. José de Acosta, agente de Felipe II en la corte romana: Un capítulo de la historia de la Compañía." In *Crítica y Humanismo*, 111–33; Madrid: Archivo Agustiniano, 1966.

Plazaola, Juan, ed. *Ignacio de Loyola y su tiempo. Congreso Internacional de Historia (9–13 Septiembre, 1991) Universidad de Deusto*. Bilbao: Ediciones Mensajero, 1991.

Pott, Anton. "Die Missionslehre des P. Joseph de Acosta, S.J." Doct. diss., Rome Pontifical Gregorian University, 1934.

Rabuske, Arthur. "A Doutrina de Juli, do Peru, como modelo inicial das reduções do antigo Paraguai." In *A Experiência Reducional No Sul Do Brasil: Anais I Simpósio Nacional de Estudos Missioneiros, Santa Rosa, 23 a 26 de outubro de 1975*, ed. Erneldo Schallenberger, 10–32; Canoas, RS, Brasil: Editora La Salle, 1982.

Randle, Guillermo. "España y Roma en el origen urbano de las misiones jesuitas guaraníes (1610–1767)." In *La Compañía de Jesús en América: Evangelización y Justicia. Siglos XVII y XVIII. Actas del Congreso Internacional de Historia*, ed. Feliciano Delgado, 275–305; Córdoba: Imprenta San Pablo, S.L., 1993.

Reites, J. W. "St. Ignatius of Loyola and the Jews." *Studies in the Spirituality of Jesuits* 13/4 (1981): 1–48.

Resines Llorente, Luis. "Catecismos Americanos de Jesuitas." In *La Compañía de Jesús en América: Evangelización y Justicia. Siglos XVII y SXVIII. Actas del Congreso Internacional de Historia,* ed. Feliciano Delgado, 315–21; Córdoba: Imprenta San Pablo, S.L., 1993.

_____. "El Catecismo Limense." In *Inculturación del Indio,* ed. Luciano Pereña Vicente et al., 191–200; Salamanca: Universidad Pontificia de Salamanca, 1988.

Rivara de Tuesta, María Luisa. *José de Acosta, un humanista reformista.* Lima: Editorial Universo, 1970.

Rivera, Luis N. *A Violent Evangelism: The Political and Religious Conquest of the Americas.* Louisville: Westminster/John Knox Press, 1992.

Rizzi, Armido. "José de Acosta. De Procuranda Indorum Salute. L'evangelizzazione degli indios: problemi e metodi." *Futuro dell'uomo* 19/2 (1992): 69–88.

Robles Ortíz, Elmer. *Educación y ciencias sociales en el pensamiento de José de Acosta.* Trujillo: Editorial Libertad, 1990.

Rodríguez Carracido, José. *El P. José de Acosta, S.J., y su importancia en la literatura científica española.* Madrid: Sucesores de Rivadeneyra, 1899.

Romero Ferrer, Raimundo. "La eclesiología de los catecismos limenses (1584–1585)." In *Evangelización y teología en América siglo XVI: Simposio internacional de teología de la Universidad de Navarra,* vol. 2, ed. Josep-Ignasi Saranyana, 1277–92; Pamplona: Universidad de Navarra, 1990.

Ruiz Jurado, Manuel. "Cronología de la vida del P. Jerónimo Nadal, S.J. (1507–1580)." *AHSI* 48 (1979): 248–76.

Sánchez-Arjona, Rodrigo. "El problema de la incorporación a la Iglesia y de la fe explícita en la teología de la colonia." *Allpanchis Phuturinqa* 4 (1972): 157–81.

Sánchez del Barrio, Antonio. *Estructura urbana de Medina del Campo.* Valladolid: Junta de Castilla y León, Consejería de Cultura y Bienestar, 1991.

Santos Hernández, Angel. *Los Jesuitas en América.* Colección Iglesia Católica en el Nuevo Mundo; Madrid: Editorial MAPFRE, 1992.

Saranyana, Josep-Ignasi. "Teología académica y teología profética americanas (S. XVI)." In *Evangelización y teología en América siglo XVI: Simposio internacional de teología de la Universidad de Navarra,* vol. 2, ed. Josep-Ignasi Saranyana, 1035–78; Pamplona: Universidad de Navarra, 1990.

Saranyana, Josep-Ignasi, ed. *Evangelización y teología en América siglo XVI: Simposio internacional de teología de la Universidad de Navarra,* 2 vols. Pamplona: Universidad de Navarra, 1990.

Shea, Daniel E. "A Defense of Small Population Estimates for the Central Andes in 1520." In *The Native Population of the Americas in 1492,* 2d ed., ed. William M. Denevan, 157–80; Madison: The University of Wisconsin Press, 1992.

Simón Díaz, José. *Bibliografía de la Literatura Hispánica*, 17 vols. Madrid: CSIC, 1950–1972.

————. *Jesuitas de los Siglos XVI y XVII: Escritos Localizados*. Madrid: Universidad Pontificia de Salamanca and Fundación Universitaria Española, 1975.

Stern, Steven J. *Peru's Indian Peoples and the Challenge of Spanish Conquest: Huamanga to 1640*, 2d ed. Madison: The University of Wisconsin Press, 1993.

Tapia, Joaquín Tapia. *Iglesia y teología en Melchor Cano (1509–1560): Un protagonista de la restauración eclesial y teológica en la España del siglo XVI*. Rome: Iglesia Nacional Española, 1989.

Trigo, Pedro. "Evangelización en la colonia. *De Procuranda Indorum Salute*: una teología patética." *Revista Latinoamericana de Teología* 20 (1990): 163–88.

Udías, Agustín. "José de Acosta (1539–1600): A pioneer of geophysics." *Eos* 67 (1986): 461–62.

Uriarte, José de, and Mariano Lecina. *Biblioteca de escritores de la Compañía de Jesús pertenecientes a la antigua Asistencia de España desde sus orígenes hasta el año 1773*, vol. 1, pt. 1, 24–33. Madrid: Sucesores de Rivadeneyra, 1925.

Urriza, Juan. *La Preclara Facultad de Artes y Filosofía de la Universidad de Alcalá de Henares en el Siglo de Oro. 1509–1621*. Madrid: CSIC, 1942.

Vargas Ugarte, Rubén. *La Elocuencia Sagrada en el Perú en los Siglos XVII y XVIII. Discurso de Recepción del R. P. Rubén Vargas Ugarte, S.J. Contestación del Director de la Academia D. José de la Riva-Agüero y Osma*. Lima: Impresores Gil, S.A., 1942.

————. *Historia de la Compañía de Jesús en el Perú*, vol 1: 1568–1618. Burgos: Imprenta de Aldecoa, 1963.

————. *Historia de la Iglesia en el Perú*. vol. 2: 1570–1640. Burgos: Imprenta de Aldecoa, 1959.

————. "Método de la Compañía de Jesús en la educación del indígena. (La doctrina de Juli)." *Mercurio Peruano* 22 (1940): 554–66.

Villegas, Juan. "El indio y su evangelización de acuerdo a los lineamientos del P. José de Acosta, S.J." In *La Compañía de Jesús en América: Evangelización y Justicia. Siglos XVII y XVIII. Actas del Congreso Internacional de Historia*, ed. Feliciano Delgado, 331–76; Córdoba: Imprenta San Pablo, S.L., 1993.

————. "El Tiempo como categoría misional en el P. José de Acosta, S.J." In *Misiones Jesuíticas en la Orinoquia (1625–1767)*, vol. 2, ed. José del Rey Fajardo, 779–99; San Cristóbal (Venezuela): Universidad Católica del Táchira, 1992.

Zevallos, Noé. "El Padre José de Acosta." In *Evangelización y Teología en el Perú: luces y sombras del siglo XVI*, ed. Pablo Nguyen Thai Hop, 179–98; Lima: CEP, 1991.

INDEX